"an **anglophone** = an English-speaking person, esp. in a country where two or more languages are spoken."

# anglophone s.a.

Montreuil-sous-Bois

**Editor-in-Chief**
David Applefield

**Assistant Editor/Communications**
Judith Rosenzweig

**Advertising/Marketing Manager**
Axelle Marais

**Graphic Design**
Christiane Charlot

**Online Editor**
Cory McCloud, Gyoza Media

**Webmaster**
Beth Boutry, Gyoza Media

**Editorial Assistance**
Angeline Kassi, Jean Rémy Lerin, Ilse Rubio

---

**Publisher**
David Applefield

**Executive Publisher**
Frank D. Cluck

Paris-Anglophone™, an Anglophone Directory, is published by Anglophone SA.

**TO ORDER**

- North American trade and individual orders should be sent to:
Mosaic Press, 1252 Speers Rd. Units 1 & 2 , Oakville, Ontario, L6L 5N9 Canada.
Toll-Free Orders may be placed by phone/fax at 1 (800) 387-8992.
Credit Cards accepted.

- UK trade sales are handled by Houghton-Mifflin: (Tel: 44 1235 833827).

- All other inquiries, corrections, comments, and orders should be addressed to:

**anglophone s.a**
32, rue Edouard Vaillant
93100 MONTREUIL / France
Tel: (33) 01 48 59 66 58  Fax: (33) 01 48 59 66 68
Email: info@paris-anglo.com
Web site: http://www.paris-anglo.com

*Directeur de la publication: David Applefield*
*Dépôt légal: 2e trimestre 1997.*
*Printed in Canada by Webcom.*
*ISBN: 2-912332-00-1*

# TABLE OF CONTENTS
## TABLE DES MATIÈRES

# TABLE OF CONTENTS
TABLE DES MATIÈRES

# LIVING & STUDYING _____143

# TABLE OF CONTENTS
## TABLE DES MATIÈRES

# INTRODUCTION/WELCOME!

## INTRODUCTION/BIENVENUE !

Dear Readers,

After several years of first testing the waters, then attempting to serve all the needs of everyone, we decided to take a tip from you – our users. Whether we looked at your comments and requests from our web site, or your letters and calls directly to our services, we noticed that your questions centered around four basic issues and we've tailored this newly designed and updated edition along these lines:

• TRAVEL: how do we get there from here? Who rents cars? Should I even dream of driving in and around Paris? Are the trains on time? Taxis cheap? Tolls expensive? What's best for getting around in the country? Interesting excursions? Where should I eat? What are the great bars and cafés to hang-out in? To meet Parisians?

• HOUSING: Where should we stay? What are rents like? Can I buy an apartment? How much will it cost me? Are loans available? Can you name a good hotel? A hide-a-way place in the country? Does student housing exist? I'm on an assignment for a year – can I get a furnished apartment? A suite hotel? English speaking agents?

• WORKING: Can I get work papers? How can I set up office or start a company or non-profit organization? I need a computer! Who has good Net access? We need English language temps... where are they? What's it cost to create a company? I need legal advice. Which is the bank for us? Can I get a loan? When do I pay taxes?

• STUDYING: Can I do an MBA in Paris? How do I extend my visa? Can I work and study? I'm transferred and need to learn French fast – where do I go? And an American school for my kids? Where can I learn French cuisine? Can I get into a French school of music or find art classes?

### FIFTH EDITION

In this fifth edition of PARIS-ANGLOPHONE, we have opted to be less comprehensive and increasingly useful. We no longer aim to provide every address; we want the best ones, those that are valuable to both our readers and our listees. Thus, we have trimmed down the number of entries in order to serve your needs better. You will find more listings organized around the new main divisions of the directory: TRAVEL & TOURISM, DOING BUSINESS & WORKING, LIVING & STUDYING. These contacts have been carefully updated and editorially selected and filtered to allow you quicker access to information and services – whether your questions concern how to get to Paris ... finding your way around when you get here ... landing a place to live ... earning your daily *baguette...* or hitting the books. You'll also find in this edition a lot more editorial content in that we've invited companies to enrich their listings with descriptive lines of text, inviting logos, and direct email and Web addresses.

Many of the classic directory entries haven't changed: what would life in Paris be without the arts, the restaurants, the boutiques and the hot spots? But there are plenty of places to find these common travel tips, and perhaps, like us, you'd rather discover your own "off-the-beaten-path" bistro. So we have limited the "pleasure" side of French life in our listings in order to better help you get down to business.

## GOOD NEWS

As an owner of this copy of PARIS-ANGLOPHONE, you automatically become a preferred member of the Franco-File Club, entitling you to a growing list of valuable Paris benefits and permanent updates on our associated web site, http://www.paris-anglo.com. (Just send in the enclosed **FF** Registration Card to receive you personal Membership Number and a list of **FF** Benefits!)

Furthermore, on the Web side of life, we are very pleased to find that so many users of PARIS ANGLOPHONE have gone "electronic" with us. We search to keep the same mix of Business and Pleasure on our Internet site as you will find here in the paper edition. Throughout the year we seek new ways to bring added value and information to our visitors – now numbering over 130,000 per week! They are the first to discover new additions to our publications list, such as Harriet Welty Rochefort's FRENCH TOAST, an amusing look at 25 years of life among the French, or the awaited new edition of PARIS INSIDE-OUT, the very practical and highly-detailed guide to life in Paris that works as the perfect complement to the PARIS-ANGLOPHONE directory. Leave us a message (by letter, phone, fax, or email) and let us know precisely your wants and needs in France!

## INTRODUCTION/WELCOME!

Finally, as old-time Anglophones in France, let us welcome you to Paris, to France and to the new PARIS-ANGLO-PHONE directory. Or if you are a returning user (client, acquaintance, friend), we thank you for your renewed confidence. If this is your first experience with us, we are delighted to be beginning a new relationship. We thank you all in advance for telling your colleagues and friends about us, and for keeping us informed on how we can be of further service.

From all the staff of Anglophone S.A. ...

ENJOY!

# TRAVEL & TOURISM

Paris – the most visited city in the world – boasts of over five million North American tourists and some twenty million travelers gliding through the Eurotunnel or sailing the English Channel each year. Paris is more than a European capital; it's a mythic place of love and style, *grande cuisine* and fine wines, fashion and beauty. Paris is a city you visit as a young adult and then come back to like an old friend or lover. Much of the pleasure of visiting Paris is the act of returning, tracking down those favorite spots and artful details, and settling-in for a *café crème* or *ballon de rouge* at that same sidewalk table.

The real joy of being in Paris is attained when you start feeling like you belong here, you know your way around, and you're no longer perceived as just another English-speaking tourist asking for ice cubes in their drinks, and their steaks overcooked. To gain that degree of intimacy, whether you're coming to Paris for a few days, a few weeks, or longer requires an understanding of Parisian habits, a host of key addresses, and a stable of quality contacts. In this spirit, PARIS-ANGLO-PHONE has gathered here a healthy selection of products and services to meet your needs as a Paris visitor, bringing together the practical with the aesthetic. The directory has collected the most useful entries in the following 13 headings.

Take note that the listings concerning Shopping are located in the Living & Studying section of the directory in that they have been selected not only for tourists but as great places to frequent often.

## A QUICK NOTE ON ARRIVING

Paris has two major international airports, Charles deGaulle (CDG), also known as Roissy, and Orly. CDG is organized into two major terminals, Aerogare 1, used by all international carriers, and Aerogare 2, which has four major wings A,B, C, and D, used primarily by Air France. Orly has two major terminals, Orly Sud, serving primarily the international carriers, and Orly Ouest, used mostly for domestic flights. Paris boasts of six major train stations: Austerlitz, Saint Lazare, Gare de Lyon, Gare du Nord, Gare de l'Est, and Gare de Montparnasse. Make sure you know where you're arriving and departing from. Greater Paris (Ile de France) is well served by the RATP, public transportation service, a dependable, safe, and efficient means of getting around.

Welcome to Paris (or welcome back)!

# AIRLINES
## COMPAGNIES AÉRIENNES

Here is a list of the principal airlines serving France to and from the United States, Canada, Great Britain, Australia, New Zealand, South Africa, India, and other anglophone countries. In addition to these updated listings we have selected the key airlines serving the most frequently-visited European destinations.

### Aer Lingus
47, ave de l'Opéra
75002 PARIS
Res: 01 47 42 12 50
Fax: 01 42 66 36 62
Frequent Flyer Program: 01 42 66 93 61
Web site: http://www.aerlingus.ie
Marketing Director: Mme Monika CASALI

### Air Canada
10, rue de la Paix
75002 PARIS
Res: 01 44 50 20 20
Toll-Free: 0 801 63 14 15
Fax: 01 42 60 99 99
Frequent Flyer Program: 01 44 50 20 55
Web site: http://www.aircanada.ca
President: M. Klaus BERG

### Air France Ticket Office
2, rue Robert Esnault Pelterie
75007 PARIS
Res: 0 802 80 28 02
Admin: 01 41 56 78 00
Frequent Flyer Program
(Fréquence Plus): 01 49 38 64 64
Roissy CDG: 01 48 62 22 80
Arrivals: 01 43 20 12 55
Orly: 01 49 75 15 15
Minitel: 3615 AF

### Air India
1, rue Auber
75009 PARIS
Res: 01 42 68 40 10
Fax: 01 42 66 22 02
Frequent Flyer Program: 01 42 68 40 21
Commercial Director: M. E. MAJRI

### Air Inter (Air France)
12, rue Provigny
94230 CACHAN
Tel: 01 45 55 07 72
Res: 01 45 46 90 00
Fax: 01 45 51 01 78
Frequent Flyer Program: 01 49 38 64 64

### Air New Zealand
66, ave des Champs Élysées
75008 PARIS
Tel: 01 53 77 13 30
Fax: 01 53 77 13 65

### Air UK
3, rue de Choiseul
75002 PARIS
Res: 01 44 56 18 08
Fax: 01 42 60 52 47
Web site: http://www.airuk.co.uk
Sales Manager: Mme Martine NERAUD

### Alitalia
69, Bd Haussmann
75008 PARIS
Tel: 01 44 94 44 00
Fax: 01 44 94 44 80
Frequent Flyer Program: 01 44 94 44 81
Public Relations: M. Jean-Pierre GAILLARD

### America West Airlines
66, ave des Champs Élysées
75008 PARIS
Res: 01 53 77 13 20
Fax: 01 53 77 13 65

## AOM

13, rue Pont des Halles
94150 RUNGIS Complexe
Tel: 0 803 00 12 34
Res: 01 49 79 10 00

## Austrian Airlines

4-14, rue Ferrus
75014 PARIS
Res: 01 45 81 11 01
Fax: 01 53 80 60 40
Frequent Flyer Program: 0 800 10 40 50
web site: http://www.aua.com.aua

## British Airways

Tour Winterthur
Immeuble Kupka A
18 , rue Hoche
92920 PARIS LA DÉFENSE Cedex
Tel: 01 46 53 73 00
Res: 0 802 80 29 02
Fax: 01 46 53 73 71
Frequent Flyer Program (British Airways
Executive Club): 0 800 90 59 79
Contact: Mme Isabelle KOCH

## British Midland Airways

4, place de Londres
Continental Square
Roissypole
95700 ROISSY CDG
Tel: 01 48 62 55 52 (Frequent Flyer Program)
Res: 01 48 62 55 65
Fax: 01 48 62 55 97
Web site: http://www.if/ybritishmidland.com
Sales Manager: M. Michel TURINI

## Canadian Airlines International

109, rue du Fbg Saint Honoré
75373 PARIS Cedex 08
Tel: 01 01 42 99 99 30 (Commercial service)
Res: 01 69 32 73 00
Fax: 01 42 99 99 33
Commercial Director: Mme KIRCHER

## Continental Airlines

92, ave des Champs Élysées
1st Floor
75008 PARIS
Res: 01 42 99 09 09
Fax: 01 42 25 31 89
Frequent Flyer Program: 01 42 99 09 10
Web site: http://www.flycontinental.com
Director: Mme Annette BRAUNER

## Delta Air Lines

Immeuble Lavoisier
4, place des Vosges
92052 PARIS LA DÉFENSE Cedex 64
Res: 01 47 68 92 92
(Also Frequent Flyer Program)
Fax: 01 47 68 52 82
Web site: http://www.delta-air.com
Director France: Mme Reine CAVEY

## Eurobelgian Airlines

Roissypole Dôme
1, rue de la Haye
BP 10928
95731 ROISSY CDG Cedex
Tel: 01 48 16 15 00
Fax: 01 48 16 15 06

## Ibéria

11, place des Cinq Martyrs du
Lycée Buffon
75014 PARIS
Res: 01 40 47 80 90
Fax: 01 42 79 11 02
Frequent Flyer Program: 0 800 30 05 40

## Island Helicopters New York

5 bis, rue du Louvre
75001 PARIS
Tel: 01 44 77 88 01
Fax: 01 42 60 05 45

## KLM Royal Dutch Airlines

16, rue Chauveau Lagarde
75008 PARIS
Res: 01 44 56 18 18
Fax: 01 44 56 19 09
Web site: http://www.klm.nl
Contact: M. BRODU

## Lufthansa

21, rue Royale
75008 PARIS
Res: 01 42 65 37 35
Toll-free: 0 801 63 38 38
Fax: 01 42 65 74 72

## Northwest Airlines

16, rue Chauveau Lagarde
75008 PARIS
Tel: 01 42 66 90 00
Toll-Free: 0 800 00 02 80
Fax: 01 42 66 94 66
Frequent Flyer Program: 01 42 66 26 16
Web site: http://www.nwa.com

## Olympic Airways

3, rue Auber
75009 PARIS
Res: 01 42 65 92 42
Fax: 01 40 07 03 04

## Qantas Airways

13, Bd de la Madeleine
75001 PARIS
Res: 01 44 55 52 00
Fax: 01 44 55 52 12
Frequent Flyer Program: 01 44 55 52 05

## Sabena - Belgian World Airlines

4-14, rue de Ferrus
75014 PARIS
Res: 01 53 80 59 49
(Also Frequent Flyer Program)
Fax: 01 45 88 48 55

## Scandinavian Airline System (SAS)

18, Bd Malesherbes
75008 PARIS
Res: 01 53 43 25 25
Fax: 01 53 43 25 29
Frequent Flyer Program: 01 53 43 25 55
Minitel: 3615 FLY/SAS
Web site: http://www.sas.se

## Swissair

4-14, rue Ferrus
75014 PARIS
Res: 01 45 81 11 01
Fax: 01 45 65 00 48
Frequent Flyer Program: 0 800 17 40 50

## TAP (Air Portugal)

11 bis, Bd Haussmann
75009 PARIS
Admin: 01 44 86 89 50
Tel: 01 44 83 60 60
Res: 01 44 86 89 54
Fax: 01 44 83 60 68
Frequent Flyer Program: 01 44 86 89 55

## TAT

17, rue de la Paix
75002 PARIS
Tel: 01 42 61 82 10
Res: 0 803 80 58 05
Fax: 01 49 27 06 65

## Tower Air

4, rue la Michodière
75002 PARIS
Res: 01 44 51 56 56
Fax: 01 42 66 67 54

## Trans World Airlines (TWA)

6, rue Christophe Colomb
75008 PARIS
Res: 01 49 19 20 00
Toll-Free: 800 892 41 41
 (Reservations-USA)
Fax: 01 40 69 70 99
Frequent Flyer Bonus Program (France):
01 49 19 20 05
Frequent Flyer Bonus Program (USA):
1 800 227 14 71
Web site: http://www.twa.com

## United Airlines Ticket Office

34, ave de l'Opéra
75002 PARIS
Res: 01 41 40 30 30
Fax: 01 47 31 27 37
Frequent Flyer Program: 01 41 40 30 35
Web site: http://www.ualfrance.fr
http://www.ual.com
Commercial Director:
Mme Jenny RUELLAND

## US Air

23 bis, rue Danjou
92100 BOULOGNE BILLANCOURT
Res: 01 49 10 29 00
Fax: 01 49 10 00 07
Frequent Flyer Program: 01 49 10 29 43
Commercial Director:
Mme Anne-Marie PECHEUR

## UTA

12, rue Chaussée d'Antin
75009 PARIS
Res: 01 48 24 73 22
Fax: 01 45 23 22 27
Frequent Flyer Program: 01 42 46 49 16

*TRAVEL & TOURISM*

15

# CAR RENTAL-BIKE RENTAL
## LOCATION VOITURES-VÉLOS

Most international car rental companies have pick-up and drop-off points in Paris and in other major French cities. Toll free numbers are available from most anglophone countries. Several companies have "fly and drive" package deals as well as combined train and car rental packages with pick-up in numerous French train stations. Hint: car rental prices vary not only from country to country but according to the country in which you make the reservation.

### CAR RENTAL
### Location de voitures

### Ace Limousine
100, rue Jean Jaurès
92270 BOIS COLOMBES
Tel: 01 47 69 96 00
Fax: 01 47 69 96 01
Email: ace-limo@calva.net
Contact: Grégory

### Avis Location de Voitures
5, rue Bixiot
75007 PARIS
Tel: 01 44 18 10 50
Fax: 01 45 51 47 97
Director: M. Christian DU TILLET

### Baron's Limousine Service
158 bis, rue Croix-Nivert
75015 PARIS
Tel: 01 45 30 21 21
Fax: 01 45 30 30 33
Email: bsl@club-internet.fr
Contact: M. Sylvain BARON

### Budget Rent-a-Car
193-197, rue de Bercy
Tour Gamma
75012 PARIS
Tel: 01 43 46 67 01
Fax: 01 43 45 84 11

### Car Rental
60, Bd Diderot
75012 PARIS
Tel: 01 44 68 89 89
Fax: 01 44 74 96 00
Minitel: 3615 CAR RENTAL

### Espace Limousines Automobiles
70, ave Gabriel Péri
92230 GENNEVILLIERS
Tel: 01 47 91 41 63
Fax: 01 47 91 41 63
Contact: M. MARTIN

### Euro-Rent
42, ave de Saxe
75007 PARIS
Tel: 01 44 38 55 50
Fax: 01 40 65 91 94
Minitel: 3615 EURORENT

### Europcar Interrent
5, ave d'Italie
75013 PARIS
Tel: 01 42 16 80 80
Fax: 01 45 86 71 97

### Executive Car
*Chauffeur-driven cars*
25, rue d'Astorg
75008 PARIS
Tel: 01 42 65 54 20
Fax: 01 42 65 25 93
President: M. Wladimir REINE

### Hertz France

27, place Saint Ferdinand
75017 PARIS
Res: 01 45 74 97 39
Fax: 01 44 09 98 41
Minitel: 3514 HERTZ

## IDCS - Limousines Service

27, place Jeanne d'Arc
75013 PARIS
Tel: 01 44 24 51 00
Fax: 01 44 24 58 00
Email: cdavi@francenet.fr

## International Limousines

182, Bd Péreire
75017 PARIS
Res: 01 53 81 14 14
Fax: 01 45 74 66 07

## Le Voiturium

68, ave de Versailles
75016 PARIS
Tel: 01 42 88 51 88
Fax: 01 45 25 47 17
Director: M. Didier HEIDET

## Prestige Limousines

165, rue de la Convention
75015 PARIS
Tel: 01 42 50 81 81
Fax: 01 42 50 87 29

## Promenades de Style

*1964 Lincoln convertible*
*Tours and events*
52, rue du Fbg Poissonnière
75010 PARIS
Tel: 01 46 71 73 35
Fax: 01 46 71 61 70
Email: 100442.423@compuserve.com
Anglophone Chauffeur: Edward

## Rual

1, Bd Pershing
75017 PARIS
Tel: 01 45 74 53 34
Fax: 01 45 74 74 53

## BIKE RENTAL
## Location de vélos

## Cyclic

19, rue Monge
75005 PARIS
Tel: 01 43 25 63 67
Fax: 01 43 25 63 67

## Paris Vélo Rent a Bike

2, rue du Fer à Moulin
75005 PARIS
Tel: 01 43 37 59 22
Fax: 01 47 07 67 45
Director: M. Olivier CATHALA

## Maison du Vélo

*Bicycle rentals, sales and repairs*
11, rue Fénelon
75010 PARIS
Tel: 01 42 81 24 72

## Paris Bike

83, rue Daguerre
75014 PARIS
Tel: 01 45 38 58 58
Fax: 01 43 20 71 93
Director: M. Thierry VINH MAU

*TRAVEL & TOURISM*

17

# EMBASSIES-CONSULATES
## AMBASSADES - CONSULATS

Here is a list of the Embassies and Consulates in France of English-speaking countries essential for obtaining passport and visa requirements, voting and tax information, security and emergency services, etc. PARIS-ANGLOPHONE also includes the principal addresses for embassy and consulate contacts for other European countries.

## ENGLISH-SPEAKING COUNTRIES
Pays anglophones

### Australia - Embassy
4, rue Jean Rey
75724 PARIS Cedex 15
Tel: 01 40 59 33 00
Fax: 01 40 59 33 10
Visas: 01 40 59 33 06
Minitel: 3614 AUSTRALIE
Web site: http://www.austgov.fr

### Canada - Embassy
35, ave Montaigne
75008 PARIS
Tel: 01 44 43 29 00
Fax: 01 44 43 29 99
Visas: 01 44 43 29 16

### Canada - Consulate
30, Bd de Strasbourg
31000 TOULOUSE
Tel: 05 61 99 30 16

### Great Britain - Embassy
35, rue du Fbg Saint Honoré
75008 PARIS
Tel: 01 44 51 31 00
Fax: 01 42 66 95 90
Fax2: 01 40 07 03 65
Minitel: 3615 GBRETAGNE

### Great Britain - Consulate
9, ave Hoche
75008 PARIS
Tel: 01 42 66 38 10
Fax: 01 40 76 02 87

### Great Britain - Consulate
24, ave Prado
13006 MARSEILLE
Tel: 04 91 15 72 10
Fax: 04 91 37 47 06

### Great Britain - Consulate
353, Bd du Président Wilson
33200 BORDEAUX
Tel: 05 57 22 21 10
Fax: 05 56 08 33 12

### Great Britain - Consulate
11, square Dutilleul
59800 LILLE
Tel: 03 20 57 87 90
Fax:03 20 54 88 16

### Great Britain - Consulate
Victoria Center
20, Chemin Laporte
31300 TOULOUSE
Tel: 05 61 15 02 02

### Great Britain - Consulate
11, rue de Paradis
06000 NICE
Tel: 04 93 82 32 04

### India - Embassy
15, rue Alfred Dehodencq
75016 PARIS
Tel: 01 40 50 70 70
Fax: 01 40 50 09 96

### India - Consulate
20-22, rue Albéric Magnard
75116 PARIS
Tel: 01 40 50 71 71
Fax: 01 40 50 09 96

### Ireland - Embassy
4, rue Rude
75116 PARIS
Tel: 01 44 17 67 00
Fax: 01 45 00 84 17
Minitel: 3615 IRLANDE

## Ireland - Consulate
4, rue Desparmet
69008 LYON
Tel: 04 78 76 44 85

## Ireland - Consulate
152, Bd John Kennedy
06600 ANTIBES
Tel: 04 93 61 50 63

## New Zealand - Embassy
7 ter, rue Léonard de Vinci
75116 PARIS
Tel: 01 45 00 24 11
Fax: 01 45 01 26 39

## South Africa - Embassy
59, quai d'Orsay
75007 PARIS
Tel: 01 45 55 92 37
Fax: 01 47 53 99 70

## United States of America - Embassy
2, ave Gabriel
75008 PARIS
Tel: 01 43 12 22 22
Fax: 01 43 12 21 72

## United States of America - Embassy Commercial Service
2, ave Gabriel
75008 PARIS
Tel: 01 43 12 21 97
Fax: 01 43 12 21 72
Minitel: 36 28 00 61
Email: ocollett@doc.gov
Director of Information and Special
Projects: M. Olivier COLLETTE

## United States of America - Consulate
2, rue Saint Florentin
75001 PARIS
Tel: 01 43 12 22 22
Fax: 01 42 86 82 91

## United States of America - Consulate
15, ave d'Alsace
67082 STRASBOURG Cedex
Tel: 03 88 24 06 95

## United States of America - Consulate
12, Bd Paul Peytral
13006 MARSEILLE Cedex 6
Tel: 04 91 54 92 00
Fax: 04 91 55 09 47

## United States of America - Consulate
31, rue du Maréchal Joffre
06000 NICE
Tel: 04 93 88 89 55
Tel2: 04 93 82 30 98

## OTHER EUROPEAN COUNTRIES
Autres pays européens

## Austria - Embassy
6, rue Fabert
75007 PARIS
Tel: 01 40 63 30 63
Fax: 01 47 20 25 80

## Belgium - Embassy
9, rue de Tilsitt
75017 PARIS
Tel: 01 44 09 39 39
Fax: 01 47 54 07 64

## Czech Republic
15, ave Charles Floquet
75007 PARIS
Tel: 01 40 65 13 00
Fax: 01 44 32 02 12

## Denmark - Embassy
77, ave Marceau
75116 PARIS
Tel: 01 44 31 21 21
Fax: 01 44 31 21 88

## Federal Republic of Germany - Embassy
13, ave Franklin Roosevelt
75008 PARIS
Tel: 01 53 83 45 00
Fax: 01 43 59 74 18

*TRAVEL & TOURISM*

19

# EMBASSIES-CONSULATES
## AMBASSADES - CONSULATS

### Federal Republic of Germany Consulate

34, ave d'Iéna
75016 PARIS
Tel: 01 53 83 46 40
Fax: 01 47 20 01 60
Visas: 01 47 20 01 60

### Finland - Embassy

39, quai d'Orsay
75007 PARIS
Tel: 01 44 18 19 20
Fax: 01 45 55 51 57

### Finland - Consulate

18 bis, rue d'Anjou
75008 PARIS
Tel: 01 44 18 19 20
Fax: 01 45 55 51 57

### Greece - Embassy

17, rue Auguste Vacquerie
75116 PARIS
Tel: 01 47 23 72 28
Fax: 01 47 23 73 85

### Hungary - Embassy

5 bis, ave Foche
75016 PARIS
Tel: 01 45 00 41 59
Fax: 01 45 01 66 00

### Iceland - Embassy

8, ave Kléber
75016 PARIS
Tel: 01 40 67 91 19
Fax: 01 40 67 99 96

### Italy - Embassy

51, rue de Varenne
75007 PARIS
Tel: 01 49 54 03 00
Fax: 01 45 49 35 81

### Luxembourg - Embassy

33, ave Rapp
75007 PARIS
Tel: 01 45 55 13 37
Fax: 01 45 51 72 29

### The Netherlands - Embassy

7-9, rue Eblé
75007 PARIS
Tel: 01 40 62 33 00
Fax: 01 40 56 01 32

### Norway - Embassy

28, rue Bayard
75008 PARIS
Tel: 01 53 67 04 00
Fax: 01 53 67 04 40

### Poland - Embassy

1, rue Talleyrand
75007 PARIS
Tel: 01 45 51 49 12
Fax: 01 45 55 72 02

### Portugal - Embassy

3, rue du Noisiel
75016 PARIS
Tel: 01 47 27 35 29
Fax:01 47 55 00 40

### Spain - Embassy

22, ave Marceau
75008 PARIS
Tel: 01 44 43 18 00
Fax: 01 47 23 59 55

### Sweden - Embassy

17, rue Barbet de Jouy
75007 PARIS
Tel: 01 44 18 88 00
Fax: 01 44 18 88 40

### Switzerland - Embassy

142, rue de Grenelle
75007 PARIS
Tel: 01 49 55 67 00
Fax: 01 45 51 34 77

# EXCHANGE BUREAUX
## POINTS DE CHANGE

Changing money in Paris is not a difficult task, and there are many options for travelers and tourists. Major credit cards are widely accepted and travelers checks in French francs pose few problems. Remember that, especially for large amounts, the exchange rates, although posted, are somewhat negotiable at exchange bureaux. Inquire about commissions at banks before changing money.

### Banque Régionale d'Escompte

*Automatic teller for converting 10 and 20 US bills into francs*
66, ave des Champs Élysées
75008 PARIS
Tel: 01 42 89 10 99
Fax: 01 49 53 90 24
Director: M. MICHEL

### Change Alliance

Alliance Française de Paris, Hall A
101, Bd Raspail
75006 PARIS
Tel: 01 45 49 18 40
Fax: 01 45 49 17 20
Director: M. Dominique DUMAND

### Change du Rond-Point

Galerie Élysées Rond-Point
47, ave Franklin Roosevelt
75008 PARIS
Tel: 01 42 25 91 36
Tel2: 01 42 25 91 37

### Change Saint Michel

5, quai Saint Michel
75005 PARIS
Tel: 01 43 54 40 10

### Chequepoint

150, ave des Champs Élysées
75008 PARIS
Tel: 01 49 53 02 51
Fax: 01 49 53 02 58
Director: M. HASSAN

### Crédit Commercial de France

115, ave des Champs Élysées
75008 PARIS
Tel: 01 40 70 70 40
Fax: 01 40 70 35 21
Director: M. Philippe DULAC

### European Exchange Office

6, rue Yvonne Le Tac
75018 PARIS
Tel: 01 42 52 67 19
Fax: 01 42 52 58 20

### Thomas Cook

Thomas Cook

8, rue Bellini
75016 PARIS
Tel: 01 47 55 52 25
Fax: 01 47 27 37 22
Web site:
http://www.thomascook.com/icentre
Public Relations Director:
M. SOISSON

### Tradex Change

74, rue Rambuteau
75001 PARIS
Tel: 01 42 36 92 01
Contact: M. Edward STEWART

### Western Union International

4, rue Cloître-Notre-Dame
75004 PARIS
Tel: 01 43 54 46 12
Director: M. Michel FAURE

# GUIDE SERVICES/TOURS
## SERVICES DE GUIDES

Although Paris is a great city to wander around on your own, there's nothing quite like a good tour to get oriented and to really get deeper into the cityscape's most revealing details. Here are a few quality options.

### Cityrama
147, rue Saint Honoré
75001 PARIS
Res: 01 44 55 60 00

### Cityscope
11 bis, Bd Haussman
75009 PARIS
Tel: 01 53 34 11 91

### French Links
29, rue Patrice de la Tour du Pin
BP 41
75020 PARIS
Tel: 01 44 64 76 26
Fax: 01 44 64 76 26
Email: kaplan@club-internet.fr
Contact: Mme Rachel KAPLAN

### Lusina I.S.G.

*Bilingual site about South West France: tourism information and emphasis on Cognac, Pineau des Charentes, Armagnac (market, prices, gossips, and results of our bi-weekly tastings). Purchase on our site with secured payment!*
7, route de Coucoussac
17160 MATHA
Tel: 05 46 26 67 01
Fax: 05 46 26 67 50
Email: cognac@msn.com
Web site: http://www.swfrance.com
Contact: M. Mac ANDREW

### Paris Contact
*Multilingual cultural guide service*
46, rue Lepic
75018 PARIS
Tel: 01 42 51 08 40
Fax: 01 42 51 08 40
Contact: Mme Jill DANEELS

### Paris International
*Guides, personal services, interpreters*
65, rue Pascal
75013 PARIS
Tel: 01 43 31 81 69
Fax: 01 43 37 11 46
Email: nagpal@magic.fr
Director: M. SINGH

### Peter & Oriel Caine
*Paris walking tours*
10, rue Samson
93200 SAINT DENIS
Tel: 01 48 09 21 40
Fax: 01 42 43 75 51

### Promenades de Style
*1964 Lincoln convertible*
*Tours and events*
52, rue du Fbg Poissonnière
75010 PARIS
Tel: 01 47 70 08 28
Fax: 01 48 24 05 60
Email: 100442.423@compuserve.com
Anglophone Chauffeur: Edward

*TRAVEL & TOURISM*

23

# HOTELS & OTHER ACCOMODATIONS
## HÔTELS & LOGEMENTS

Paris has hundreds of large and small hotels, offering diverse services at varying prices. This list is not intended to be exhaustive, but rather offers a useful selection of quality hotels at different catagories and price ranges, ranging from exclusive four-star *luxe,* and major chains with international reservation services, to small and charming out of the way hotels, while not forgetting simpler but well-situated bed & breakfasts and a few youth hostels. Note that hotels have been listed according to number of stars from \*\*\*\* to \*. The Paris Tourist Office offers an extensive accomodations service. You can also consult http://www.paris-anglo.com/housing for up-to-date hotel suggestions.

## HOTELS
Hôtels

## \*\*\*\* LUXE

### Groupe Hôtels Intercontinental
\*\*\*\* *luxe*

Toll-Free: 01 81 847 22 77
(Reservations-UK)
Toll-Free: 1 800 327 02 00
(Reservations-USA/Canada)
Toll-Free: 05 90 85 55
(Reservations-France)
Toll-Free: 232 11 99
(Reservations-Australia)
Email: parha@interconti.com
Web site: http://www.interconti.com

### Hôtel Meurice \*\*\*\* *luxe*

228, rue de Rivoli
75001 PARIS
Tel: 01 44 58 10 10
Fax: 01 44 58 10 16
Director: M. ROCHE

### Hôtel Plaza Athénée \*\*\*\* *luxe*

25, ave Montaigne
75008 PARIS
Tel: 01 53 67 66 65
Fax: 01 53 67 66 66

### Hôtel Prince de Galles \*\*\*\*
*luxe*

33, ave Georges V
75008 PARIS
Tel: 01 53 23 77 77
Fax: 01 53 23 78 78
Web site:
http://www.calvacom/princedegalles
Sales director: Mme KERG

### Hôtel Ritz \*\*\*\* *luxe*

15, place Vendôme
75041 PARIS Cedex 01
Tel: 01 43 16 30 30
Fax: 01 43 16 31 78
Res: 01 43 16 36 69
Commercial Director: Mme HOLTMANN

### Le Warwick Champs Élysées \*\*\*\* *luxe*

5, rue de Berri
75008 PARIS
Tel: 01 45 63 14 11
Fax: 01 42 57 77 59
Sales Marketing Manager:
M. Dominic HAWKINS

### Groupe Hôtels Concorde \*\*\*\*
*luxe* & \*\*\*\*

Toll-Free: 0 800 05 00 11
(Reservations-France)
Toll-Free: 0 800 181 591
(Reservations-UK)
Toll-Free: 0 800 888 47 47
(Reservations-USA/Canada)
Web site: http://www.concorde-hotels.com

## ****

### Hilton Paris ****
18, ave de Suffren
75740 PARIS Cedex 15
Tel: 01 44 38 56 00
Fax: 01 44 38 56 10
Director:
M. Oskar von KRETSCHMANN

### Hôtel de Castiglione ****
40, rue du Fbg Saint Honoré
75008 PARIS
Tel: 01 44 94 25 25
Fax: 01 42 65 12 27
Director: M. Eric MOUEZ

### Hôtel George V ****
31, ave George V
75008 PARIS
Tel: 01 47 23 92 40
Fax: 01 47 20 06 49

### Hôtel Westminster ****
13, rue de la Paix
75002 PARIS
Tel: 01 42 61 57 46
Res: 01 42 61 75 67
Fax: 01 42 60 30 66
Email: sales@westminster.hepta.fr
Web site: http://www.hepta.fr/westminster
Contact: Mlle Isabelle LANGLOIS

### Hyatt Regency Paris Roissy
****

351, ave du Bois de la Pie
BP 40048
95912 ROISSY CDG Cedex
Tel: 01 48 17 18 19
Toll-Free: 0 800 90 85 29
Fax: 01 48 63 00 81
Web site: http://www.hyatt.com
Sales Director: Mme Florence LAROCHE

### Le Bristol ****
112, rue du Fbg Saint Honoré
75008 PARIS
Tel: 01 53 43 43 00
Fax: 01 53 43 43 01

### Le Méridien Hotels ****
Toll-Free: 0 800 40 22 15
(Reservations-France)
Toll-Free: 0 800 40 40 40
(Reservations-UK)
Toll-Free: 1 800 225 58 43
(Reservations-USA/Canada)
Web site: http://www.forte-hotels.com

### Relais Hotel du Vieux Paris****
*First-class hotel, built in 1480*
9, rue Gît-le-Coeur
75006 PARIS
Tel: 01 44 32 15 9
Fax: 01 43 26 00 15
Email: vieuxpar@worldnet.fr
Web site:
http://www.travel2000.com/h/Europe/
France/Paris/relaispa.fr/1.htm
Manager: M. Claude ODILLARD

### Saint James Paris ****
43, ave Bugeaud
75116 PARIS
Tel: 01 44 05 81 81
Fax: 01 44 05 81 82
Web site: http://www.slh.com/slh
Director: M. Tim GODDARD

### Sofitel ****
*See Resinter Hotel Reservations*

### Best Western Hotels
#### **** & ***

Tel: 01 44 87 40 31
Fax: 01 44 87 40 84/39
Toll-Free: 0 800 90 44 90
(Reservations-France)
Toll-Free: 0 800 39 31 30
(Reservations-UK)
Toll-Free: 1 800 528 1234
(Reservations-USA/Canada)
Toll-Free: 131 779
(Reservations-Australia)
Toll-Free: 1 800 709 101
(Reservations-Ireland)
Web site:
http://www.bestwestern.com/best.html

### Holiday Inn Worldwide
#### **** & ***

45, rue Anatole France
92300 LEVALLOIS PERRET
Toll-Free: 0 800 905 999
(Reservations-France)
Toll-Free: 0 800 897 121
(Reservations-UK)
Toll-Free: 1 800 465 4329
(Reservations-USA/Canada)
Web site: http://www.holiday-inn.com

*TRAVEL & TOURISM*

25

# HOTELS & OTHER ACCOMODATIONS
## HÔTELS & LOGEMENTS

### ★★★

### Château Golf des 7 Tours ★★★
37330 COURCELLES DE TOURAINE
Tel: 02 47 24 69 75
Tel2: 02 47 24 90 34
Fax: 02 47 24 23 74
Director: M. Daniel PERRY

### Claridge Bellman ★★★
37, rue François 1er
75008 PARIS
Tel: 01 47 23 54 42
Fax: 01 47 23 08 84

### Flatotel Expo ★★★
52, rue d'Oradour sur Glane
75015 PARIS
Tel: 01 45 54 93 45
Fax: 01 45 54 93 07
General Manager: Mme Cécile QUILEZ

### Hôtel Alésia Montparnasse ★★★
84, rue Raymond Losserand
75014 PARIS
Tel: 01 45 42 16 03
Fax: 01 45 42 11 60
Email: alesiamont@3and1hotels
Director: Mme Marie-Hélène LOCHET

### Hôtel Britannique ★★★

★ ★ ★

*A charming hotel in the heart of Paris. Friendly staff, quiet setting, extremely comfortable rooms, and all-around quality service*
20, ave Victoria
75001 PARIS
Tel: 01 42 33 74 59
Fax: 01 42 33 82 65
Email: britannique@unimedia.fr
Web site:
  http://www.unimedia.fr/britannic
Director: M. J.F. DANJOU

### Hôtel des États-Unis ★★★
16, rue d'Antin
75002 PARIS
Tel: 01 47 42 43 25
Fax: 01 47 42 82 83

### Hôtel Excelsior Opéra ★★★
5, rue Lafayette
75009 PARIS
Tel: 01 48 74 99 30
Fax: 01 48 74 21 93
Directors:
MM. Gérard & François DEROSSI

### Hôtel Holiday Inn Garden Court Paris Tolbiac ★★★
*Well-situated on the Left Bank, just a few steps from the new National Library, a lovely hotel with a convivial and warm atmosphere*
21, rue de Tolbiac
75013 PARIS
Tel: 01 45 84 61 61
Fax: 01 45 84 43 38
Contact: M. Hervé MARACHE

### Hôtel Les Jardins d'Eiffel ★★★
8, rue Amélie
75007 PARIS
Tel: 01 47 05 46 21
Fax: 01 45 55 28 08
Email: eiffel@unimédia.fr
Web site: http://www.unimédia.fr/eiffel
Contact: M. RECH

### Hôtel Mercure Paris Tour Eiffel ★★★
64, Bd de Grenelle
75015 PARIS
Tel: 01 45 78 90 90
Fax: 01 45 78 95 55
Contact: Dominique RUCHAUD

### Hôtel Queen Mary ★★★
9, rue Greffulhe
75008 PARIS
Tel: 01 42 66 40 50
Fax: 01 42 66 94 92
Commercial Director:
M. Olivier TARRON

## Hôtel Ternes Arc de Triomphe ***

97, ave des Ternes
75017 PARIS
Tel: 01 53 81 94 94
Fax: 01 53 81 94 95
Contact: M. Arnaud SAUVE

## Mercure ***
## Novotel ***

*See Resinter Hotel Reservations*

**\*\***

## A l'Hôtel du Bois **

11, rue du Dôme
75116 PARIS
Tel: 01 45 00 31 96
Fax: 01 45 00 90 05
Commercial Director:
M. Olivier TARRON

## Au Palais de Chaillot **

*Charming hotel, close to Eiffel Tower and the Champs Élysées, fully renovated in 1996. Moderate prices, close to public parking*

35, ave Raymond Poincarré
75116 PARIS
Tel: 01 53 70 09 09
Fax: 01 53 70 09 08
Manager: M. Cyrille PIEN

## Eden Hôtel **

7, rue Jean-Baptiste Dumay
75020 PARIS
Tel: 01 46 36 64 22
Fax: 01 46 36 01 11

## Hôtel Beaumarchais **

3, rue Oberkampf
75011 PARIS
Tel: 01 53 36 86 86
Fax: 01 43 38 32 86

## Hôtel du Vieux Pont **

Rue du Pont de la Légende
64390 SAUVETERRE DE BEARN
Tel: 05 59 38 95 11
Fax: 05 59 38 99 10
Email: info@adhoc-fr.com

## Hôtel Tour Eiffel Dupleix **

*Near the Eiffel Tower, the hotel has 4 comfortable bedrooms with private bathroom, cable TV and buffet-breakfast*

11, rue Juge
75015 PARIS
Tel: 01 45 78 29 29
Fax: 01 45 78 60 60
Contact: M. Frédéric LEBAILLY

## Ibis**

*See Resinter Hotel Reservations*

**\***

## Hôtel Saint Honoré *

*Hôtel Saint-Honoré*

*In the heart of Paris: Louvre, Opéra, Notre-Dame. Spacious rooms: direct phone & TV, economic prices start at 320 FF (for 2), 450 FF (for 3/4). Friendly English-speaking staff*

85, rue Saint Honoré
75001 PARIS
Tel: 01 42 36 20 38
Fax: 01 42 21 44 08
Manager: Brice

## Hôtel de la Herse d'Or *

20, rue Saint Antoine
75004 PARIS
Tel: 01 48 87 84 09

## CENTRAL RESERVATIONS

### Centrale Internet

37, rue de Gergovie
75014 PARIS
Tel: 01 40 44 74 60
Fax: 01 40 44 74 77
Email: pmelloul@adi.fr
Web site: http://www.hotels.fr

### Paris-Anglophone

Web site: http://www.paris-anglo.com/housing

# HOTELS & OTHER ACCOMODATIONS
## HÔTELS & LOGEMENTS

### Resinter Hotel Reservations

*All Sofitel \*\*\*\*, Novotel \*\*\*,
Mercure \*\*\*, Ibis \*\* hotels*

Tel: 01 60 77 27 27
(Reservations-France)
Tel: 44 171 724 10 00
(Reservations-UK)
Toll-Free: 1 800 221 45 42
(Reservations-USA)
Toll-Free: 1 800 64 22 44
(Reservations-Australia)
Fax: 01 69 91 05 63
(Reservations-France)
Web site: http://www.hotelweb.fr

### Sphère International

*All Etap & Formule 1 hotels
reservation center*

6-8, rue du Bois Briard
91021 ÉVRY Cedex
Tel: 01 69 36 75 00
(Reservations-France)
Fax: 01 69 36 76 00
Web site: http://www.hotelweb.fr

### BED & BREAKFAST-RURAL HOUSES
Bed & breakfast - Gîtes

### France Lodge

41, rue Lafayette
75009 PARIS
Tel: 01 53 20 09 09
Fax: 01 53 20 01 25

### Gîte l'Oasis

*Year around, fully equipped gîte
(rural houses) with hiking and
mountaineering programs. Half-
board available.*

65120 BAREGES
Tel: 05 62 92 69 47
Fax: 05 62 92 65 17
Owners:
M. & Mme Phillipe & Andréa TREY

### Le Mistral B&B

8, rue Frédéric Mistral
13122 VENTABREN
Fax: 01 42 28 87 37
Email: lynnmcd@pacwan.mm-soft.fr
Owner: Mme Lynn MCDONALD

### Les Sarments

Allée de Clotomont
77183 CROISSY BEAUBOURG
Tel: 01 64 62 99 86
Fax: 01 64 05 03 45
Contact:
Mme Christine SCARANO

### RENTAL (SHORT TERM / FURNISHED)
Locations (court terme / meublées)

See Living & Studying:
Housing

### YOUTH HOSTELS /
Auberges de Jeunesse

### Fédération des Auberges de Jeunesse

27, rue Pajol
75018 PARIS
Tel: 01 44 89 87 27

### Le Fauconnier

11, rue Fauconnier
75004 PARIS
Tel: 01 42 74 23 45
Fax: 01 40 27 81 64

### Ligue française pour les auberges de jeunesse

38, Bd Raspail
75007 PARIS
Tel: 01 45 48 69 84
Fax: 01 45 44 57 47

### The Three Ducks Hostel

*Youth hostel for foreign students*

6, place Etienne Pernet
75015 PARIS
Tel: 01 48 42 04 05
Fax: 01 48 42 99 99
Director: M. Éric CHECHE

# MINITEL DIRECTORY
## SERVEURS MINITEL

The French household online computer, the Minitel, provides a vast choice of free and pay-per-view information sources and commercial and cultural services. Here is a selection of Minitel services that could help you in your travel needs in France. For commercial services, see Minitel Directory in the Doing Business & Working section.

### 3614 A LA CARTE
*Everything on the USA: maps of states and cities, video guides, national parks..., info on UK, Scotland, Ireland*

### 3614 G7
*Taxi reservation service (Paris & suburbs)*

### 3615 AIRFRANCE - 3615 AF
*Air France information*

### 3615 AIRTEL
*National and international airline schedules and fares*

### 3615 AVIS
*Rental of cars and professional vehicles*

### 3615 BISONFUTE
*Weather reports, traffic conditions*

### 3615 BR
*British Rail*

### 3615 CANADA
*Information released by the Canadian Embassy: tourism, formalities, travel, immigration*

### 3615 CORUS
*Information on 150 mountain resorts*

### 3615 COUNCIL
*Council Travel Services agency: prices of regular and charter flights*

### 3615 DEGRIFTOUR
*Reduced travel tickets*

### 3615 EUROPCAR
*Rental of cars and professional vehicles*

### 3615 EUROTUNNEL
*Information on the Channel tunnel*

### 3615 FERRIES
*Sea crossings and package tours available from Brittany Ferries*

### 3615 FUAJ
*Information on French youth hostels*

### 3615 GBRETAGNE
*Practical information on Great Britain*

### 3615 GLISS
*Skiing information*

### 3615 GO
*Discount rates for charters and regular flights*

### 3615 HERTZ
*Rental of cars and professional vehicles*

### 3615 HORAV
*Airport English-speaking guide: flight departure and arrival times, hotels, car parks, services*

### 3615 HOVER
*Hoverspeed offers information about Channel crossings*

### 3615 IRISHFERRI
*Sea crossings and package tours available from Irish Ferries*

### 3615 IRLANDE
*Information on Ireland*

### 3615 ITOUR
*National directory of tourist offices by region, department and town*

### 3615 METEO
*Regular update on the weather situation in France*

### 3615 MICHELIN
*Road itineraries in France and Europe, information on tires, hotels and restaurants*

### 3615 RANDO
*Guide to walking trips in France*

### 3615 RATP
*This connection is helpful in determining the best means of transport to use (RER, métro, bus) and how long it will take you*

### 3615 ROUTARD
*International travel information for small budgets*

### 3615 ROUTE
*Traffic conditions and highway information*

### 3615 SEALINK
*Times and prices for ferries to England and Ireland*

### 3615 SNCF
*French National Railway information. Train times, reservations, sleeping compartments, etc. + Eurostar information*

### 3615 STATES
*Tourist information about the United States and about American activities in France*

### 3616 AMEXTC
*Limited service for ordering American Express traveler's checks*

## RESTAURANTS / BARS

PARIS-ANGLOPHONE offers you here an eclectic selection of interesting dining options, organized via price range and ambiance, delineated by the sub-headings Upscale/*Chic*, Mid-Range/*Prix moyens*, and Good Value/*Bon Marché*. Note that the information listed below has been provided respectively by each establishment. An effort has been made to include selections of not only French culinary venue but from Paris' wide-range of international cuisines. For nostalgic readers, Anglo-American restaurants and bars in Paris are amply listed in the section Living & Studying. The editors of PARIS-ANGLOPHONE are interested in receiving suggestions of favorite eating places and watering-holes, great experiences, and ones to avoid.

*TRAVEL & TOURISM*

## RESTAURANTS
Restaurants

### UPSCALE/*CHIC*

**Chez Georges**
273, Bd Pereire
75017 PARIS
Tel: 01 45 74 31 00
Fax: 01 45 74 02 56

**Closerie des Lilas**
171, Bd Montparnasse
75006 PARIS
Tel: 01 43 54 21 68

**Flora Danica**
*Scandinavian cuisine*
142, ave des Champs Élysées
75008 PARIS
Tel: 01 44 13 86 26

**Fouquet's**
99, ave des Champs Élysées
75008 PARIS
Tel: 01 47 23 70 60
Director: M. Joel MINOT

**Lasserre**
17, ave Franklin Roosevelt
75008 PARIS
Tel: 01 43 59 53 43
Fax: 01 45 63 72 23

**La Tour d'Argent**
15-17, quai de la Tournelle
75005 PARIS
Tel: 01 43 54 23 31

**Le Petit Bedon**
38, rue Pergolèse
75016 PARIS
Tel: 01 45 00 23 66
Fax: 01 45 00 44 03
Contact: M. Claude GUIBERT

**Maxim's Restaurant**
3, rue Royale
75008 PARIS
Tel: 01 42 65 27 94
Fax: 01 40 17 02 91

**Restaurant Copenhague**
142, ave des Champs Élysées
75008 PARIS
Tel: 01 44 13 86 26
Fax: 01 42 25 83 10
Email: bocar@mail.club-internet.fr
Contact: M. ENGSTRÖM

**Taillevent**
15, rue Lamennais
75008 PARIS
Tel: 01 44 95 15 01
Fax: 01 42 25 95 18

## MID-RANGE/*PRIX MOYENS*

### 404 Restaurant Familial
*Authentic Moroccan cuisine*
69, rue des Gravilliers
75003 PARIS
Tel: 01 42 74 57 81
Fax: 01 42 74 03 41

### Au Pied de Cochon
6, rue Coquillière
75001 PARIS
Tel: 01 40 13 77 00
Fax: 01 40 13 77 09
Manager: M. VIGOUREUX

### Aux Délices de Szechuen
*Chinese restaurant*
40, ave Duquesne
75007 PARIS
Tel: 01 43 06 22 55

### Aux Iles Philippines
9, rue de Pontoise
75005 PARIS
Tel: 01 43 29 39 00
Tel: 01 46 47 56 68
Contact: Mme Nora V. DAZA

### Brasserie Le Grand Colbert
2, rue Vivienne
75002 PARIS
Tel: 01 42 86 87 88
Fax: 01 42 86 82 65

### ChantAirelle Restaurant
17, rue Laplace
75005 PARIS
Tel: 01 46 33 18 59
Fax: 01 46 33 18 59
Email: asterion@worldnet.fr
Web site: http://www.asterion.fr/chantairelle
Manager: M. Frédéric BETHE

### Chez André
12, rue Marbeuf
75008 PARIS
Tel: 01 47 20 59 57

### Chez Gégène
*Open-air dance restaurant on the banks of the Marne*
Allée des Guinguettes
162 bis, quai de Polangis
94340 JOINVILLE LE PONT
Tel: 01 48 83 29 43
Fax: 01 48 83 72 62

### Chez Jenny
39, Bd du Temple
75003 PARIS
Tel: 01 42 74 75 75
Fax: 01 42 74 38 69

### Chez Julien
1, rue du Pont Louis Philippe
75004 PARIS
Tel: 01 42 78 31 64
Fax: 01 42 74 39 30

### Congrès Auteuil
144, Bd Exelmans
75016 PARIS
Tel: 01 46 51 15 75

### Congrès Maillot
80, ave de la Grande Armée
75017 PARIS
Tel: 01 45 74 17 24

### Dominique
*Russian restaurant*
19, rue Bréa
75006 PARIS
Tel: 01 43 27 08 80

### Du Côté 7ème
29, rue Surcouf
75007 PARIS
Tel: 01 47 05 81 65
Contact: Mme RENAUD

### L'Auberge Dab
161, ave de Malakoff
75016 PARIS
Tel: 01 45 00 32 22

32

# ADVANTAGE INSURANCE
## • ASSOCIATES •

## INSURANCE MADE EASY... IN ENGLISH

### Dedicated To Serving
### Americans in France

When you call Advantage, you'll find the answers to all your questions about insurance in France.
Clear, detailed explanations - in English.

And as we are completely independent, accredited by over 40 French, American and International Insurance companies, we can find the best contract at the best price for you.

Your policy documents come complete with full summaries of cover in English...translations of the claims forms... and information on exactly what to do should the worst happen.

You'll also be able to call on our full claims service which will give you all the back-up and assistance you may need.

Whether you need health, motor, home contents, life, personal injury coverage, business insurance - or simply want an impartial view on your current arrangements, call now at 01 53 20 03 33. And don't hesitate to call before you arrive in France at 33 1 53 20 03 33

### Advantage Insurance Associates
17, rue Chateaudun
75009 PARIS / France
Tel: 01 53 20 03 33   Fax: 01 44 63 00 97
Email: advantag@easynet.fr
Web site: http://www.paris-anglo.com/housing

CITADINES

Paris' prime
all-suites
hotels.

anglophone/Charlot

For Reservations and Information call:
01 41 05 79 79
or
visit the Citidines web site at
www.citadines.com

### L'Auberge Nicolas Flamel

*Charming and romantic restaurant in Paris' oldest house. Specializes in medieval cuisine. Your host is Nathan*
51, rue de Montmorency
75003 PARIS
Tel: 01 42 71 77 78
Email: info@paris-anglo.com

### La Belle Epoque
*New Orleans buffet*
10, place de la République
75011 PARIS
Tel: 01 43 55 44 34
Fax: 01 47 00 39 14

### La Coupole
102, Bd Montparnasse
75014 PARIS
Tel: 43 20 14 20

### La Fermette Marbeuf
5, rue Marbeuf
75008 PARIS
Tel: 01 53 23 08 00
Fax: 01 53 23 08 09

### La Gare
Chaussée de la Muette
75016 PARIS
Tel: 01 42 15 15 31
Fax: 01 42 15 15 23

### Les Grandes Marches
6, place de la Bastille
75012 PARIS
Tel: 01 43 42 90 32

### Le Grenier
34, rue de Penthièvre
75008 PARIS
Tel: 01 42 25 07 90
Owner: Mme BURGIO

### La Maison d'Alsace
39, ave des Champs Élysées
75008 PARIS
Tel: 01 53 93 97 00

### Les Ministères
30, rue du Bac
75007 PARIS
Tel: 01 42 61 22 37

### Le Moulin de la Galette
83, rue Lepic
75018 PARIS
Tel: 01 46 06 84 77
Fax: 01 42 58 11 91

### Le Muniche
9, rue Saint-Benoît
75006 PARIS
Tel: 01 42 61 12 70
Fax: 01 42 61 22 04

### Le Procope
13, rue de l'Ancienne Comédie
75006 PARIS
Tel: 01 40 46 79 00
Fax: 01 40 46 79 09

### La Robe et le Palais
13, rue des Lavandières Sainte Opportune
75001 PARIS
Tel: 01 45 08 07 41
Manager: M. Olivier SCHVIRTZ

### La Route du Fleuve
*One-day cruises, bar and restaurant on board*
Place Proslin
77000 MEULIN
Tel: 01 64 37 83 18
Fax: 01 64 37 84 53

### Le Totem
17, place du Trocadéro
75016 PARIS
Tel: 01 47 27 28 29
Fax: 01 47 27 53 01

### Pitchi Poï
*Jewish-Polish cuisine*
7, rue Caron
75004 PARIS
Tel: 01 42 77 46 15

### Restaurant Toupary
### Samaritaine

2, quai du Louvre
Magasin n°2, Samaritaine, 5th Floor
75001 PARIS
Tel: 01 40 41 29 29

### Restaurant Fauchon

26-30, place de la Madeleine
75008 PARIS
Tel: 01 47 42 60 11
Fax: 01 47 42 96 02

### Sebillon Élysées

66, rue Pierre Charon
75008 PARIS
Tel: 01 43 59 28 15
Fax: 01 43 59 30 00

### Sebillon Neuilly

20, ave Charles de Gaulle
92200 NEUILLY SUR SEINE
Tel: 01 46 24 71 31

### Thai Elephant

43-45, rue de la Roquette
75011 PARIS
Tel: 01 47 00 42 00
Fax: 01 47 00 45 44

### Tokaj

*Hungarian specialties*
57, rue du Chemin Vert
75011 PARIS
Tel: 01 47 00 64 56

### Villa Médicis

*Italian family restaurant*
11 bis, rue Saint Placide
75006 PARIS
Tel: 01 42 22 51 96
Fax: 01 45 48 47 57
Manager: M. Michel NAPOLI

### GOOD VALUE/*BON MARCHÉ*

### Aquarius

*Gastronomic vegetarian restaurant*
40, rue de Gergovie
75014 PARIS
Tel: 01 45 41 36 88

### Aux Lyonnais

32, rue Saint Marc
75002 PARIS
Tel: 01 42 96 65 04
Fax: 01 42 97 42 95
President: M. Pierre VALLEE

### Batifol Maillot

135, ave de Malakoff
75016 PARIS
Tel: 01 45 00 36 73

### Brasserie Lipp

151, Bd Saint Germain
75006 PARIS
Tel: 01 45 48 53 91

### Café du Commerce

51, rue du Commerce
75015 PARIS
Tel: 01 45 75 03 27
Fax: 01 45 75 27 40

### Chartier

7, rue du Fbg Montmartre
75009 PARIS
Tel: 01 47 70 86 29

### Chez Lucie

*Martinique and Caribbean specialties*
15, rue Augereau
75007 PARIS
Tel: 01 45 55 08 74

---

Chez Marianne

# *Chez Marianne*

*Great deli and hospitality plus art gallery (See advertisement)*
2, rue des Hospitalières Saint Gervais
75004 PARIS
Tel: 01 42 72 18 86
Web site: http://www.paris-anglo.com

---

### Cubana Café

47, rue Vavin
75006 PARIS
Tel: 01 40 46 80 81
Fax: 01 40 46 98 00

## Au Gamin de Paris

51, rue Vieille du Temple
75004 PARIS
Tel: 01 42 78 97 24

## Higuma

*Japanese restaurant*
32 bis, rue Sainte Anne
75001 PARIS
Tel: 01 47 03 38 59

## Jo Goldenberg

*Jewish delicatessen*
7, rue des Rosiers
75004 PARIS
Tel: 01 48 87 20 16

## La Petite Légume

*Vegetarian food*
36, rue des Boulangers
75005 PARIS
Tel: 01 40 46 06 85

## La Rotonde

105, Bd Montparnasse
75006 PARIS
Tel: 01 43 26 48 26
Fax: 01 43 26 68 84

## La Truffe

*Natural cuisine*
31, rue Vieille du Temple
75004 PARIS
Tel: 01 42 71 08 39

## Layali Phoenicia

*Lebanese restaurant*
170, rue Saint Martin
75003 PARIS
Tel: 01 42 77 07 77

## Le Balzar

*French traditional*
49, rue des Écoles
75005 PARIS
Tel: 01 43 54 13 67

## Le Drouot

103, rue Richelieu
75002 PARIS
Tel: 01 42 96 68 23

## Le Maharajah

*Indian cuisine*
72, Bd Saint Germain
75005 PARIS
Tel: 01 43 54 26 07
Fax: 01 40 46 08 18

## Le Pot au Feu

59, Bd Pasteur
75015 PARIS
Tel: 01 43 20 79 80

## Le Refuge des Fondues

17, rue des Trois Frères
75018 PARIS
Tel: 01 42 55 22 65
Fax: 01 42 55 22 65

## Millesimes

7, rue Lobineau
75006 PARIS
Tel: 01 46 34 22 15
Contacts: Diana et Max BRAUD

## Pub et Atelier Mustang

41, ave Lénine
92000 NANTERRE
Tel: 01 47 24 35 78
Fax: 01 47 29 07 27
Contacts: Patrick & Vincent

## Restaurant Pooja

*Authentic Indian restaurant. 85 F evening menu, lunch menu at 30 F. Vegetarian food available. Recommended in Le Monde and Gault & Millau*
91, passage Brady
75010 PARIS
Tel: 01 48 24 00 83
Owner: M. UMESHBHAT

## Trattoria Via Curti

*Italian cuisine*
79, rue de la Plaine
75020 PARIS
Tel: 01 43 73 22 78
Owner: M. Ermogene
LOSENGO

## BARS/CAFÉS
Bars/cafés

### Au Diable des Lombards

64, rue des Lombards
75001 PARIS
Tel: 01 42 33 81 84
Fax: 01 42 33 28 22

### Au Père Tranquille

16, rue Pierre Lescot
75001 PARIS
Tel: 01 45 08 00 34

### Café de Flore

172, Bd Saint Germain
75006 PARIS
Tel: 01 45 48 55 26

### Café de la Paix

12, Bd des Capucines
75009 PARIS
Tel: 01 40 07 30 20

### Coffee Parisien

5 & 8, rue Perronet
75007 PARIS
Tel: 01 40 49 08 08
Tel: 01 45 44 92 93

### Coffee Parisien

4, rue Princesse
75006 PARIS
Tel: 01 43 54 18 18

### La Tartine

24, rue de Rivoli
75004 PARIS
Tel: 01 42 72 76 8

### Le Baragouin

*Located in the heart of the Montorgueil area, Le Baragouin welcomes music, sports & pool fans with its rock, pop, trip-hop atmosphere. Cheapest Happy Hour in Paris !*
*5 pm to 2 am every day*

17, rue Tiquetonne
75002 PARIS
Tel: 01 42 36 18 93
Contact: Pascal

### Le Port d'Amsterdam

20, rue du Croissant
75002 PARIS
Tel: 01 40 39 02 63
Contact: M. Richard RODURICK

### Les Deux Magots

170, Bd Saint Germain
75006 PARIS
Tel: 01 45 48 55 25
Manager: M. DUPIN

### Les Mousquetaires

77, ave du Maine
75014 PARIS
Tel: 01 43 22 50 46
Fax: 01 40 47 67 37

### Lire Entre Les Vignes

38, rue Sedaine
75011 PARIS
Tel: 01 43 55 69 49
Contact: Mme Michelle O'BRIEN

### Willi's Wine Bar

*Fine dining with extensive wine list*

13, rue des Petits-Champs
75001 PARIS
Tel: 01 42 61 05 09
Fax: 01 47 03 36 93
Web site: http://www.aawine.com/willis

# TAXI SERVICES
## SERVICES DE TAXI

When not traveling by Metro or by foot in Paris, you'll want to grab a taxi. Note that Paris taxis are found most easily at marked Taxi Stands, train stations, and airports. Don't try to hail a taxi in the middle of the street. When you order a taxi, remember that the meter usually starts at the point in which the taxi heads to fetch you, not when you get in.

### Alpha
Tel: 01 45 85 85 85

### Business Link Taxis
*Multilingual*
Tel: 06 07 43 71 63

### London Cab in Paris
*Picks up at airports & train stations*
16, rue Chevreul
75011 PARIS
Tel: 01 43 70 18 18
Fax: 01 43 56 78 35

### Taxi Artisanal
*Personalized service*
Tel: 01 43 45 91 71
Portable: 06 11 40 19 26
Contact: Jean-Pierre RAVA

### Taxis Bleus
*Bilingual*
Tel: 01 49 36 10 10

### Taxis G7
*Credit cards accepted for more than 50 FF*
Tel: 01 47 39 47 39

List your local Taxi stands here

37

# TOURIST OFFICES
## OFFICES DE TOURISM

Here are the key tourist offices in Paris for French regions as well as European and others anglophone countries.

## FRENCH TOURIST OFFICES
### Offices de tourisme français

### Alpes Dauphiné Tourist Office

2, place André Malraux
75001 PARIS
Tel: 01 42 96 08 43
Fax: 01 42 96 08 56

### Aveyron Tourist Office

46, rue Berger
75001 PARIS
Tel: 01 42 36 84 63
Fax: 01 40 39 01 35

### Cannes Tourist Office

3, rue du Fbg Saint Honoré
75008 PARIS
Tel: 01 42 68 05 58
Fax: 01 42 68 05 56

### France Tourist Office

8, ave de l'Opéra
75001 PARIS
Tel: 01 42 96 10 23

### Franche Comté Tourist Office

2, Bd de la Madeleine
75009 PARIS
Tel: 01 42 66 26 28
Fax: 01 49 24 96 56

### Hautes Alpes Tourist Office

4, ave de l'Opéra
75001 PARIS
Tel: 01 42 96 05 08
Fax: 01 40 15 04 82

### Limousin Tourist Office

30, rue Caumartin
75009 PARIS
Tel: 01 40 07 04 67
Fax: 01 40 07 04 64

### Lorraine Tourist Office

182, rue de Rivoli
75001 PARIS
Tel: 01 44 58 94 00
Fax: 01 44 58 94 17

### Lozère Tourist Office

194 bis, rue de Rivoli
75001 PARIS
Tel: 01 44 55 33 33
Fax: 01 44 55 33 34

### Nord-Pas de Calais Tourist Office

25, rue Bleue
75009 PARIS
Tel: 01 48 00 59 62
Fax: 01 48 00 59 61

### Office du Tourisme et des Congrès de Paris

127, ave des Champs Élysées
75008 PARIS
Tel: 01 49 52 53 54
English Recording: 01 49 52 53 56
Press: 01 49 52 53 66
Fax: 01 49 52 53 00

### Périgord Tourist Office

6, rue Gomboust
75001 PARIS
Tel: 01 42 60 38 77
Fax: 01 42 60 10 09

### Poitou-Charentes Tourist Office

68, rue du Cherche Midi
75006 PARIS
Tel: 01 42 22 83 74

### Savoie Tourist Office

31, ave de l'Opéra
75001 PARIS
Tel: 01 42 61 74 73
Fax: 01 42 61 06 83

# TOURIST OFFICES

## OTHER TOURIST OFFICES
## Autres offices de tourisme

### Australian Tourist Commission
*Tourist information on Australia*
4, rue Jean Rey
75015 PARIS
Tel: 01 45 79 10 64
Fax: 01 45 79 19 07

### Austria Tourist Office
BP 475
75336 PARIS Cedex 08
Tel: 01 53 83 95 20
Fax: 01 45 61 97 67
Minitel: 3615 AUTRICHE
Web site: http://www.austria-info.at/

### Bahamas Tourist Office
60, rue Saint Lazare
75009 PARIS
Tel: 01 45 26 62 62
Fax: 01 48 74 06 05

### Belgium Tourist Office
21, Bd des Capucines
75002 PARIS
Tel: 01 47 42 41 18
Fax: 01 47 42 71 83

### Boston and Massachusetts Massport Information Center
5 bis, rue du Louvre
75001 PARIS
Tel: 01 44 77 88 07

### Canada Tourist Office
35, ave Montaigne
75008 PARIS
Tel: 01 44 43 29 00
Visas: 01 44 43 29 16
Fax: 01 44 43 29 99
Minitel: 3615 OTCAN

### Cyprus Tourist Office
15, rue de la Paix
75002 PARIS
Tel: 01 42 61 42 49
Fax: 01 42 61 65 13

### Czech Republic Tourist Office
32, ave de l'Opéra
75002 PARIS
Tel: 01 44 94 87 50
Fax: 01 49 24 99 46

### Danish Tourist Office
18, Bd Malesherbes
75008 PARIS
Tel: 01 53 43 26 26
Fax: 01 53 43 26 23

### Federal Republic of Germany Tourist Office
9, Bd de la Madeleine
75001 PARIS
Tel: 01 40 20 01 88
Fax: 01 40 20 17 00

### Finland Tourist Office
13, rue Auber
75009 PARIS
Tel: 01 42 66 40 13
Fax: 01 47 42 87 22

### Great Britain Tourist Office
19, rue des Mathurins
75009 PARIS
Tel: 01 44 51 56 20
Fax: 01 44 51 56 21
Minitel: 3615 BRITISH

### Greece Tourist Office
3, ave de l'Opéra
75001 PARIS
Tel: 01 42 60 65 75
Fax: 01 42 60 10 28

### Hong Kong Tourist Association
53, rue François Ier
75008 PARIS
Tel: 01 47 20 39 54
Fax: 01 47 23 09 65

### India Tourist Office
13, Bd Hausmann
75009 PARIS
Tel: 01 45 23 30 45
Fax: 01 45 23 33 45

# TOURIST OFFICES
OFFICES DE TOURISM

## Irish Tourist Board
33, rue de Miromesnil
75008 PARIS
Tel: 01 53 43 12 12

## Israel Tourist Office
22, rue des Capucines
75008 PARIS
Tel: 01 42 61 01 97
Fax: 01 49 27 09 46

## Italy Tourist Office
23, rue de la Paix
75002 PARIS
Tel: 01 42 66 03 96
Info: 08 36 68 26 28
Fax: 01 47 42 19 74

## Jersey Island Information Center
Tel: 03 88 94 10 20

## Monaco Tourist Office
9, rue de la Paix
75002 PARIS
Tel:  01 42 96 12 23
Fax: 01 42 61 31 52

## Morocco Tourist Office
161, rue Saint Honoré
75001 PARIS
Tel: 01 42 60 63 50
Fax: 01 40 15 97 34

## New Orleans et Puerto Rico Information Center
5 bis, rue du Louvre
75001 PARIS
Tel: 01 44 88 05 (New Orleans)
Tel: 01 44 77 88 06 (Puerto Rico)

## Northern Ireland Tourist Office
3, rue de Pontoise
78100 SAINT GERMAIN EN LAYE
Tel: 01 39 21 93 80
Fax: 01 39 21 93 90

## Poland Tourist Office
49, ave de l'Opéra
75002 PARIS
Tel: 01 47 42 07 42
Fax: 01 49 24 94 36

## Portugal Tourist Office
7, rue Scribe
75009 PARIS
Tel: 01 47 42  55  57
Fax: 01 42 66 06 89

## Singapore Tourist Office
2, place du Palais Royal
75001 PARIS
Tel: 01 42 97 16 16
Fax: 01 42 97 16 17

## South African Tourist Board
61, rue La Boétie
75008 PARIS
Tel: 01 45 61 01 97
Fax: 01 45 61 01 96

## Spain Tourist Office
43, rue Decamps
75116 PARIS
Tel: 01 45 03 82 50
Fax: 01 45 03 82 51

## Sweden Tourist Office
18, Bd Malesherbes
75008 PARIS
Tel: 01 53 43 26 27
Fax: 01 53 43 26 24

## Switzerland Tourist Office
11 bis, rue Scribe
75009 PARIS
Tel: 01 44 51 65 51
Fax: 01 47 42 43 88
Email: stparis@switzerlandtourism.ch
Web site: http://
www.switzerlandtourism.ch

## The Netherlands Tourist Office
9, rue Scribe
75009 PARIS
Tel: 01 42 25 41 25
Fax: 01 43 12 34 20

## Tunisia Tourist Office
32, ave de l'Opéra
75002 PARIS
Tel: 01 47 42 72 67
Fax: 01 47 42 52 68

## Turkish Tourist Office
102, ave des Champs Élysées
75008 PARIS
Tel: 01 45 62 78 68
Fax: 01 45 63 81 05

## United States Tourist Office
Tel: 01 42 60 57 15

# TRANSPORTATION
## TRANSPORTS

For making travel plans and reservations, whether by train, bus, ferry, barge or hot-air balloon, here's a quick reference list of key addresses.

## Aéroports de Paris
*Administration of airport authorities*
291, Bd Raspail
75675 PARIS Cedex 14
Tel: 01 43 35 70 00
Fax: 01 43 35 74 27

## Aviation Methods France
*Private planes*
Aéroport de Paris - Le Bourget
Pavillon Paul Bert
93350 LE BOURGET
Tel: 01 49 92 19 92
Fax: 01 49 92 19 90
Director: M. HOLTER

## Bateaux Mouches
*Tourist boat tours*
Port Conférence
75008 PARIS
Tel: 01 42 25 96 10
Fax: 01 42 25 02 28

## Bateaux Parisiens
*Tourist boat tours*
Port La Bourdonnais
75007 PARIS
Tel: 01 44 11 33 44

## Bombard Balloon Adventures
*Hot air balloon visits of the Loire region*
Château de Laborde
Laborde au Château
21200 BEAUNE
Tel: 03 80 26 63 30
Res: 03 80 26 63 30
Fax: 03 80 26 69 20
President: M. Buddy BOMBARD

## British Rail International
19, rue des Mathurins
75009 PARIS
Tel: 01 44 51 06 00
Fax: 01 42 66 40 43
Minitel: 3615 BRI
Contact: M. Michael CHESWORTH

## Canadian National Railway
*Canadian & US trips information & reservations*
1, rue Scribe
75009 PARIS
Tel: 01 47 42 76 50
Fax: 01 47 42 24 39

## Compagnie Transair
Zone Nord Aéroport
BP 174
93352 LE BOURGET Cedex
Tel: 01 49 92 75 75
Fax: 01 49 92 75 00
Sales Assistant: Mme Annie LEBARS

## Continental Waterways
*Barge trips in Burgundy*
1, promenade du Rhin
21000 DIJON
Tel: 03 80 53 15 45
Fax: 03 80 41 67 73
Email: cw@magic.fr
Director: M. Guy BARDET

## Deutsche Bahn
*German Railway*
13, rue d'Alsace
75010 PARIS
Tel: 01 46 07 13 40
Fax: 01 40 37 26 64

## Eurolines
*International bus and coach station in Paris*
Gare Internationale de Paris-Gallieni
28, ave du Général de Gaulle
BP 313
93170 BAGNOLET
Tel: 01 49 72 51 51
Fax: 01 49 72 51 61

## Eurostar

*High-speed passenger train linking
Paris to London via the Channel
Tunnel*
Tel: 08 36 35 35 39
Tel2: 01 42 66 40 43
Fax: 01 44 51 06 02

## Eurotunnel

*Calais headquarters*
*Information for travel through
Eurotunnel*
BP 69
62904 COQUELLES Cedex
Tel: 03 21 00 61 00
(Service Auto-Crossing)
Info: 03 21 00 69 14

## Eurotunnel

*Travel through Eurotunnel
information*
112, ave Kléber
BP 166
75770 PARIS
Tel: 01 44 05 62 00
Fax: 01 44 05 62 90
Communications Director:
Mme Dominique MAIRE

## France Montgolfières

*Hot air balloon trips, canoeing
weekends*
76, rue Balard
75015 PARIS
Tel: 01 40 60 11 23
Fax: 01 45 58 60 73
Web site: http://www.franceballoons.com
Contact: M. David LA BEAUME

## HeliFrance

*Public helicopter transport and
tourist trips*
4, ave de la Porte de Sèvres
75015 PARIS
Tel: 01 45 54 95 11
Fax: 01 45 54 18 81

## Hoverspeed

*Hydrofoil to U.K.*
165, ave de Clichy
75017 PARIS
Tel: 01 40 25 22 00
Info: 03 21 46 14 00
Toll-Free: 0 800 90 17 77

## Irish Ferries

*Crossing information & reservations*
32, rue du Quatre Septembre
75002 PARIS
Tel: 01 42 66 90 90
Fax: 01 42 66 15 80

## Northrop and Johnson

*Sale and rental of luxury boats*
13, rue Pasteur
06400 CANNES
Tel: 04 93 94 20 08
Fax: 04 93 94 42 29
Email: northrop@riviera.fr
President: M. Cornelis VAN VLIET

## P & O European Ferries

*Ferry information & reservations*
Maison de Grande-Bretagne
19, rue des Mathurins
75009 PARIS
Tel: 01 44 51 00 51

## Pullman Orient Express

*Compagnie Internationale des
Wagons-Lits et du Tourisme*
87, rue du Charolais
75012 PARIS
Tel: 01 40 19 21 21
Tel2: 01 40 19 21 02
Fax: 01 40 19 21 99
Contact: Mme Pascale CHEVALIER

## RATP

*Parisian Transport Authority*
52, quai de la Rapée
75012 PARIS
Tel: 01 44 68 20 20
Time schedules : 08 36 68 77 14
Route Info: 01 36 68 77 14
Minitel: 3615 RATP

### Sealink Voyages
*Ferry crossing information &
reservation*
23, rue Louis le Grand
75002 PARIS
Tel: 01 44 94 40 40
Fax: 01 42 65 10 17

## SNCF
23, ave de la Porte d'Aubervilliers
75018 PARIS
Admin: 01 40 37 17 76
Info: 01 53 90 20 20 (Ile de France)
Info: 08 36 35 35 35 (Grandes lignes)
Minitel: 3615 SNCF

## Vedettes de Paris
*Tourist boat tours and rentals*
Port de Suffren
75007 PARIS
Tel: 01 47 05 71 29
Fax: 01 47 05 74 53

## Vedettes du Pont-Neuf
*Tourist boat tours*
1, Square du Vert Galant
75001 PARIS
Tel: 01 46 33 98 38

*TRAVEL & TOURISM*

43

# TRAVEL AGENCIES
## AGENCES DE VOYAGE

Travel agencies in Paris that can respond to your travel needs are highly valuable addresses. Whether you need tickets to get to France or to fly home or are simply looking for great travel ideas from Paris, these contacts are dedicated to providing quality solutions for all budgets.

### Access Voyages
6, rue Pierre Lescot
75001 PARIS
Tel: 01 44 76 84 50
Fax: 01 42 21 44 20
Minitel: 3615 ACCESSVOYAGE

### Aclat Multitour
202, rue de Rivoli
75001 PARIS
Tel: 01 42 60 82 09
Fax: 01 49 27 94 32
Director: M. CHARPENTIER

### African Safari Club
13, rue des Pyramides
75001 PARIS
Tel: 01 42 86 53 55
Fax: 01 42 86 53 64
Director: Mme Marie-France CANZANO

### Agence Airliner
14, rue Crussol
75011 PARIS
Tel: 01 43 38 34 34
Fax: 01 43 38 01 65
Director: M. MEZRAHI

### Agence Solari
111, ave Victor Hugo
75016 PARIS
Tel: 01 47 04 93 93
Fax: 01 47 27 48 54
Director: Mme Martine DELCOURT

### Antipodes Découvertes
16, rue Notre Dame de Lorette
75009 PARIS
Tel: 01 44 91 99 00
Fax: 01 44 91 92 49
Director: M. BOITIER

### Any Way
46, rue des Lombards
75001 PARIS
Tel: 01 40 28 00 74
Fax: 01 42 36 11 41
Communications Director:
Mme Patricia AVELINE

### Association France-Ontario
Allée de Clotemont
77183 CROISSY BEAUBOURG
Tel: 01 60 06 44 50
Fax: 01 60 05 03 45
Contact: Mme Christine SCARANO

### Australie Tours
129, rue Lauriston
75016 PARIS
Tel: 01 45 53 58 39
Fax: 01 47 55 95 93
Director: M. RIDET

### Blue Marble Travel
2, rue Dussoubs
75002 PARIS
Tel: 01 42 36 02 34
Fax: 01 42 21 14 77
Director: M. Nicolas CLIFFORD

### Canada Welcome
24, Bd Port Royal
75005 PARIS
Tel: 01 43 37 43 96
Fax: 01 47 07 16 96
Contact: Mme Nathalie SAUREL

### Canadien National
1, rue Scribe
75009 PARIS
Tel: 01 47 42 76 50
Fax: 01 47 42 24 39
Director: M. Pierre BRICOUT

### Carlson Wagonlit Travel
168, rue du Fbg Saint Honoré
75904 PARIS Cedex 15
Tel: 01 41 33 68 66
Info: 01 41 33 64 64
Minitel: 3615 CARLSON
President: M. PLLARUELUO

### Cash & Go
34, ave des Champs Élysées
75009 PARIS
Tel: 01 53 93 63 63
Fax: 01 42 89 65 33
Director: M. FUMAT

# TRAVEL AGENCIES
## AGENCES DE VOYAGE

### CIT

3, Bd des Capucines
75002 PARIS
Tel: 01 44 51 39 51
Fax: 01 42 66 54 57
Email: natale.Gjordano@wanadoo.fr
Director: Mme Adriana MOUGENOT

### Club Méditerranée

25, rue de Cambrais
75597 PARIS Cedex 19
Tel: 01 53 35 35 53
Fax: 01 53 35 36 16
Minitel: 3615 CLUB MED
Web site: http://www.clubmed.com

### Council Travel Services

22, rue des Pyramides
75001 PARIS
Tel: 01 44 55 55 65
Fax: 01 44 55 55 56
Minitel: 3615 COUNCIL
Web site: http://www.ctfciee.org

### CTS Voyages

20, rue des Carmes
75005 PARIS
Tel: 01 43 25 00 76
Fax: 01 43 54 48 98

### Fédération des Pourvoyeurs du Québec

20, rue du Château
95320 SAINT LEU LA FORET
Tel: 01 34 18 18 18
Fax: 01 34 18 18 00
Director: M. René POITRAS

### Fram Voyages

128, rue de Rivoli
75001 PARIS
Tel: 01 40 26 30 31
Fax: 01 40 26 30 32
Director: M. Claude RAIMBAULT

### Frantour

7, rue Pablo Neruda
92532 LEVALLOIS PERRET Cedex
Tel: 01 45 19 12 00
Fax: 01 45 19 14 41

### Forum Voyages

Headquarters
113, ave de Verdun
92441 ISSY LES MOULINEAUX
Tel: 01 46 43 71 43
Fax: 01 46 43 71 77
Minitel: 3615 FV

### Gulliver's Travel Agency

80, ave Marceau
75008 PARIS
Tel: 01 47 23 53 03
Fax: 01 47 23 53 55
Director: Mme SHEPPARD

### Holt Paris Welcome Service

12, rue Helder
75009 PARIS
Tel: 01 45 23 08 14
Fax: 01 42 47 19 89
Email: holt@club-internet.fr
Directors: Susan & Alan HOLT

### Intairline

*Message to future travelers: you can afford our lite air fares from France to USA or 5 continents. Call!*
28, rue Delambre
75014 PARIS
Tel: 01 43 20 90 46
Fax:01 43 21 85 15
Minitel: 3615 RLINES
Email: interline@magic.fr
Web site:
http://www.//interresa.ca/ta/rlines//fr//
Director: M. Robert GIARRATANO

### Jet Set Voyage

41-45, rue de Galilée
75116 PARIS
Tel: 01 53 67 13 00
Fax: 01 53 67 13 29
Director: M. Fici ERMANO

### Jet Tours

19, ave de Tourville
75007 PARIS
Tel: 01 47 05 01 95
Fax: 01 45 50 41 57
Director: Mme Annie BOSIO

## La Balade du Monde

99, rue de Sèvres
75006 PARIS
Tel: 01 45 49 47 49
Fax: 01 45 49 37 87
Contact: Mme Tonthat HONG LANG

## Look Voyages

6, rue Marbeuf
75008 PARIS
Tel: 01 44 31 84 22
Fax: 01 44 31 84 40
Minitel: 3615 LOOK
Director: Mme Valérie ROUET

## Maison des Amériques

4, rue Chapon
75003 PARIS
Tel: 01 42 77 50 50
Fax:01 42 77 50 60
Minitel: 3615 MDA
Director: M. ANTAS

## Non Stop USA

*For all your business and leisure travel. Specialists in travel arrangements to the USA. Attractive prices and quality service*
7, rue Berryer
75008 PARIS
Tel: 01 53 93 75 00
Fax: 01 45 62 02 10
Director: M. Mario CASSUTO

## Nouveau Monde

8, rue Mabillon
75006 PARIS
Tel: 01 43 29 40 80
Fax:01 53 73 78 81
Director: M. François MOREAU

## Pacific Holidays

34, ave du Général Leclerc
75014 PARIS
Tel: 01 45 41 52 58
Fax: 01 45 39 49 06
Director: M. François GUSTINI

## Planète Havas

26, ave de l'Opéra
75001 PARIS
Tel: 01 53 29 40 00
Fax: 01 47 03 32 13
Director: M. GUIVARC'H

## The French Company - Creative Tour

*Specialized in tours to France*
37, rue Chanzy
75011 PARIS
Tel: 01 40 09 07 10
Fax: 01 43 79 70 99
Email: info@creativetour.com
Director: Mme Catherine LONGEAU

## Tourism Consulting Group

34, ave Général Leclerc
75014 PARIS
Tel: 01 45 39 61 10
Fax: 01 45 39 49 06
Director: M. François AGIUSTINI

## Travel Store

14, Bd de la Madeleine
75009 PARIS
Tel: 01 53 05 20 00

## Usit Voyages

85, Bd Saint Michel
75005 PARIS
Tel: 01 43 29 69 50
Fax: 01 43 25 29 85
Minitel: 3615 USIT
Communications Director:
Mme Corinne COTTEBRUNE

## Usit Voyages

12, rue Vivienne
75002 PARIS
Tel: 01 42 44 14 00
Minitel: 3615 USIT
Contact: Mme Jane WHIBLEY

## Vacances Air Canada

10, rue de la Paix
75002 PARIS
Tel: 01 40 15 15 15
Fax: 01 42 61 68 81
Commercial Director:
Mme Rose-Marie FARRUGIA

## Vacances Air Transat

43, Bd Richard Lenoir
75011 PARIS
Tel: 01 43 55 44 11
Fax: 01 43 55 41 59
Director: M. Jean-Marc BATTA

*TRAVEL & TOURISM*

47

### Venise Simplon Orient Express

75, ave des Champs Elysées
75008 PARIS
Tel: 01 45 62 00 69

### Via Voyages

26, rue de la Pépinière
75008 PARIS
Tel: 01 44 70 03 61
Fax: 01 43 87 50 94
Director: M. Christian MARTIN

### Voyageurs aux USA/ Voyageurs au Canada

55, rue Sainte Anne
75002 PARIS
Tel: 01 42 86 17 30
Voyageurs en Australie: 01 42 86 16 00
Voyageurs en Inde: 01 42 86 16 90
Fax: 01 42 60 35 44
Web site: http://www.vdm.com

### Wingate Travel

19 bis, rue du Mont Thabor
75001 PARIS
Tel: 01 44 77 30 16
Fax: 01 44 77 30 26
Director: M. SPATAFORA

### World Media

*Online travel information*
82, rue Beaubourg
75003 PARIS
Tel: 01 44 54 27 80
Fax: 01 42 72 95 01
Email: info@worldmedia.fr
Web site: http://www.worldmedia.fr/travel
Director: M. Bertrand PEQERIE

48

# USEFUL NUMBERS
## RENSEIGNEMENTS PRATIQUES

Here's a quick reference page for your Travel & Tourism needs in Paris. Don't hesitate to add your own numbers or to share with the Editors your most reliable numbers. For emergencies, see Emergency Numbers at the back of directory.

### Air France Inter-Airport Bus Service
Tel: 01 41 56 78 00

### Air France Vaccination Center
Tel: 01 41 56 66 00

---

### Boutique Michelin, Maps and Guides

32, ave de l'Opéra
75002 PARIS
Tel: 01 42 68 05 20
Web site: http://www.michelin.fr
Contac: M. Philippe DUMONCEAU

---

### Élysées 1212
*Free booking service for hotels, restaurants, cabarets and cruises*
Tel: 01 43 59 12 12

### Lost Eurocard/Mastercard/ Mastercharge
Tel: 01 45 67 47 67

### Lost/Stolen American Express Card
Tel: 01 47 77 72 00

### Lost/Stolen Carte Bleue or Visa Card
Tel: 01 42 77 11 90

### Lost/Stolen Diner's Club Card
Tel: 01 47 62 75 75

### Objets Trouvés - Lost and Found
36, rue des Morillons
75015 PARIS
Tel: 01 45 31 14 80

### Orly Airport Information
Tel: 01 49 75 15 15
Info: 01 49 75 52 52

### Roissy Charles de Gaulle Airport
Tel: 01 48 62 12 12

### Tourist Office of Paris
*Recording in English*
Tel: 01 49 52 53 56

### Train Info SNCF
Info: 01 53 90 20 20
Res: 3615 SNCF

### W.T.A.
*Runs French Travel Gallery Website, publisher of FAQ Travel in France Net-letter*
1, place Alphonse Jourdain
31000 TOULOUSE
Tel: 05 63 40 17 47
Fax: 05 63 41 83 80
Email: webmaster@bonjour.com
Web site: http://www.bonjour.com
Director: M. Thierry TONIUTTI

### Youth Hostel Office
Tel: 01 43 57 55 60
Fax: 01 40 21 79 92

# DOING BUSINESS & WORKING

Whether you have visited France a little or a lot as a tourist, you are in for a whole new French experience if you have decided to work here or do business with the French. Besides the obvious language and monetary differences, you will have to navigate in very deep cultural waters, and stir through complex tides of administrative structures, fiscal eddies and financial whirlpools. On the whole, for those of you used to an Anglo-American commercial environment, be prepared for some heavy turbulence, as you learn the ups and downs of Doing Business in France. On the cultural side, remember a few key points: the French are motivated by a lot more than money. Being too fast, too abrupt, too hasty, and too direct will not necessarily help you make lasting and valuable business relationships, close on contracts, or gain success. French business culture has its own logic: so learn it – you are not at home.

## GOOD NEWS

Here is some good news and bad news on Doing Business and Working in France.

On the upside, the French, it can be said, have excellent schools including those highly prestigous *grandes écoles*. The bad news is that the French tend to lack initiative and an entrepreneurial spirit. Fiscally and administratively, the good news is that the system here offers greater protection for its employees, and reflects greater respect for the basic needs of its citizens. The bad news is that taxes are high, hidden fees are prevalent, and compliance is expensive and heavy on paperwork. Be prepared to spend a lot more time and money for accounting and administrative tasks than you have been used to alloting elsewhere. Financially, the good news is that French society offers a lot of security, protection, and stability. The bad news is that the French take little capital risk and bankers tend to lend only to those who don't really need it.

To help you get through it, PARIS-ANGLOPHONE has brought together a battery of valuable contacts, services, leads, and solution-providers in the 27 areas that follow.

Whether you're here to start your own company or are working for someone else, adapting to the larger cultural differences will be the key to prospering in your professional endeavors in France.

# ACCOUNTING
## EXPERTISE COMPTABLE

Much of French commercial activity revolves around issues concerning accounting. Thus, the importance of the accountant in France should not be underestimated. Here is a mixed list of large and less-large accounting firms in Paris handling diverse issues including standard bookkeeping, annual reports, tax issues, value-added tax, social security and employment formalities, etc.

## Accountemps
17, rue Jean Mermoz
75008 PARIS
Tel: 01 45 63 08 01
Fax: 01 45 63 08 45
Director: M. VAN DE VOORDE

## Anderson Consulting et Cie
55, ave Georges V
75008 PARIS Cedex 379
Tel: 01 53 23 55 55
Fax: 01 53 23 53 23

## Arthur D. Little France
15, rue Galvani
75017 PARIS
Tel: 01 40 55 29 00
Fax: 01 40 55 08 80
Director: M. Éric BELOT

## Cabinet Cassien
6, rue de Sfax
75116 PARIS
Tel: 01 45 00 10 10
Fax: 01 45 01 98 77
Contact: M. Olivier CASSIEN

## Cantor, Gary
*Bilingual financial consultant*
6, rue Crétet
75009 PARIS
Tel: 01 48 78 08 47
Fax: 01 42 85 45 59

## CCAS (Cabinet Angleys Saint Pierre International)
12, rue de Madrid
75008 PARIS
Tel: 01 53 42 41 00
Fax: 01 45 22 78 87
Partner: M. ANGLEYS

## Coopers & Lybrand
32, rue Guersant
75017 PARIS
Tel: 01 45 72 80 00
Fax: 01 45 72 22 19
President: M. P. B. ANGLADE

## Deloitte Touche Tohmatsu
185, ave Charles de Gaulle
92200 NEUILLY SUR SEINE
Tel: 01 40 88 28 00
Fax: 01 40 88 28 28
Contact: M. Hervé BARDON

## Ernst & Young
Tour Manhattan
6, place de l'Iris
92095 PARIS LA DÉFENSE 2 Cedex 21
Tel: 01 46 93 60 00
Fax: 01 47 76 20 33

## Ex Com
48, Bd des Batignolles
75017 PARIS
Tel: 01 44 90 84 00
Fax: 01 44 70 96 10

## Factofrance Heller
Tour Facto
18, rue Hoche
92988 PARIS LA DÉFENSE Cedex 88
Tel: 01 46 35 70 00
Fax: 01 46 35 69 00
President: M. Michel AUSSAVY

## Gregory Smith & Associates
*US accounting tax returns. 13 yrs. experience w/ IRS + Big Six firms. Solid references*
10, rue Duphot
75001 PARIS
Tel: 01 42 60 89 89
Fax: 01 42 60 27 77
Director: M. Gregory SMITH

# ACCOUNTING
## EXPERTISE COMPTABLE

### Inter Audit
21 bis, rue Lord Byron
75008 PARIS
Tel: 01 43 59 58 73
Fax: 01 42 89 14 02
Director: M. R. J. TWIST

### Lavigne Cogéval et Associés
159, rue de Rome
75017 PARIS
Tel: 01 42 27 24 10
Fax: 01 42 27 80 15

### Okoshken, Samuel
*Income tax, property, setting up a business in France*
51, ave Montaigne
75008 PARIS
Tel: 01 44 13 69 50
Fax: 01 45 63 24 96

### Price Waterhouse
Tour AIG
34, place des Corolles
92908 PARIS LA DÉFENSE Cedex 105
Tel: 01 41 26 16 00
Fax: 01 41 26 16 16
President: M. Joël GARLOT

### Raymond Chabot International
Tour Framatome
La Défense 6
92084 PARIS LA DÉFENSE Cedex 16
Tel: 01 47 96 63 90
Fax: 01 47 96 63 96
Director: M. Yves LABAT

### Richard A. Van Ham
74, ave Marceau
75008 PARIS
Tel: 01 47 23 89 12
Fax: 01 47 20 15 07

### Sefico
65, ave Kléber
75116 PARIS
Tel: 01 47 27 65 98
Fax: 01 47 04 97 84
Manager: M. Yves-Marie MORIN

### Smith Barney
7, place Vendôme
75001 PARIS
Tel: 01 42 96 10 66
Fax: 01 42 96 22 81
Manager: M. PINCHART-DENY

### Sogecc
12, rue Yves Toudic
75010 PARIS
Tel: 01 53 72 72 72
Fax: 01 53 72 72 73
President: M. Jean-Claude HAGEGE

### Tucker Anthony Inc.
5 bis, rue du Louvre
75001 PARIS
Tel: 01 42 61 57 68
Fax: 01 40 20 96 88
Manager: M. Hilary Gordon EDWARDS

54

# ADVERTISING/MARKETING
## PUBLICITÉ/MARKETING

Under the large banner of advertising and marketing PARIS-ANGLOPHONE brings together most of the key firms creating advertising and communications campaigns as well as companies specializing in advertising representation, direct marketing, cross-cultural communications, strategy planning, media buying, and public relations and promotion. For reference purposes, the publications *Stratégies* and *CB News* specialize in covering these fields.

### Agence Alabama
11, rue Moreau Vauthier
92100 BOULOGNE BILLANCOURT
Tel: 01 46 04 45 04
Tel2: 01 46 04 28 18

### Agence Annie Schneider
110-114, rue Jules Guesde
92300 LEVALLOIS PERRET
Tel: 01 47 31 46 47
Fax: 01 47 31 99 05

### Agence Marketbase

## MARKETBASE

*Marketing + communications -
Research, promotional campaigns,
trade rep, PR, direct mail,
advertising*
107, ave La Bourdonnais
75007 PARIS
Tel: 01 45 51 36 03
Fax: 01 47 53 72 85
Email: 100744.2447@compuserve
Director: Mme Johanna STOBBS

### Agence Transatlantique
170, rue du Fbg Saint Antoine
75012 PARIS
Tel: 01 40 09 89 62
Fax: 01 40 09 92 66

### AJIF

*Production of customised
marketing publications, marketing
events and electronic databases
for use on the Internet*
44, rue de Laborde
75008 PARIS
Tel: 01 43 87 19 41
Fax: 01 43 87 00 46
Email: furtado@ibm.net
Web site: http://www.ajif.com
Director: M. Adrian FURTADO

### Ammirati-Puris-Lintas
22, rue Faidherbe
75011 PARIS
Tel: 01 55 25 55 25
Fax: 01 55 25 55 55
President: M. Alain LAURENS

### Austin Knight
26, ave de l'Opéra
75001 PARIS
Tel: 01 53 45 11 11
Fax: 01 53 45 11 39

### Bates France
11, rue Galvani
75017 PARIS
Tel: 01 44 09 59 59
Fax: 01 45 74 08 06

## BDDP

162, rue de Billancourt
92100 BOULOGNE BILLANCOURT
Tel: 01 49 09 70 10
Fax: 01 48 25 04 19
Web site: http://www.bddp.fr
Chairman Worlwide: Jean-Marie DRU

## Bell Treasure Halas (B.T.H.)

14, Bd Sébastopol
75004 PARIS
Tel: 01 42 71 40 90
Fax: 01 42 71 10 12

## Bood & Partners

152, rue Saint Honoré
75001 PARIS
Tel: 01 42 96 62 27
Fax: 01 42 86 92 14
Director: M. Maurice BOOD

## Bordelais Lemeunier Leo Burnett (B.L.L.B.)

122, rue Édouard Vaillant
92300 LEVALLOIS PERRET
Tel: 01 41 49 73 00
Fax: 01 41 05 09 99
President: M. Jacques BORDELAIS

## Bureau International de Relations Publiques (B.I.R.P.)

17, ave Ledru Rollin
75012 PARIS
Tel: 01 53 17 11 40
Fax: 01 53 17 11 45
Director: M. Jean-Pascal JEGU

## Burson-Marsteller

*PR/communication agency*
11, rue Paul Baudry
75008 PARIS
Tel: 01 42 99 93 93
Fax: 01 40 74 07 14
President: Mme S. SAUVAGE

## CLM-BBDO

2, allée Moulineaux
92130 ISSY LES MOULINEAUX
Tel: 01 41 23 41 23
Fax: 01 41 23 43 70
Web site: http://www.bll.com
President: M. Alain POIREE

56

## CM&O

MARKETING OPERATIONNEL

Vélizy Espace
Immeuble Nungesser
13, ave Morane-Saulnier BP 259
78147 VÉLIZY Cedex
Tel: 01 34 58 29 29
Fax: 01 34 58 29 20
Email: gch@cmeo.com
Web site: http://www.cmeo.com
Director: M. Gilles CHAUVEAUX

## Colorado

71, rue Chardon Lagache
75016 PARIS
Tel: 01 45 27 80 00
Fax: 01 45 27 49 39

## Company Revolver

8, Bd de la Madeleine
75009 PARIS
Tel: 01 53 43 89 09
Fax: 01 53 43 89 00

## Copywrite

1, passage Brady
75010 PARIS
Tel: 01 42 02 48 53
Fax: 01 42 38 14 08
Director: M. John FARR

## D.D.B. Needham Worldwide

55, rue d'Amsterdam
75391 PARIS Cedex 08
Tel: 01 53 32 60 00
Fax: 01 45 26 43 51
President: M. BROSSARD

## D'Arcy Masius Benton & Bowles (DMB&B)

20, rue des Jardins
92601 ASNIERES Cedex
Tel: 01 46 88 10 10
Fax: 01 46 88 10 19

## Data Research Publications

6, rue Mignard
75116 PARIS
Tel: 01 45 03 02 72
Fax: 01 45 03 02 96
Manager: M. Pascal DUMAS

## Duboi

22, rue Paul Vaillant-Couturier
92300 LEVALLOIS PERRET
Tel: 01 47 57 69 69
Fax: 01 47 57 69 64
Email: asimkine@imaginet.fr
Web site: http://www.imaginet.fr/~duboi
Contact: M. Antoine SIMKINE

## Dun & Bradstreet International

Immeuble Défense Bergères
345, ave Georges Clémenceau
92882 NANTERRE Cedex 9
Tel: 01 41 35 17 00
Fax: 01 41 35 17 77
Director:
M. Bruno LEPROU DE LA RIVIERE

## Essentiel Communication

*Public Relations*
6, rue de la Victoire 75009 PARIS
Tel: 01 49 95 96 96
Fax: 01 49 95 97 16
Director: M. Oliver WOOTON

## Euro RSCG Havas Advertising

84, rue de Villiers
92683 LEVALLOIS PERRET Cedex
Tel: 01 41 34 34 34
Fax: 01 41 34 45 67
President: M. Alain DE POUZILHAC

## Gallaher France

77-79, rue Marcel Dassault
92773 BOULOGNE Cedex
Tel: 01 47 61 97 97
Fax: 01 47 61 93 95
Director: M. BIEHLER

## Grey Promotion

63 bis, rue de Sèvres
92514 BOULOGNE Cedex
Tel: 01 46 84 85 00
Fax: 01 46 84 00 18
Director: Mme LÉCUYER

## Havas Media International

78, ave Raymond Poincaré
75016 PARIS
Tel: 01 45 01 54 55
Fax: 01 45 01 64 02

## Hill and Knowlton

*Public relations*
42, ave Raymond Poincaré
75116 PARIS
Tel: 01 44 05 28 00
Fax: 01 45 00 23 69

## IDSI Novaction

Le Doublon, Bâtiment A
11, ave Dubonnet
92407 COURBEVOIE Cedex
Tel: 01 49 04 43 33
Fax: 01 43 34 81 39
Email: amaury.debeaumont@novaction.
infonet.com

## Image & Fonction

*Corporate communications, sales
tools, clients: Kroll, Société Générale, American Club*
6, rue des Bauches
75016 PARIS
Tel: 01 40 50 03 26
Fax: 01 42 24 18 43
Email:
100071.2312@compuserve.com
Owner: Mme Pamela WESSON

## Information et Entreprise

*Public relations*
7, rue du Pasteur Wagner
75011 PARIS
Tel: 01 49 29 12 12
Fax: 01 48 06 55 65
Director: M. BEAUDOIN

## Infratest Burke

78-80, ave du Général de Gaulle
Tour Galliéni 1
93174 BAGNOLET Cedex
Tel: 01 49 72 51 00
Fax: 01 49 72 51 06

## J. Walter Thompson

35, rue Baudin
92593 LEVALLOIS PERRET
Tel: 01 41 05 80 00
Fax: 01 41 05 80 05
Director: M. Daniel COLÉ

## LLI Promotion

11 bis, rue Baliat
92400 COURBEVOIE
Tel: 01 47 68 50 54
Fax: 01 43 34 18 24

## Louis Harris France

*US polling institute*
46, rue de l'Échiquier
75010 PARIS
Tel: 01 55 33 20 00
Fax: 01 55 33 20 20

## Madison

3, rue Troyon
75017 PARIS
Tel: 01 47 64 04 45
Fax: 01 47 66 43 69

## McCann-Erikson

48, rue de Villiers
92309 LEVALLOIS PERRET Cedex
Tel: 01 47 59 34 56
Fax: 01 47 48 07 57
President: M. Claude DOUCE

## Nielsen

9, ave des Trois Fontaines
95007 CERGY PONTOISE Cedex
Tel: 01 34 41 44 44
Fax: 01 30 38 60 77
President: M. Jean-Jacques MEYER

## ODA - Régie Publicitaire des Annuaires France -Télécom

7, ave de la Cristallerie
92317 SÈVRES Cedex
Tel: 01 46 23 30 00
Fax: 01 46 23 32 86

## Ogilvy & Mather

40, ave George V
75008 PARIS
Tel: 01 53 23 30 00
Fax: 01 53 23 30 20
Email: ogilvy@club-internet.fr
President: M. Daniel SICOURI

## Paul Krob Media Representation

*Foreign publications Media repre-
sentative and advertising advisor
Rep for Time Magazine classifieds*
20, allée Darius Milhaud
75019 PARIS
Tel: 01 42 41 22 64
Fax: 01 42 41 22 64
Director: M. Paul KROB

## Payrat & Associé

9, rue Denis Poisson
75017 PARIS
Tel: 01 53 26 21 21
Fax: 01 41 10 47 47

## Peaux Rouges

17, rue Hermel
75018 PARIS
Tel: 01 42 59 19 00
Fax: 01 42 59 18 48
Web site: http://www.didactique.com

## Promosalons

45, ave George V
75008 PARIS
Tel: 01 47 20 93 79
Fax: 01 40 70 11 31
Email: 106137.1077@compuserve.com

## Publicis

133, ave des Champs Élysées
75008 PARIS
Tel: 01 44 43 70 00
Fax: 01 44 43 75 25
Web site: http://www.publicis.fr
Communications Director:
Mme Laurence REY

## Ray Lampard International Media

*Media consultant and publications
advertising representation*
6, rue Bertin-Poirée
75001 PARIS
Tel: 01 40 28 01 19
Tel2: 01 40 28 91 84
Fax: 01 40 26 34 33
Email: intmedia@worldnet.fr
Director: M. Ray LAMPARD

### Romance, Alan
97, rue Vieille du Temple
75003 PARIS
Tel: 01 42 71 71 32
Fax: 01 42 71 12 86
Director: M. Alan ROMANCE

### Rouge Comme Une Pivoine
1, rue Chabanais
75002 PARIS
Tel: 01 42 97 42 87
Fax: 01 42 74 63 01
Contact: M. Gérald MORALES

### Saatchi & Saatchi Advertising
30, Bd Vital-Bouhot
92521 NEUILLY SUR SEINE Cedex
Tel: 01 40 88 40 00
Fax: 01 47 47 97 99

### Saatchi & Saatchi Business Communications Group
3, Bd Georges Seurat
92523 NEUILLY SUR SEINE Cedex
Tel: 01 40 88 80 00
Fax: 01 46 40 19 41
Director: M. Christian LARGER

### Smartech Company
54, rue Moxouris
78150 LE CHESNAY
Tel: 01 39 63 30 60
Fax: 01 39 55 10 02
Director: Mme Martine MANDAR

### Spinnaker Communication
96, ave du Géneral Leclerc
92100 BOULOGNE
Tel: 01 48 25 44 55
Email: silber@spinnaker.fr
Web site: http://www.spinnaker.fr
President: Mme Denise SILBER

### TBWA
25, rue du Pont-Neuf
75001 PARIS
Tel: 01 40 41 58 59
Fax: 01 40 26 62 50
Chairman: M. Jacques LEVY

### Teatime Communications
43 bis, rue d'Hautpoul
75019 PARIS
Tel: 01 42 40 14 00
Fax: 01 42 40 77 67
Director: M. Daniel BISSON

### Text Appeal International
113, rue des Pyrénées
75020 PARIS
Tel: 01 43 56 74 75
Fax: 01 43 56 80 84
President: M. Elliot H. POLAK

### The Media Partnership France
149, quai Stalingrad
92130 ISSY LES MOULINEAUX
Tel: 01 40 93 08 09
Fax: 01 40 93 08 21

### William H. Wainwright Business and Financial Communication
*Communication, advertising*
9, rue de la Croix Blanche
78610 SAINT LÉGER EN YVELINES
Tel: 01 34 86 36 12
Fax: 01 34 86 36 13
Managing Partner: M. W.H. WAINWRIGHT

### Work in Progress
57, rue Labrouste
75015 PARIS
Tel: 01 48 28 44 44
Fax: 01 48 28 31 31

### World Gold Council
1, ave Bertie Albrecht
75008 PARIS
Tel: 01 49 53 04 61
Fax: 01 49 53 04 67
Manager: M. François DE LASSUS

### Young & Rubicam France
23, allée Maillasson
BP 73
92105 BOULOGNE Cedex
Tel: 01 46 84 33 33
Fax: 01 46 84 32 70
Fax: 01 46 84 32 72
Director: M. Etienne BOISROND

# BANKING
## BANQUES

Banking in France, perhaps even more so than elsewhere, is facilitated by reliable contacts. Here, PARIS-ANGLOPHONE has assembled many of the most important banking institutions working with the anglophone community, organized separately under the sub-headings Commercial Banking and Retail Banking.

### COMMERCIAL BANKING
### Banques d'affaires

### ABN Amro Bank
3, ave Hoche
75008 PARIS
Tel: 01 42 67 50 50
Fax: 01 42 67 48 40
Director: M. Maggiel SCALONGNE

### Australia & New Zealand Banking Group
6, rue de Berri
75008 PARIS
Tel: 01 40 75 05 37
Fax: 01 40 75 05 46
General Manager:
M. Maurice LEMOINE

### Bank of America
43-47, ave de la Grande Armée
75782 PARIS Cedex 16
Tel: 01 45 02 68 00
Fax: 01 45 01 77 89
Senior Vice-President:
M. Christian BARTHOLIN

### Bank of Boston
104, ave des Champs Élysées
75008 PARIS
Tel: 01 40 76 75 00
Fax: 01 40 76 75 95
Director: M. Peter JETON

### Bank of India
3, rue Scribe
75009 PARIS
Tel: 01 42 66 50 04
Fax: 01 42 66 50 06
Director: M. S. GOEL

### Bank of New York
36, Bd Haussmann
75009 PARIS
Tel: 01 42 46 26 25
Fax: 01 42 47 02 36
Director: Mme Deirdre PEYROUX

### Bankers Trust Company
12-14, Rond-Point des Champs Élysées
BP 649-08
75367 PARIS Cedex 08
Tel: 01 42 99 30 00
Fax: 01 42 89 02 92
President: M. ATTALI

### Banque Audi France
73, ave des Champs Élysées
75008 PARIS
Tel: 01 42 25 75 00
Fax: 01 42 56 09 74
Director: M. Yves KUEHN

### Banque Française Du Commerce Extérieur
21, Bd Haussmann
75009 PARIS
Tel: 01 48 00 48 00
Fax: 01 45 23 10 56
International Director: M. Erik LESCAR

### Banque de France
39, rue Croix-des-Petits-Champs
75001 PARIS
Tel: 01 42 92 42 92
Fax: 01 42 96 04 23
Governor: M. Jean-Claude TRICHET

### Banque Indosuez
96, Bd Haussmann
75008 PARIS
Tel: 01 44 20 20 20
Fax: 01 44 20 29 56
Vice-President: M. M. MAURIN

### Banque Paribas
3, rue d'Antin
75002 PARIS
Tel: 01 42 98 12 34
Fax: 01 42 98 11 42
Communications Director:
Mme Véronique GUILLOT-PELPEL

## Banque Sanpaolo

52, ave Hoche
75382 PARIS Cedex 08
Tel: 01 47 54 40 40
Fax: 01 47 54 46 57
Mkt Director: M. CHEDVILLE

## Banque Woolwich

Headquarters
9, rue Boudreau
75009 PARIS
Tel: 01 42 68 42 68
Fax: 01 47 42 72 72
Director: M. Alain MARCEL

## Banque Wormser Frères

11 bis, Bd Haussmann
75009 PARIS
Tel: 01 47 70 90 80
Fax: 01 47 70 37 79
President: M. André WORMSER

## Barclays Bank

21, rue Laffitte
75009 PARIS
Tel: 01 44 79 79 79
Fax: 01 44 79 72 52
Intl Deputy Director:
M. Arnaud DE MASCAREL

## Baring Brothers

49, ave d'Iéna
75116 PARIS
Tel: 01 53 67 11 11
Fax: 01 53 67 11 22

## Chase Manhattan Bank

Washington Plaza
40-42, rue de Washington
75408 PARIS Cedex 08
Tel: 01 53 77 10 00
Fax: 01 53 77 10 50
President: M. BARTHOLIN

## Citibank International plc

Citicenter
19, Le Parvis
92073 PARIS LA DÉFENSE
Tel: 01 49 06 10 10
Minitel: 3615 CITIBANK

## Commerzbank

3, place de l'Opéra
75002 PARIS
Tel: 01 44 94 17 00
Fax: 01 44 94 18 00

## Deutsche Bank

3, ave de Friedland
75008 PARIS
Tel: 01 44 95 64 00
Fax: 01 53 75 07 01

## Deutsche Morgan Grenfell

3, ave Friedland
75008 PARIS
Tel: 01 53 75 05 90
Fax: 01 44 95 67 00
Directors:
 MM. CHENARD & PANDRAUD

## Discount Bank

16, ave Kléber
75016 PARIS
Tel: 01 45 01 23 00
Fax: 01 45 01 58 10

## Goldman Sachs Paris Inc & Cie

2, rue de Thann
75017 PARIS
Tel: 01 42 12 11 00
Fax: 01 42 12 11 99
Web site: http://www.gs.com
Contact: M. HEFES

## J.P. Morgan & Cie

14, place Vendôme
75001 PARIS
Tel: 01 40 15 45 00
Fax: 01 40 15 44 77
President: M. J. AIGRAIN

## Kleinwort Benson France

11, ave Myron Herrick
75008 PARIS
Tel: 01 44 95 05 05
Fax: 01 42 89 87 36

## Lazard Frères et Cie

121, Bd Haussmann
75008 PARIS
Tel: 01 44 13 01 11
Fax: 01 44 13 01 01

## Legal and General Bank

58, rue de la Victoire
75009 PARIS
Tel: 01 48 74 35 72
Fax: 01 45 26 65 60

# BANKING
BANQUES

## Lehman Brothers Bank
21, rue Balzac
75008 PARIS
Tel: 01 53 89 30 00
Fax: 01 53 89 31 30
President: M. JEORGER

## Louis Dreyfus France
87, ave de la Grande Armée
75016 PARIS
Tel: 01 40 66 11 11
Fax: 01 40 67 14 19

## Midland
20 bis, ave Rapp
75332 PARIS Cedex 07
Tel: 01 44 42 70 00
Fax: 01 44 42 77 77
Director: M. Richard MOSLEY

## Morgan Stanley
25, rue Balzac
75008 PARIS
Tel: 01 53 77 70 00
Fax: 01 53 77 70 99

## National Bank of Canada
123, ave des Champs Élysées
75008 PARIS
Tel: 01 47 20 37 52
Fax: 01 47 23 31 04
Director: M. Jean-Luc ALIMONDO

## Republic National Bank of New York
20, place Vendôme
75001 PARIS
Tel: 01 44 86 18 61
Fax: 01 42 60 05 62
President: M. Elo ROZENCWAJG

## Riggs National Bank (Europe)
US Embassy Office
2, ave Gabriel
75382 PARIS Cedex 08
Tel: 01 47 42 37 22
Fax: 01 47 42 38 10
President: M. Christopher WELTON

## Royal Bank of Canada
29, rue de la Bienfaisance
75008 PARIS
Tel: 01 40 08 42 00
Fax: 01 42 93 32 11
Director: M. Hugues DE GUITAUT

## Rothschild et Cie
17, ave Matignon
75008 PARIS
Tel: 01 40 74 40 74
Fax: 01 45 61 48 52

## Salomon Brothers
4, ave Hoche
75008 PARIS
Tel: 01 42 12 78 00
Fax: 01 42 12 78 09

## S.G. Warburg Securities Sas
65, rue de Courcelles
75008 PARIS
Tel: 01 48 88 33 44
Fax: 01 40 53 07 07
Email: sbc warburg@gb.swissbank.com
Director: M. François BACOT

## Société Générale
29, Bd Haussmann
75009 PARIS
Tel: 01 53 43 57 00
Fax: 01 53 43 59 49
Director: M. Marc VIENOT

## RETAIL BANKING
## Banques de dépôts

## Abbey National Bank
163, Bd Haussmann
75008 PARIS
Tel: 01 44 95 00 95
Free-call: 0 800 10 10 11
Fax: 01 44 95 00 99

## American Express Bank
*Foreign currency and traveler's checks*
11, rue Scribe
75009 PARIS
Tel: 01 47 14 50 00
Fax: 01 47 14 51 99
Director: M. Pierrot GRANDI

## American Express Carte France
4, rue Louis Blériot
92561 RUEIL MALMAISON Cedex
Tel: 01 47 77 77 07
Fax: 01 47 77 74 57
President: M. Charles PETRUCCELLI

## Banque Audi France

73, ave des Champs Élysées
75008 PARIS
Tel: 01 42 25 75 00
Fax: 01 42 56 09 74
Director: M. Yves KUEHN

## Banque Nationale de Paris (BNP)

16, Bd des Italiens
75009 PARIS
Tel: 01 40 14 45 46
Minitel: 3614 BNP
Communications Director:
Mme Françoise MONARD

## Banque Sanpaolo

52, ave Hoche
75382 PARIS Cedex 08
Tel: 01 47 54 40 40
Fax: 01 47 54 46 57
Mkt Director: M. CHEDVILLE

## Banque Transatlantique

17, Bd Haussmann
75009 PARIS
Tel: 01 40 22 80 00
Fax: 01 48 24 01 75
Manager: M. Anthony STONE

## Barclays

183, ave Daumesnil
75012 PARIS
Tel: 01 44 79 79 79
Fax: 01 44 79 72 52

---

## Citibank Consumer Banking Services

**CITIBAN🌐®**

*Citiphone: 01 49 05 49 05 (24
hours a day, Monday through
Saturday). **Anywhere**, the most
international bank in the world.
**Anytime**, 24 hours a day 7 days
per week, Citibank is there for you.
**Anyhow**, Citibank means
convenience (See advertisement)*
30, ave des Champs Élysées
75008 PARIS
Tel: 01 40 76 33 79
Fax: 01 40 76 33 70
Gen. Info: 01 40 76 33 77
Minitel: 3615 CITIBANK
Contact: Mme Judith DAVIS

---

## Citibank Private Bank

*Private retail banking. Large initial
deposit required*
17-19, ave Montaigne
75008 PARIS
Tel: 01 44 43 45 10
Fax: 01 40 70 90 55
Director: M. HERVÉ

## Cortal

*Banking by telephone*
131, ave Charles de Gaulle
92571 NEUILLY SUR SEINE Cedex
Free call: 0 800 10 15 20

## Kiosque American Express

*American Express cash dispenser*
19, ave George V
75008 PARIS
Tel: 01 53 67 03 15
Fax: 01 47 20 24 01

## Lloyds Bank

15, ave d'Iéna
75016 PARIS
Tel: 0144 43 42 41
Fax: 01 44 43 42 05
Director: M. Claude DEMARIA

## National Bank of Canada

123, ave des Champs Élysées
75008 PARIS
Tel: 01 47 20 37 52
Fax: 01 47 23 31 04
Director: M. Jean-Luc ALIMONDO

## Société Générale

29, Bd Haussmann
75009 PARIS
Tel: 01 53 43 57 00
Fax: 01 53 43 59 49
Director: M. Marc VIENOT

## State Street Banque

21-25, rue Balzac
75008 PARIS
Tel: 01 53 75 80 80
Fax: 01 53 75 80 09
Director: Mme Monique BOURVEN

## Thomas Cook Bankers France

8, rue Bellini
75016 PARIS
Tel: 01 47 55 52 25
Fax: 01 47 27 37 22
Web site: http://www.thomascook.com
Public Relations Director: M. SOSSON

# BUSINESS CENTERS
## CENTRE D'AFFAIRES

There are lots of practical solutions for setting up offices and grouping secretarial and commercial services in Paris. Here are several solution providers.

### Anglo-American Business and Culture Center

20, rue Godot de Mauroy
75009 PARIS
Tel: 01 42 66 14 11
Fax: 01 42 66 31 89

### CNIT - Centre des Nouvelles Technologies et Industries

2-4, place de la Défense
92053 PARIS LA DÉFENSE
Tel: 01 46 92 12 12
Fax: 01 46 92 24 49

### P.E.P. Action Business Center

*Answering service, secretarial assistance, conference rooms*

16, rue Christophe Colomb
75008 PARIS
Tel: 01 44 43 88 00
Fax: 01 44 43 88 10

### Startup

22, rue Robert de Flers
75015 PARIS
Tel: 01 45 78 65 28
Fax: 01 45 75 87 27

# CHAMBERS OF COMMERCE
## CHAMBRES DE COMMERCE

These organizations provide a wide range of services and activities designed to facilitate commerce and communications between the Anglo and Franco communities. Most publish their own newsletters and directories of industrial leaders in France and organize regular meetings and conferences. Good places to plug-in.

## American Chamber of Commerce

*Publishes yearly a directory of American businesses in Paris. Library services, etc.*

21, ave George V
75008 PARIS
Tel: 01 40 73 89 90
Fax: 01 47 20 18 62
Minitel: 36 17 CECOM
Email: amchamfr@club-internet.fr
Executive Director:
M. W. Barret DOWER

## British Overseas Trade Board

British Embassy
35, rue du Fbg Saint Honoré
75008 PARIS
Tel: 01 44 51 31 00
Contact: M. Brian WEST

## Chambre de Commerce France-Canada

9-11, ave Franklin Roosevelt
75008 PARIS
Tel: 01 43 59 32 38
Fax: 01 42 56 25 62

---

## Chambre de Commerce et d'Industrie de Paris (C.C.I.P.)

CHAMBRE DE COMMERCE ET D'INDUSTRIE DE PARIS

*See advertisement*
27, ave de Friedland
75008 PARIS
Tel: 01 42 89 70 00
Info: 01 42 89 78 36
Fax: 01 42 89 78 68
Web site: http://www.ccip.fr
Contact: Georges FISCHER

---

## Chambre de Commerce Internationale (I.C.C.)

38, cours Albert Ier
75008 PARIS
Tel: 01 49 53 28 28
Fax: 01 49 53 29 42
Email: icc@iccwbo.org
Web site: http://www.iccwbo.org

## Conseillers du Commerce Extérieur

22, ave Franklin Roosevelt
75008 PARIS
Tel: 01 43 59 66 24
Fax: 01 42 25 29 87
Contact:
Mme Véronique PEYRELONGUE

## Embassy of Australia Commercial Services

4, rue Jean Rey
75724 PARIS Cedex 15
Tel: 01 40 59 33 00
Fax: 01 40 59 33 22
Web site: http://www.austgov.fr

## French-American Chamber of Commerce

104, rue de Miromesnil
75008 PARIS
Tel: 01 53 89 11 00
Fax: 01 53 89 11 09
Director: Mme SERRE

## Franco-British Chamber of Commerce

31, rue Boissy d'Anglas
75008 PARIS
Tel: 01 53 30 81 30
Fax: 01 53 30 81 35

# CHAMBERS OF COMMERCE
CHAMBRES DE COMMERCE

## Franco-Irish Chamber of Commerce

33, rue de Miromesnil
75008 PARIS
Tel: 01 53 43 12 00
Fax: 01 47 42 84 76

## Irish Food Board

*Promotion of all Irish food & drinks*

33, rue de Miromesnil
75008 PARIS
Tel: 01 42 66 22 93
Fax: 01 42 66 22 88

## United States of America - Embassy Commercial Service

2, ave Gabriel
75008 PARIS
Tel: 01 43 12 21 97
Fax: 01 43 12 21 72
Minitel: 36 28 00 61
Email: ocollett@doc.gov
Director of Information and Special Projects: M. Olivier COLLETTE

For the complete list of French-American Chambers of Commerce in the United States, see page 141

This huge area of commercial activity includes many, but not all, of the major computer hardware and software companies present in the Paris area, especially those who offer hotlines and customer services for anglophones working in France. A limited selection of dealers and service-providers have been included to assist you in your computing needs.

## HARDWARE/SOFTWARE
Constructeurs

### Adobe Systems France
2, rue du Centre
93885 NOISY LE GRAND Cedex
Tel: 01 43 04 10 00
Fax: 01 43 04 10 20
Director: M. BOURDON

### American Software France
54, ave Victor Hugo
92500 RUEIL MALMAISON
Tel: 01 47 10 08 50
Fax: 01 47 16 00 74
Web site: http://www.amsoftware.com
Director: M. CHETTLE

### Apple Computer France
12, ave de l'Océanie
ZA de Courtaboeuf
91956 LES ULIS Cedex
Tel: 01 69 86 34 00
Fax: 01 69 28 74 32
Web site: http://www.fr.euro.apple.com
Director: M. Georges BONGI

### Cabletron Systems
ZAC Nanteuil
Bâtiment Paul Henri Spaak
12, rue Jules Ferry
93561 ROSNY SOUS BOIS
Tel: 01 48 94 70 72
Fax: 01 48 94 44 89
Web site: http://www.cabletron.com
Communications Dir.: M. CLOTEAUX

### Candle France
13, ave de la Porte d'Italie
75013 PARIS
Tel: 01 53 61 60 00
Fax: 01 53 61 05 15
President: M. LABANT

### Compaq
5, allée Gustave Eiffel
92442 ISSY LES MOULINEAUX
Tel: 01 41 33 41 00
Fax: 01 41 33 44 00
Director: M. MANIGLIER

### Dell Computer France
*Micro-computer manufacturer*
BP 9646
34054 MONTPELLIER
Tel: 01 47 62 69 00
Fax: 01 47 62 69 01

### Digital Equipment France
Parc du Bois Briard
9-11-13, ave du Lac Courcouronnes
91004 ÉVRY Cedex
Tel: 01 69 87 51 11
Fax: 01 69 87 54 44
Director: M. RUFFAT

### Hewlett Packard France
Parc du Bois Briard
2, ave du Lac Courcouronnes
91040 ÉVRY Cedex
Tel: 01 69 82 60 60
Fax: 01 69 91 84 32
Web site: http://www.france.hp.com
President: M. Yves COUILLARD

### IBM France
Direction Générale
Tour Septentrion
20, ave André Prothin
92081 PARIS LA DÉFENSE
Tel: 01 49 05 70 70
President: M. Bernard DUFAU

### Intel Corporation
1, quai de Grenelle
75015 PARIS
Tel: 01 45 71 71 71
Minitel: 3616 INTEL
Web site: http://www.intel.com

## International French Business

73, Bd Clichy
75009 PARIS
Tel: 01 49 70 08 08
Fax: 01 49 70 00 04

## Lotus Development

Hotline: 01 30 12 55 00

## Microsoft France

18, ave du Québec
ZA de Courtaboeuf 1
91957 COURTABOEUF Cedex
Tel: 01 69 86 46 46
Technical support: 01 69 86 10 20
Hotline: 01 69 86 10 20
Fax: 01 64 46 06 60
Web site:
http://www.microsoft.com/france
Director: M. Jean-Philippe COURTOIS

## Novell Wordperfect

Tour Framatome
1, place de la Coupole
92084 PARIS LA DÉFENSE Cedex
Tel: 01 47 96 60 00
Fax: 01 40 90 92 83
President: M. Jean-Loup
DESAMAISON-COGNET

## Oracle France

*Software publisher for businesses*
65, rue des Trois Fontanot
92732 NANTERRE
Tel: 01 47 62 20 20
Fax: 01 47 62 21 15
Web site: http://www.oracle.com

## Rank Xerox

7, rue Touzet
93586 SAINT OUEN Cedex
Tel: 01 49 48 47 46
Fax: 01 49 48 43 21
President: M. J.M. MACHON

## Softimage

6, rue de l'Est
92100 BOULOGNE BILLANCOURT
Tel: 01 46 04 33 00
Fax: 01 46 04 39 61
Email: imartin@microsoft.com
Director: Mme Irène MARTIN

## Speedware France S.A.

*Software publisher Internet for
businesses*
92, ave des Champs Élysées
75008 PARIS
Tel: 01 40 74 01 10
Fax: 01 45 62 85 16
Email: guye@speedware.com
President: M. Guy EICHELBRENNER

## Ubi Soft Entertainment

28, rue Armand Carrel
93108 MONTREUIL SOUS BOIS
Cedex
Tel: 01 48 18 50 00
Fax: 01 48 57 23 77
Web site: http://www.ubisoft.fr
President: M. Yves GUILLEMOT

## COMPUTER DEALERS/ SERVICES
## Vente/Services informatique

## Alex Informatique

51, route de Thônes
74940 ANNECY LE VIEUX
Tel: 04 50 64 08 97
Fax: 04 50 64 09 02
Email: info@alex.fr
Manager: M. Patrice FONTAINE

## AMAC

4, rue de la Sorbonne
75005 PARIS
Tel: 01 44 07 11 75
Fax: 01 44 07 01 21

## Andyne France

66, rue Escudier
92774 BOULOGNE Cedex
Tel: 01 41 10 05 05
Hotline: 01 41 10 05 16
Fax: 01 41 10 05 00
President: M. Philippe COUP-JAMBET

# COMPUTERS
INFORMATIQUE

## AWS

*Apple dealership and self-service bureau*
7, rue Gay Lussac
75005 PARIS
Tel: 01 43 25 09 09
Fax: 01 43 29 68 78
Director: M. William SETRUCK

## Cabinet Derek Erb

99-103, rue de Sèvres
75006 PARIS
Tel: 01 40 61 90 03
Fax: 01 40 61 90 51
Email: erb@erb.com
Web site: http://www.erb.com
President: M. Derek ERB

## DAP Technologies

6, place du Village des Barbanniers
92632 GENNEVILLIERS Cedex
Tel: 01 41 21 95 95
Fax: 01 41 21 95 65
Email: dap-mktg@i-t.fr
Director: M. Alexis BOUCHEZ

## David Anteby

*Computer applications for small and medium-sized businesses*
15, rue Georges Lafenestre
92340 BOURG LA REINE
Tel: 01 46 61 06 47
Email: anteby@club-internet.fr

## Digitco

*Apple dealership specializing in service to the anglophone community. 15% off rentals & repairs by simply mentioning Paris-Anglophone*
*(See advertisement)*
29, Bd Henri IV
75004 PARIS
Tel: 01 42 72 90 04
Fax: 01 42 72 58 63
Contact: Mme Soheila ANQUETIL

## DMR

35, rue d'Artois
75008 PARIS
Tel: 01 53 89 16 60
Fax: 01 45 61 25 09
Director: M. J.P. SAURIN

## Euro Soft

15, rue Danielle Casanova
75001 PARIS
Tel: 01 40 20 98 00
Fax: 01 40 20 98 22
Email: 100070.3555@compuserve.com

## Facilite Informatique

72-74, ave Édouard Vaillant
92100 BOULOGNE BILLANCOURT
Tel: 01 46 04 84 84
Fax: 01 46 04 03 30
Email: facilite@club-internet.fr
Financial Director: M. Alain GIROUX

## Fire Mountain Services

31, rue de la Princerie
91470 FORGES LES BAINS
Tel: 01 64 59 03 18
Fax: 01 64 59 00 44
Email: montaigne@fms.host.org.
Contact: Mme Beverly LAFLAMME

## FNAC Micro

71, Bd.Saint Germain
75005 PARIS
Tel: 01 44 41 31 50
Hotline: 01 41 70 77 77
Fax: 01 44 41 31 79
Web site: http://www.fnac.fr

## Info Matic

36, rue de Washington
75008 PARIS
Tel: 01 42 56 81 00
Fax: 01 42 56 07 65

## Info Zéro Un

Port Van Gogh Paris
2, quai Aulagnier
92600 ASNIÈRES
Tel: 01 47 93 33 83
Fax: 01 47 93 44 47

### Jal Technologie

4, allée de la Toison d'Or
Bureau 2
94000 CRÉTEIL
Tel: 01 40 33 26 23
Fax: 01 43 99 25 37
President: M. Albert LASRY

### Matrox

2, rue de la Couture
94528 RUNGIS Cedex
Tel: 01 45 60 62 00
Fax: 01 45 60 62 05
Email: matrox.france@matrox.com
Web site: http://www.matrox.com
Director: M. Gilles RAFFIER

### Self-Computer

7, Bd St Germain
75005 PARIS
Tel: 01 46 34 80 90
Fax: 01 46 34 80 91

### Surcouf Informatique

139, ave Daumesnil
75012 PARIS
Tel: 01 53 33 20 00
Fax: 01 53 33 21 01

### Terminal Image

*3-D computer graphics and animation technology*
54, rue David d'Angers
75019 PARIS
Tel: 01 42 49 21 06
Fax: 01 42 02 40 65
Email: terminal@mail.club-internet.fr
Director: M. Eric SALES

### Vera Informatique

105, rue de l'Abbé Groult
75015 PARIS
Tel: 01 45 87 33 39
Fax: 01 40 45 74 16
Email: 100625.1442@compuserve.com
Contact: Mme Brigitte DEFOORT

**DOING BUSINESS & WORKING**

71

# CONSULTING/MANAGEMENT
## CONSEIL/AUDIT

Although the lines between consulting, management, marketing and communications sometimes converge, PARIS-ANGLOPHONE has attempted to group here a list of consulting groups and consultants from a broad range of specific areas of competence to satisfy all needs.

### ABC Groupe

*International management consulting founded in 1979 in Paris. Specializes in corporate strategy, organization & turn-arounds*

9, rue Beaujon
75008 PARIS
Tel: 01 44 29 95 00
Fax: 01 44 29 95 29
Email: jbojin@groupeabc.com
Chairman: M. Jacques BOJIN

### Alaska Seafood Marketing Institute

58, rue Pottier
78150 LE CHESNAY
Tel: 01 39 23 20 07
Fax: 01 39 23 20 17
Email: 101716,2420@compuserve.com
Director: Mme Nelly MASSON

### Allen et Associés

11, rue La Boétie
75008 PARIS
Tel: 01 42 65 88 57
Fax: 01 42 65 02 80
Director: M. Ross ALLEN

### Arthur Andersen et Associés

55, ave Georges V
75008 PARIS
Tel: 01 53 23 55 55
Fax: 01 53 23 53 23
President: M. Gérard VAN KEMMEL

### Arthur D. Little France

15, rue Galvani
75017 PARIS
Tel: 01 40 55 29 00
Fax: 01 40 55 08 80
Director: M. Éric BELOT

### B.L.I.T.S. (Business Language International Training Services)

41, rue Dauphine
75006 PARIS
Tel: 01 43 54 79 61

### Bain & Co.

21, Bd de la Madeleine
75001 PARIS
Tel: 01 44 55 75 75
Fax: 01 44 55 76 00
Director: M. Jean-Marie PEAN

### BC2

Parc Evolic Villebon Bâtiment H6
12, ave du Québec
BP 738
91962 COURTABOEUF Cedex
Tel: 01 69 86 03 03
Fax: 01 69 86 98 91
Manager: M. Bruno CÈZARD

### Bearware Engineering

*IT, Internet and Intranet consulting*

25, place Georges Pompidou
92300 LEVALLOIS PERRET
Tel: 01 47 59 96 19
Fax: 01 47 48 09 64
Email: info@bearware.net
Web site: http://www.bearware.net
Director: M. Tapani TUOMINEN

### Bechtel France

38, rue Bassano
75008 PARIS
Tel: 01 47 20 53 04
Fax: 01 47 20 55 06
Director: M. CORI

### Bernard Krief Consultants

26, Bd Malesherbes
75008 PARIS
Tel: 01 42 66 44 44
Fax: 01 42 66 02 01
Contact: M. Louis PETIET

### Boole & Babbage Europe

Valmy Espace 21 Bâtiment 6
3, place Ronde Puteaux Défense 7
92686 PARIS LA DÉFENSE Cedex
Tel: 01 47 75 55 98
Fax: 01 47 75 55 41

## Booz Allen & Hamilton, Inc.

112, ave Kléber
BP 165 Trocadéro
75770 PARIS Cedex 16
Tel: 01 44 34 31 31
Fax: 01 44 34 30 00
Senior Vice-President:
M. Pierre RODOCANACHI

## Boston Consulting Group (The)

4, rue d'Aguesseau
75008 PARIS
Tel: 01 40 17 10 10
Fax: 01 40 17 10 15
Vice-President: M. GARAIALDE

## Bourse Européenne pour le Commerce et l'Industrie (BECI)

15-17, ave de Ségur
75007 PARIS
Tel: 01 45 55 71 27
Fax: 01 45 51 27 48

## Boyden Global Executive Search

1, Rond-Point des Champs Élysées
75008 PARIS
Tel: 01 44 13 67 00
Fax: 01 44 13 67 13
President: M. LAMY

## Braxton Associés

185, ave Charles de Gaulle
92200 NEUILLY SUR SEINE
Tel: 01 46 37 16 16
Fax: 01 46 37 59 90
Director: M. Bruno LANNES

## Broadmark

20, ave Kléber
75016 PARIS
Tel: 01 45 00 00 01
Fax: 01 45 00 82 82

## Buck Consultants

*Compensation and benefits advice*
18, Bd Malesherbes
75008 PARIS
Tel: 01 44 51 16 96
Fax: 01 44 51 16 99
Director: M. Claude VALA

## Business Development Network International

*Seminar "How to Attract New Clients Easily". Individual sessions. Low cost for tight budgets. In French/English*
4, ave des Jonchères
78121 CRESPIERES
Tel: 01 30 54 94 66
Fax: 01 30 54 94 67
Contact:
Mme Élisabeth de VULPILLIERES

## C.S.C. France

63 ter, ave Édouard Vaillant
92517 BOULOGNE BILLANCOURT
Cedex
Tel: 01 46 10 29 00
Fax: 01 46 10 29 10

## Caldwell Consulting

18, rue Rambuteau
75003 PARIS
Tel: 01 48 04 03 56
Fax: 01 42 72 88 09
Director: Mme Nancy CALDWELL

## Cantor, Gary

*Bilingual financial consultant*
6, rue Crétet
75009 PARIS
Tel: 01 48 78 08 47
Fax: 01 42 85 45 59

## CH2M Hill

*Environmental consulting*
104, ave Albert 1er
92563 RUEIL MALMAISON Cedex
Tel: 01 47 51 75 15
Fax: 01 47 08 25 78
Director: M. LEVADOUX

## Connell Speirs & Associates

10, place de la Madeleine
75008 PARIS
Tel: 01 40 15 98 98
Fax: 01 40 15 99 66
Director: M. James SPEIRS

## Coopers & Lybrand

32, rue Guersant
75017 PARIS
Tel: 01 45 72 80 00
Fax: 01 45 72 22 19
President: M. P.B. ANGLADE

73

## Dames and Moore

*Consulting engineers in earth and environmental sciences*
2, rue de Marly le Roi
78150 LE CHESNAY
Tel: 01 39 23 80 80
Fax: 01 39 55 35 71
Managing Director: M. VERMERSCH

## Datura

42, rue de Chezy
92200 NEUILLY SUR SEINE
Tel: 01 46 37 09 36
Fax: (44) 171 681 1194
Email: rc@datura.com
Web site: http://www.datura.com
Manager: M. Robert CHELSETH

## Deloitte Touche Tohmatsu

185, ave Charles de Gaulle
92200 NEUILLY SUR SEINE
Tel: 01 40 88 28 00
Fax: 01 40 88 28 28
Contact: M. Hervé BARDON

## Dun & Bradstreet International

Immeuble Défense Bergères
345, ave Georges Clémenceau
92882 NANTERRE Cedex 9
Tel: 01 41 35 17 00
Fax: 01 41 35 17 77
Director:
M. Bruno LEPROU DE LA RIVIERE

## Ernst & Young Audit

Tour Manhattan
6, place de l'Iris
92095 PARIS LA DÉFENSE 2 Cedex 21
Tel: 01 46 93 60 00
Fax: 01 47 76 20 33
President: M. Antoine BRACCHI

## Ernst & Young Conseil

*Advice about information technologies*
Tour Manhattan
6, place de l'Iris
92095 PARIS LA DÉFENSE 2 Cedex 21
Tel: 01 46 93 60 00
Fax: 01 47 76 20 33
Partner: M. B. CARLING

## Eurokhi

*Organize seminars and conferences. Create made-to-measure foreign language programs*
18, ave des Champs Élysées
75008 PARIS
Tel: 01 43 06 16 06
Fax: 01 45 67 10 89
Email: eurokhi@worldnet.net
Director: Mme Karen HARTUNG

## Expatriate Management Consultants (EMC)

62, ave Foch
92250 LA GARENNE COLOMBES
Tel: 01 47 81 12 85
Fax: 01 42 42 39 63
Director: Mme Patricia DIRLIK

## Fidulor

65, rue de Bercy
75012 PARIS
Tel: 01 43 63 72 73
Fax: 01 43 63 02 55
Contact: M. Hervé GOHIN

## Frankenhuis, Jean-Pierre

*Computer consulting*
4, rue Jasmin
75016 PARIS
Tel: 01 45 25 97 64
Fax: 01 45 20 62 94
Email: 763473565@compuserve.com

## Frost & Sullivan

24, rue de Londres
75009 PARIS
Tel: 01 42 81 54 50
Fax: 01 42 81 54 52
Manager: M. Ian RUTHERFORD

## Gauntlett Europe

89, rue de la Boëtie
75008 PARIS
Tel: 01 45 61 18 60
Fax: 01 45 61 18 61
Email: gauntlett.europe@hol.fr
Director: M. Paul CHAPON

## Gavin Anderson & Company France

29, rue de Lisbonne
75008 PARIS
Tel: 01 53 83 93 18
Fax: 01 53 83 93 23
Contact: Mme I. VIRY

## Gray Matters

*Artist management*
14, rue de Birague
75004 PARIS
Tel: 01 42 77 03 03
Fax: 01 42 77 82 36
Director: Mme Alexandra GRAY

## Horwath France

*Hotel, catering, tourism and leisure industries*
12, rue de Madrid
75008 PARIS
Tel: 01 53 42 41 00
Fax: 01 45 22 78 87
President: M. René AMIRKHANIAN

## Hospitality Management Consulting

18, rue Maubeuge
75009 PARIS
Tel: 01 42 80 34 56
Fax: 01 42 80 34 56
Email: bipinman@hotmail.com
Contact: M. Bipin SHRESTHA

## IDC

*Computer consulting*
2, place des Vosges
92051 PARIS LA DÉFENSE
Tel: 01 49 04 80 00
Fax: 01 49 04 80 80
Web site: http://www.idcresearch.com

## ICME

154, Bd Haussmann
75008 PARIS
Tel: 01 53 93 70 80
Fax: 01 45 61 05 30
Email: 100547,3571@compuserve.com
Director: M. Denis LEBREC

## IDC France

*Market studies*
2, place des Vosges
immeuble La Fayette
92051 PARIS LA DÉFENSE Cedex 65
Tel: 01 49 04 80 00
Fax: 01 49 04 80 80
Web site: http://www.idcresearch.com
Director: M. BIDAL

## Institut de Gestion Sociale

25, rue François Ier
75008 PARIS
Tel: 01 53 67 84 00
Fax: 01 40 70 10 74

## John Hardman Associates

*Franco-British and US marketing strategies*
BP 03
24210 AZERAT
Tel: 05 53 05 28 74
Fax: 05 53 05 28 73
Email: hardman@perigord.com
Director: M. John HARDMAN

## John Taylor

*Real estate*
86, ave Victor Hugo
75016 PARIS
Tel: 01 45 53 25 25
Fax: 01 47 55 63 97

Kelly, Russel

# RUSSEL KELLY

*Management services for anglophone Business-to-Business companies. Individual consulting tasks or complete operation*
36, rue Chauveau
92200 NEUILLY SUR SEINE
Tel: 01 47 22 35 67
Fax: 01 47 22 35 67
Email:
106137.3220@compuserve.com
Contact: M. Russel KELLY

*DOING BUSINESS & WORKING*

# CONSULTING/MANAGEMENT
## CONSEIL/AUDIT

## Kepner Tregoe
*Management and training
consultants*
91, rue du Fbg Saint Honoré
75008 PARIS
Tel: 0 800 90 87 03
Fax: 0 800 90 87 10
Partner: M. VERDINA-HENCHIOZ

## Leaders Trust International
32, ave Kléber
75116 PARIS
Tel: 01 45 02 17 00
Fax: 01 45 00 56 07
Director: M. Gérard SAKAKINI

## Louis Berger
71, rue Fondary
75015 PARIS
Tel: 01 45 78 39 39
Fax: 01 45 77 74 69
Manager: M. François FARHI

## Manex International
20, rue du Général Appert
75116 PARIS
Tel: 01 47 04 50 24
Fax: 01 47 04 80 44
Director: M. Jack FINLAY

## McKinsey & Company
79, ave des Champs Élysées
75008 PARIS
Tel: 01 40 69 14 00
Fax: 01 40 69 93 93
Director: M. Peter KRALJIC

## Multi Services International
2, rue Marc Sangnier
94240 L'HAY LES ROSES
Tel: 01 46 86 26 58
Fax: 01 46 86 02 61
Email: 101460.2164@compuserve.com
General Manager:
M. Albert HAMMOND

## Oxo Consultants
10, rue Royale
75008 PARIS
Tel: 01 42 60 39 52
Fax: 01 42 60 33 21
Email: cyberoxo@oxo.fr
Contact: M. PROUHET

## Pab Consultants
5, rue Vercingétorix
75014 PARIS
Tel: 01 43 35 57 20
Fax: 01 43 22 21 16

## Price Waterhouse
Tour AIG
34, place des Corolles
92908 PARIS LA DÉFENSE Cedex 105
Tel: 01 41 26 10 00
Fax: 01 41 26 16 16
President: M. Joël GARLOT

## Proudfoot Crosby France
9, ave Franklin Roosevelt
75008 PARIS
Tel: 01 45 61 09 20
Fax: 01 45 61 09 21

## Guestrel International
*Building Consultants*
12 bis, rue Duphot
75001 PARIS
Tel: 01 42 96 17 93
Fax: 01 42 96 17 94
President: M. Norman JACKSON

## Raymond Chabot International
Tour Framatome
La Défense 6
92084 PARIS LA DÉFENSE Cedex 16
Tel: 01 47 96 63 90
Fax: 01 47 96 63 96
Director: M. Yves LABAT

## Research & Business Partners
8, rue Halévy
75009 PARIS
Tel: 01 44 51 14 30
Fax: 01 44 51 14 31

## Robins Communications
*Business to Business communications*
7, rue Campagne Première
75014 PARIS
Tel: 01 43 22 43 81
Fax: 01 43 21 84 89
Director: Mme ROBINS

### Sahni, Deep

1, place de l'Odéon
75006 PARIS
Tel: 01 43 44 30 20
Email: deep@easynet.fr

### Schroeder-Wertheim

137, rue du Fbg Saint Honoré
75001 PARIS
Tel: 01 44 20 65 00
Fax: 01 44 20 65 01
President: M. Geoffrey DE FARAMOND

### Technology Applications Group

69, rue de Paris
91400 ORSAY
Tel: 01 69 07 32 27
Tel2: 01 48 10 99 89
Fax: 01 69 07 83 93
Email:
dominiqueroussel@compuserve.com
Contact: M. Dominique ROUSSEL

### Tocqueville International Finances

16, ave de Friedland
75008 PARIS
Tel: 01 53 77 20 00
Fax: 01 45 63 05 04

### Travôtel Concept

*Prepares business reports: market research, planning, feasibility studies for project development, market representation in Paris*
18, rue Maubeuge
75009 PARIS
Tel: 01 42 80 34 56
Fax: 01 42 80 34 56
Email: bipinman@hotmail.com
Contact: M. Bipin SHRESTHA

### Workplace Association

*Career management, job hunting*
17, rue Emile Dubois
75014 PARIS
Tel: 01 45 65 23 43
Fax: 01 53 62 00 79
Contact: Mme Brenda DEAN

### Write Angle

*Business communications services*
10, rue Chaudron
75010 PARIS
Tel: 01 40 35 96 69
Fax: 01 40 35 98 89
Email: 100042.2175@compuserve.com
Director: M. Henry BLOUNT

*DOING BUSINESS & WORKING*

77

# COURIER SERVICES
## COURSIERS INTERNATIONAUX

Keep your thumb in this page. All anglophones working in or with France need a reliable international courier service. For local couriers, consult the Minitel. Let the Editors know about great service you encounter.

### Air Borne Express
9, Bd Ney
75018 PARIS
Tel: 01 44 89 82 20
Fax: 01 42 05 95 56

### Air Express International
BP 10406, Zone Roissytech
1, rue du Pré
Bâtiment 3317
95707 ROISSY CDG
Tel: 01 49 19 68 68
Fax: 01 48 62 49 94
President: M. Marcel ETIEN

### Burlington Air Express France
Aéroport Charles de Gaulle
BP 10287
95704 Roissy CDG Cedex
Tel: 01 48 64 63 63
Fax: 01 49 38 85 27

### Chronopost
14, rue des Frères-Voisin
92795 ISSY LES MOULINEAUX
Cedex 9
Tel: 01 46 48 10 00
Fax: 01 46 48 10 50
President: M. Frédéric TIBERGHIEN

### Federal Express France

Federal Express

125-135, ave Louis Roche
92230 GENNEVILLIERS
Tel: 01 40 85 38 00
Free-call: 0 800 12 38 00
Fax: 01 47 94 21 52
Director: M. J. PUTZEYS

### Jet Services Courier
BP 10136
95701 ROISSY CDG
Tel: 01 48 62 62 22
Fax: 01 49 19 81 90
Director: M. Gilles SOCOLOWSKI

### May Courier International
13, rue Oberkampf
75011 PARIS
Tel: 01 49 29 56 00
Fax: 01 43 38 51 44

### TNT-IPEC
3 bis, ave Evarice Gallois
93592 LE BLANC MESNIL Cedex
Tel: 01 48 14 48 14
Fax: 01 48 14 49 99

### United Parcel Service (UPS)
87, ave de l'Aérodrome
BP 39
94310 ORLY VILLE
Tel: 0 800 877 877
Fax: 01 48 92 51 07

### DHL International

WORLDWIDE EXPRESS

ZI Paris Nord II
241, rue de la Belle Etoile
95957 ROISSY CDG
Tel: 01 49 38 70 70
Free-call: 0 800 20 25 25
Fax: 01 49 38 72 69
President: M. GARIN

78

# FINANCIAL SERVICES
## ÉTABLISSEMENTS FINANCIERS

For managing your money, placing funds, playing the stock market in France and abroad, and investment counseling, here is a host of local contacts.

## 3i Group
168, ave Charles de Gaulle
92521 NEUILLY SUR SEINE Cedex
Tel: 01 47 15 11 00
Fax: 01 47 45 31 24
Director: M. Frédéric DE BROGLIE

## Arnoult, Samina
26, Bd de Clichy
75018 PARIS
Tel: 01 42 57 37 17
Fax: 01 42 59 58 19

## Bowne International France
5, rue Royale
75008 PARIS
Tel: 01 44 94 32 80
Fax: 01 44 94 32 95
Manager: M. Antoine ANTAKI

## Brink's France
49, rue Réaumur
75003 PARIS
Tel: 01 42 71 27 70
Fax: 01 42 71 63 71

## Business Group Consultants
60, ave de New York
75016 PARIS
Tel: 01 45 24 50 09
Fax: 01 45 24 40 49

## Business Perspectives
22, rue de Lubeck
75116 PARIS
Tel: 01 47 27 28 00
Fax: 01 47 27 22 80

## Centur Conseils
85-87, ave du Général De Gaulle
94017 CRÉTEIL Cedex
Tel: 01 48 98 45 45
Fax: 01 48 99 53 15

## Coopers & Lybrand Corporation Finance
32, rue Guersant
75017 PARIS
Tel: 01 45 72 80 00
Fax: 01 45 72 22 19
President: M. P.B. ANGLADE

## Datastream International
*Economical & financial databases*
25, ave Marceau
75116 PARIS
Tel: 01 44 43 85 10
Fax: 01 40 70 92 08
Director: M. GUFFROY

## De Saxce, Frank
*Tax consultant*
103, ave Émile Zola
75015 PARIS
Tel: 01 45 77 58 54

## Donaldson, Lufkin & Jenrette
6, rue Christophe Colomb
75008 PARIS
Tel: 01 49 52 69 00
Fax: 01 40 70 16 96
Director: M. GONNEAU

## Dow Jones Telerate
*Real time financial data*
128, rue du Fbg Saint Honoré
75008 PARIS
Tel: 01 42 89 05 09
Fax: 01 42 25 04 97

## Downer & Company
370, rue Saint Honoré
75001 PARIS
Tel: 01 42 61 47 47
Fax: 01 42 61 48 48
President: M. Ashley ROUNTREE

## Du Pasquier & Cie
*American financing and investments*
31, ave des Champs Élysées
75008 PARIS
Tel: 01 40 76 03 03
Fax: 01 40 74 03 32
Manager: M. Philippe DE MONTMARIN

## Dun & Bradstreet International
Immeuble Défense Bergères
345, ave Georges Clémenceau
92882 NANTERRE Cedex 9
Tel: 01 41 35 17 00
Fax: 01 41 35 17 77
Chairman:
M. Bruno LEPROU DE LA RIVIERE

# FINANCIAL SERVICES
## ÉTABLISSEMENTS FINANCIERS

### Exco Paris
7, rue de Madrid
75008 PARIS
Tel: 01 44 70 30 00
Fax: 01 42 93 31 76

### Financial & Offshore Consultants
*Raising of finance, venture capital*
18, ave Victor Cresson
92130 ISSY LES MOULINEAUX
Tel: 01 41 08 84 17
Fax: 01 41 08 84 17
Contact: M. Sharjeel MUFTY

### France Capital
*Portfolio management for individuals*
4, rue Saint Augustin
75002 PARIS
Tel: 01 45 00 42 53
Fax: 01 45 00 02 38
Contact: M. Roger CRUISE

### Frank Russell
*Venture capital company*
42, ave Kléber
75016 PARIS
Tel: 01 44 05 92 92
Fax: 01 44 05 92 93
Director: Mme Frédérique JOLY

### Gordon Capital Corporation
10, rue de la Paix
75002 PARIS
Tel: 01 49 27 08 08
Fax: 01 42 60 59 36
Contact: M. Jean-Yves LE FLOCH

### Hambros France S.A.
16, place Vendôme
75001 PARIS
Tel: 01 42 60 57 17
Fax: 01 42 86 90 19
Director: M. DE NADAILLAC

### Laidlaw International

**Laidlaw & Co.** <sup>SM</sup>

5, rue Royale
75008 PARIS
Tel: 01 47 42 97 82
Fax: 01 47 42 39 58
Financial Consultant:
M Christopher BELL

### Loewen, Ondaatje, McCutcheon & Company Ltd
16, ave George V
75008 PARIS
Tel: 01 40 73 81 00
Fax: 01 49 52 04 72

### Merrill Lynch, Pierce, Fenner & Smith
96, ave d'Iéna
75116 PARIS
Tel: 01 40 69 10 00
Tel: 01 40 69 15 00
Director: M. Jeronimo VILLALBA

### Parfinance
1, Rond-Point des Champs Élysées
75008 PARIS
Tel: 01 42 25 34 40
Fax: 01 42 89 14 20

### Porter & Reeves
5, rue Cambon
75001 PARIS
Tel: 01 42 61 55 77
Fax: 01 42 86 94 07

### Price Waterhouse Moisand et Associés
Tour AIG
34, place des Corolles
92908 PARIS LA DÉFENSE Cedex 105
Tel: 01 41 26 16 00
Fax: 01 41 26 16 16
President: M. Joël GARLOT

## RBC Dominion Securities

29, rue de la Bienfaisance
75008 PARIS
Tel: 01 53 42 11 33
Fax: 01 43 87 57 90
Director: M. Alain CORBANI

## Rem Finance

20, rue Léonard de Vinci
75116 PARIS
Tel: 01 45 00 07 50
Fax: 01 45 00 20 17
President: M. Ely Michel RUIMY

## Robertson Taylor France

94, rue Saint Lazare
75009 PARIS
Tel: 01 48 74 41 37
Fax: 01 48 74 41 27

## S.B.C. Warburg

65, rue de Courcelles
75008 PARIS
Tel: 01 48 88 33 44
Fax: 01 48 88 33 10

## Schneider

64-70, ave Jean-Baptiste Clément
92646 BOULOGNE
Tel: 01 46 99 70 00
Fax: 01 48 25 51 28
Director:
M. Didier PINEAU-VALENCIENNE

## Schroders Partenaires

41, ave George V
75008 PARIS
Tel: 01 40 73 85 00
Fax: 01 40 70 11 08

## Schroeder-Wertheim

137, rue du Fbg Saint Honoré
75001 PARIS
Tel: 01 44 20 65 00
Fax: 01 44 20 65 01
President:
M. Geoffrey DE FARAMOND

## SHJ Invest

*Franchise consulting*
Immeuble Conquistador
112, rue des Moines
75017 PARIS
Tel: 01 47 64 32 88
Fax: 01 46 22 18 46
Email: 101623,133@compuserve.com
Directeur: M. Houston JONES

## Smith Barney

7, place Vendôme
75001 PARIS
Tel: 01 42 96 10 66
Fax: 01 42 96 22 81
Director: M. PINCHART-DENY

## Technology Investment Partners

15, rue du Grand Veneur
75003 PARIS
Tel: 01 48 87 91 47
Fax: 01 48 87 91 42

## Tendler Beretz International

72, rue du Fbg Saint Honoré
75008 PARIS
Tel: 01 40 07 86 98
Fax: 01 40 07 80 40
Managing Director:
M. Anthony Boeck ACAMPORA

## The Europe Company

26, rue de la Pépinière
75008 PARIS
Tel: 01 45 22 13 77
Fax: 01 45 22 13 70

## Yorkton Securities

42, ave de la Grande Armée
75017 PARIS
Tel: 01 40 68 96 08
Fax: 01 40 68 96 09
Director: M. Daniel P. BROOKS

# FRENCH ADMINISTRATION
## ADMINISTRATION FRANÇAISE

France has lots of government, and here are listings for the administrations and ministries that you might need to contact when conducting business and commercial activities in France. The names of ministers have been left off in that names have a tendency to change. Also find the addresses of the head offices of the administrations regulating the various categories of labor and employment status as well as international organizations based in France.

### FRENCH GOVERNMENT
### Administration française

### Centre de Renseignements des Douanes
*Customs Information Service*
23, rue de l'Université
75007 PARIS
Tel: 01 40 24 65 10
Fax: 01 40 24 65 30

### Centre Français du Commerce Extérieur
*French Foreign Trade Board*
10, ave d'Iéna
75783 PARIS Cedex 16
Tel: 01 40 73 30 00
Euro Info: 01 40 73 34 67
(European trade regulations)
Fax: 01 40 73 39 79
Web site: http://www.cfce.fr

### D.A.T.A.R. (Délégation à l'Aménagement du Territoire et à l'Action Régionale)
1, ave Charles Floquet
75007 PARIS
Tel: 01 40 65 10 06
Fax: 01 40 65 12 40
General Secretary: M. Paul BEYZELON

### Greffe et Registre du Commerce
*French companies registration office*
1, quai de Corse
75004 PARIS
Tel: 01 43 29 06 75
Minitel: 3614 INFOGREFFE

### Hôtel Matignon
*Prime Minister's office*
57, rue de Varenne
75007 PARIS
Tel: 01 42 75 80 00
Fax: 01 45 44 15 72
Web site:
http://www.premier-ministre.gouv.fr

### INPI
*National Bureau of Patents and Trademarks*
26 bis, rue Saint Petersbourg
75008 PARIS
Tel: 01 53 04 53 04
Fax: 01 42 93 59 30

### Mairie de Paris
*City of Paris Town Hall*
Place de l'Hôtel de Ville
75196 PARIS R.P.
Tel: 01 42 76 40 40
Fax: 01 42 76 58 15

### Ministère de la Culture
*Ministry of Culture*
3, rue de Valois
75001 PARIS
Tel: 01 40 15 80 00
Fax: 01 40 15 37 40
Web site: http://www.culture.gouv.fr

### Ministère de l'Économie et du Budget
*Ministry of the Economy and Budget*
139, rue de Bercy
75012 PARIS
Tel: 01 40 04 04 04
Fax: 01 43 45 73 35
Web site: http://www.finances.gouv.fr

## Ministère de l'Éducation Nationale

*Ministry of Education*
110, rue de Grenelle
75007 PARIS
Tel: 01 49 55 10 10
Fax: 01 40 65 67 54 (Foreign Students)
Web site: http://www.education.gouv.fr
http://www.recherche.gouv.fr

## Ministère de l'Équipement, du Logement, des Transports et du Tourisme

*Ministry of Housing, Transportation, and Tourism*
Parvis de la Défense
92055 LA DÉFENSE Cedex
Tel: 01 40 81 21 22
Web site: http://www.equip.gouv.fr

## Ministère de l'Industrie

*Ministry of Industry*
101, ave de Grenelle
75007 PARIS
Tel: 01 43 19 36 36
Web site: http://www.industrie.gouv.fr

## Ministère de l'Intérieur

*Ministry of the Interior*
Place Beauvau
75008 PARIS
Tel: 01 40 07 60 60

## Ministère de la Défense

*Ministry of Defense*
14, rue Saint Dominique
75007 PARIS
Tel: 01 42 19 30 11
Tel: 01 47 05 55 85

## Ministère de la Jeunesse et des Sports

*Ministry of Youth and Sports*
78, rue Olivier de Serres
75015 PARIS
Tel: 01 40 45 90 00
Fax: 01 42 50 42 49
Web site:
http://www.jeunesse-sports.gouv.fr

## Ministère de la Justice

*Ministry of Justice*
13, place Vendôme
75001 PARIS
Tel: 01 44 77 60 60
Fax: 01 44 77 60 00
Web site: http://www.justice.gouv.fr

## Ministère des Affaires Étrangères

*Ministry of Foreign Affairs*
37, quai d'Orsay
75007 PARIS
Tel: 01 43 17 53 53
Web site: http://www.diplomatie.gouv.fr

## Ministère des Petites et Moyennes Entreprises, du Commerce et de l'Artisanat

*French equivalent of Small Business Administration*
80, rue de Lille
75007 PARIS
Tel: 01 43 19 24 24

## Ministère du Travail et des Affaires Sociales

*Ministry of Labor*
127, rue de Grenelle
75007 PARIS
Tel: 01 44 38 38 38
Tel: 01 44 38 21 50

## Port Autonome de Paris

2, quai de Grenelle
75732 PARIS Cedex 15
Tel: 01 40 58 29 99
Fax: 01 45 78 08 57
Contact: M. CHENEVEZ

## Préfecture de Police

*Central police authority*
7, Bd du Palais
75004 PARIS
Tel: 01 53 71 53 71
Admin: 01 53 71 31 11
Lost/Found: 01 55 76 20 00
Cartes Grises: 01 53 71 39 00
(car registry)

*DOING BUSINESS & WORKING*

83

## EMPLOYMENT ADMINISTRATIONS
### Organismes professionnels

### ADAMI
*Administration of authors' royalites*
10 a, rue de la Paix
75002 PARIS
Tel: 01 40 15 10 00
Fax: 01 40 15 10 30
General Director: M. Patrick BOIRON

### AGESSA
*Social Security office for authors*
21 bis, rue de Bruxelles
75009 PARIS
Tel: 01 48 78 25 00
Fax: 01 48 78 60 00

### ANPE
*National Employment Agency*
123, rue Oberkampf
75011 PARIS
Tel: 01 49 23 33 00
Fax: 01 43 55 99 02

### ASSEDIC de Paris
*Employment agency for industry and trade*
4, rue Traversière
75012 PARIS
Tel: 01 40 19 25 00
Fax: 01 43 42 53 53

### Chambre Syndicale de la Couture Parisienne
*Organization of Parisian fashion houses*
100, rue du Fbg Saint Honoré
75008 PARIS
Tel: 01 42 66 64 44
Fax: 01 42 66 94 63

### Inter Europe Emploi-ANPE
*Helps French people find work in other European countries*
69, rue Jean-Baptiste Pigalle
75009 PARIS
Tel: 01 44 53 16 16
Fax: 01 48 74 42 53

### La Maison des Artistes
*Social Security office for artists*
11, rue Berryer
75008 PARIS
Tel: 01 45 63 32 82
Fax: 01 45 63 94 97

### SACD
*Organization of authors and composers for the theater*
11 bis, rue Ballu
75009 PARIS
Tel: 01 40 23 44 44
Fax: 01 45 26 74 28
Email: infosacd@sacd.fr
Web site: http://www.sacd.fr
President: M. YOURI

### SACEM
*Organization of authors, composers et music publishers*
225, ave Charles de Gaulle
92221 NEUILLY SUR SEINE Cedex
Tel: 01 47 15 47 15
Fax: 01 47 45 12 94
President: M. Jacques DEMARNY

### SCAM
*Organization of multimedia authors*
38, rue du Fbg Saint Jacques
75014 PARIS
Tel: 01 40 51 33 00
Fax: 01 43 54 92 99
Communications Director:
M. Stéphane JOSEPH

### URSSAF
*Social Security office for self-employed workers*
3, rue Franklin
93518 MONTREUIL SOUS BOIS Cedex
Info: 01 49 20 40 80
Tel: 01 49 20 10 10
Fax: 01 48 51 75 75
Minitel: 3615 UR75

84

## OECD (Organization for Economic Cooperation and Development)
2, rue André Pascal
75016 PARIS Cedex 16
Tel: 01 45 24 82 00
Fax: 01 45 24 85 00
General Secretary: M. Jean-Claude PAYE

## OECD British Delegation
2, rue André Pascal
75116 PARIS
Tel: 01 45 24 98 28

## OECD Canadian Delegation
15 bis, rue de Franqueville
75016 PARIS
Tel: 01 44 43 20 90

## OECD US Delegation
19, rue de Franqueville
75016 PARIS
Tel: 01 45 24 74 77

## UNESCO
7, place de Fontenoy
75007 PARIS
Tel: 01 45 68 10 00
Fax: 01 45 67 16 90
Director:
M. Federico MAYOR-ZARAGOZA

## World Bank (Banque Mondiale)
64, ave d'Iéna
75116 PARIS
Tel: 01 40 69 30 00
Fax: 01 40 69 30 66
Web site: http://www.worldbank.org

*DOING BUSINESS & WORKING*

85

# INSURANCE
## ASSURANCES

Getting informed as to the ins and outs of insurance coverage in France requires a good broker. Here's a place to start when it comes to homeowner, automobile, life, office, and health insurance packages.

### Advantage Insurance Associates

**ADVANTAGE INSURANCE**
**• ASSOCIATES •**

*The only insurance brokers dedicated to serving Americans in France*
*(See advertisement)*
17, rue de Chateaudun
75009 PARIS
Tel: 01 53 20 03 33
Fax: 01 44 63 00 97
Email: advantag@easynet.fr
Web site: http://www.paris-anglo.com/housing
Manager: M. Vincent KUHN

### Allianz Via Assurances

2-4, ave du Général de Gaulle
94672 CHARENTON LE PONT Cedex
Tel: 01 46 76 76 76
Fax: 01 46 76 76 13
Group Communications Director:
M. Rémi CAUMONT

### Anglo-French Underwriters

25, rue de Liège
75008 PARIS
Tel: 01 44 70 71 00
Fax: 01 42 93 47 42
Contact: M. Thierry GUYONNET

### British Continental and Overseas Agencies Assurances

174, Bd Saint Germain
75006 PARIS
Tel: 01 44 39 25 00
Fax: 01 44 39 25 19
Web site: http://www.aon.com
Director: M. PAYNE

### Cabinet Vasseur

79, route de la Reine
92100 BOULOGNE
Tel: 01 46 04 41 03
Fax: 01 46 03 11 26

### Cerise Assurances

199, rue des Pyrénées
75020 PARIS
Tel: 01 47 97 64 80
Tel2: 01 47 97 95 42
Contact: M. Reuben GILES

### Chubb Insurance Company of Europe

16, ave Matignon
75008 PARIS
Tel: 01 45 61 73 00
Fax: 01 45 61 98 51
Mkt Director: Mme Marie BAZETOUX

### Cigna International

14, rue Ballu
75009 PARIS
Tel: 01 44 53 64 06
Fax: 01 42 80 69 85
Contacts: Mmes Catherine VAUTRIN & Madeleine LEODDI

### Columbus Health Care

Le Mentet
24610 CARSAC DE GURSON
Tel: 05 53 81 78 79
Fax: 05 53 81 78 79
Contact: M. John STEVENS

### Continent Assurances

62, rue de Richelieu
75002 PARIS
Tel: 01 43 16 65 00
Fax: 01 43 16 69 00
Web site:
http://www.continent-assurances.tm.fr

## Continental Insurance Company

16, rue de Vienne
75008 PARIS
Tel: 01 40 08 09 04
Fax: 01 40 08 06 94

## Credit Insurance Association France

35, rue Washington
75008 PARIS
Tel: 01 45 63 09 62
Fax: 01 53 75 06 76

## Eagle Star Vie

12, rue Torricelli
75017 PARIS
Tel: 01 44 09 44 09
Fax: 01 44 09 44 99
Director: M. Ghislain BEDUNEAU

## Eurofil

3, rue Eugène et Armand Peugeot
92505 RUEIL MALMAISON Cedex
Tel: 01 47 14 59 00
Fax: 01 47 14 59 32

## Europ Assistance

1, promenade de la Bonnette
92633 GENNEVILLIERS Cedex
Tel: 01 41 85 85 85
Fax: 01 41 85 85 71

## European Benefits Administrators

59, rue de Châteaudun
75009 PARIS
Tel: 01 42 81 97 00
Fax: 01 42 81 99 03
Email: euroben@euroben.com
Contact: Mme CHATELLIER

## F.A.C.

56, rue de Londres
75008 PARIS
Tel: 01 44 70 77 77
Fax: 01 42 93 44 93
Contact: Mme DJIDER

## Factory Mutual International

21, rue du Pré Faucon
Parc des Glaisins
BP 117
74941 ANNECY LE VIEUX Cedex
Tel: 04 50 65 50 65
Fax: 04 50 64 10 85
Engineering Manager:
M. Marc SURLERAUX

## Faugere & Jutheau

54, quai Michelet
92681 LEVALLOIS PERRET Cedex
Tel: 01 41 34 50 00
Fax: 01 41 34 55 00
Contact: M. Stanislas CHAPRON

## Guardian Risque

20, rue Jacques Daguerre
92568 RUEIL MALMAISON Cedex
Tel: 01 47 10 20 00
Fax: 01 47 10 20 10
Director: M. Robin G. MORLEY

## Lloyds of London

4, rue des Petits Pères
75002 PARIS
Tel: 01 42 60 43 43
Fax: 01 42 60 14 41

## Norwich Union France

1, rue de l'Union
92843 RUEIL MALMAISON Cedex
Tel: 01 41 39 40 23
Fax: 01 47 49 41 51
Commercial Director: M. CHOPLET

## Owa Insurance Services France

66, cours de Vincennes
75020 PARIS
Tel: 01 44 75 22 00
Fax: 01 44 75 22 10

## Sant and Co.

8, rue Halévy
75009 PARIS
Tel: 01 47 42 79 44
Fax: 01 42 68 31 70
Director: M. BEULLENS

# INSURANCE
## ASSURANCES

### Secco France
20, Bd de Courcelles
75017 PARIS
Tel: 01 42 27 51 53
Fax: 01 43 80 14 10
Director: M. C.M. WILSON

### Skandia International
4, rue Cambon
4th Floor
75001 PARIS
Tel: 01 42 61 51 45
Fax: 01 42 60 24 17

### Société Générale de Courtage d'Assurances
7-9, rue Belgrand
92309 LEVALLOIS PERRET
Tel: 01 47 56 60 60
Fax: 01 47 30 94 00
Chairman: M. Christian ROCHETEAU

### Société Intercontinentale d'Assurances pour le Commerce et l'Industrie
46, rue Pierre Charon
75008 PARIS
Tel: 01 40 69 74 74
Fax: 01 47 20 47 18
Contact: M. Roderic UPTON

### Taylor Sagassur
36, rue Laffitte
75009 PARIS
Tel: 01 44 79 04 04
Fax: 01 44 79 01 47
Contact: M. Philippe CONSOLI

### The Independent Consultancy Group France
Le Wilson 1, La Défense
70, ave du Président Wilson
92800 PUTEAUX
Tel: 01 47 78 17 34
Fax: 01 47 78 17 35
Contact: M. Stephan SMART

### Toplis et Harding
80, Bd Haussmann
75008 PARIS
Tel: 01 44 70 66 10
Fax: 01 43 87 40 16
Director: M. Peter HALL

### Tyler and Co.
12, rue de la Paix
75002 PARIS
Tel: 01 42 61 63 31
Fax: 01 42 61 95 71
Director: M. B. ISITT

# INTERNET/NEW MEDIA
## INTERNET/NOUVEAUX MÉDIAS

PARIS-ANGLOPHONE enthusiastically endorses the use of the Internet for both business and pleasure. Grouped here are Paris-based access providers and online services, followed by a concise list of multimedia and Web developers and related multimedia companies. Lastly, here are a few suggestions on Paris-oriented newsgroups, and Web sites. For Web bars, see the Living & Studying section of the directory. Otherwise, log on at http://www.paris-anglo.com

### ACCESS PROVIDERS/ ON LINE SERVICES
Fournisseurs d'accès/ Services en ligne

### ABC Internet
18, rue Pradier
75019 PARIS
Tel: 01 42 40 57 21
Fax: 01 42 40 57 51
Email: info@inp.fr
Web site: http://www.inp.fr
Contact: M. Patrick SINZ

### Adi
9, Villa Brune
75014 PARIS
Tel: 01 45 45 50 68
Fax: 01 45 41 72 74
Email: magre@adi.fr
Web site: http://www.adi.fr
Contact: M. Dominique MAGRE

### AOL/Bertelsmann Online
*Expanding America On Line in Europe*
4, rue de la Bourse
75002 PARIS
Tel: 01 69 19 94 51
Hotline: 0 800 903 910
Minitel: 3615 AOL
Web site: http://www.france.aol.com

### CalvaCom
8-10, rue Nieuport
78140 VELIZY
Tel: 01 34 63 19 19
Fax: 01 34 63 19 48
Email: scom@calva.net
Web site: http://www.calvacom.fr

### CompuServe
Centre Atria Rueil 2000
21, ave Édouard Belin
92566 RUEIL MALMAISON
Tel: 08 01 63 81 31 (technical support)
Tel: 08 01 63 81 22 (commercial service)
Fax: 01 47 14 21 51
Email: 70006,101@compuserve.com
Web site: http://www.compuserve.com
Director: M. Bernard USUNIER

### Easynet

**easynet**
*Call for all your Internet connections and mention Paris-Anglophone*
23, rue du Renard
75004 PARIS
Tel: 01 44 54 53 33
Fax: 01 44 54 53 39
Email: info@easynet.fr
Web site: http://www.easynet.fr
Contact: M. Guillaume TOUCHAIS

89

## EUnet France

# ≡EUnet≡

*Leading Internet and Intranet access provider specializing in institutional networks and online services for companies and organizations*

52, ave de la Grande Armée
75017 PARIS
Tel: 01 53 81 60 60
Fax: 01 45 74 52 79
Email: contact@eunet.fr
Web site: http://www.eunet.fr
Director: M. Eric
LAURENT-RICARD

## Grolier Interactive Europe Online Group

131, ave Charles de Gaulle
92200 NEUILLY SUR SEINE
Tel: 01 47 45 96 07
Fax: 01 47 45 99 30
Web site: http://www.club-internet.fr
General Director: M. Fabrice SERGENT

## Havas Online

31, rue du Colisée
75008 PARIS
Tel: 08 36 69 13 00
Fax: 01 53 53 89 54
Web site: http://www.havas.fr

## Internet Francenet

28, rue Desaix
75015 PARIS
Tel: 01 43 92 14 49
Fax: 01 43 92 14 45
Minitel: 3615 FRANCENET
Email: info-english@francenet.fr
Web site: http://www.francenet.fr

## Internet (Service Plus)

13, rue du Centre
78650 BEYNES
Tel: 01 44 19 66 49
Fax: 01 34 89 00 98
Email: info@isp.fr
Web site: http://www.isp.fr
Contact: Mme Corinne KLUCIK

## Internet Way

204, Bd Bineau
92200 NEUILLY SUR SEINE
Tel: 01 41 43 21 10
Fax: 01 41 43 21 11
Email: info@iway.fr
Web site: http://www.iway.fr
Director: M. Jérôme LECAT

## Internet-Micronet

28, rue Desaix
75015 PARIS
Tel: 01 43 92 12 12
Fax: 01 43 92 12 13
Email: info@micronet.fr
Web site: http://www.micronet.fr

## MSN Microsoft France

*Microsoft's Internet navigation software and network*

18, ave du Québec
91957 COURTABOEUF Cedex
Tel: 01 69 86 46 46
Tel: 01 69 86 10 20 (technical support)
Hotline: 01 69 86 47 47
Fax: 01 69 86 47 99
Web site: http://www.msn.fr
Director of dev.:
M. Jean-Christophe DEFLINE

## Netscape Communications

CNIT BP 370
2, place de la Défense
92053 PARIS LA DÉFENSE
Tel: 01 41 97 55 55
Fax: 01 41 97 55 00
Web site: http://www.netscape.com
European Mkt & Comm. Dir.:
Mme Sophie CALLIES

## Syntel

12 ter, rue Jonquoy
75014 PARIS
Tel: 01 40 52 07 17
Fax: 01 45 41 57 13
Email: syntel@syntel.fr
Contact: M. CURS

## Worldnet
11-13, rue L'Escaut
75019 PARIS
Tel: 01 40 37 90 90
Fax: 01 40 37 90 89
Email: sales@worldnet.fr
Web site: http://www.worldnet.fr

## Yahoo France
*Major search engine for French web sites*
14, place Marie-Jeanne Bassot
92593 LEVALLOIS PERRET Cedex
Tel: 01 46 39 55 32
Fax: 01 46 39 00 70
Email: webmaster@yahoo.fr
Web site: http://www.yahoo.fr
Chief Editor: M. Denis JAMET

## MULTIMEDIA/ WEB DEVELOPERS
### Constructeurs de sites web

## Ad Hoc Informatique
Le Cloitre
Rue Pannecau
64390 SAUVETERRE DE BEARN
Tel: 05 59 38 59 60
Fax: 05 59 38 92 50
Email: adhoc@adhoc-fr.com
Web site: http://www.adhoc.com
M. Neil McCARTHY

## AJIF

*Based on your needs, AJIF defines, designs, creates, updates, manages and names your multilingual website*
44, rue de Laborde
75008 PARIS
Tel: 01 43 87 19 41
Fax: 01 43 87 00 46
Email: furtado@ibm.net
Web site: http://www.ajif.com
Director: M. Adrian FURTADO

## Artinternet
1, ave Alphand
75116 PARIS
Tel: 01 43 45 49 56
Fax: 01 43 45 50 91
Email: info@artinternet.fr
Web site: http://www.artinternet.fr
Contact: M. Cédric LOISON

## Biagi Consulting
30, rue Sedaine
75011 PARIS
Tel: 01 43 38 53 47
Email: paul.biagi@hol.fr
Web site: http://ourworld.compuserve.com/homepages/pbiagi
President: M. Paul BIAGI

## Cyberion/Studi
BP 1123
86062 POITIERS Cedex 9
Tel: 05 49 88 81 25
Fax: 05 49 55 33 24
Email: jmoore@cyberion.fr
Web site: http://www.cyberion.fr
Contact: M. James MOORE

## G.T. Interactive
*Distributor of CD-Rom interactive video games*
26, Bd Malesherbes
75008 PARIS
Tel: 01 43 12 31 00
Fax: 01 43 12 31 19
Web site: http://www./gtinteractive.com

## Gyoza Media

*World Wide Web development and consulting*
9, rue aux Ours
75003 PARIS
Tel: 01 44 54 32 90
Fax: 01 44 54 32 99
Email: cory@gyoza.com
Web site: http://www.gyoza.com
Contact: M. Cory McCLOUD

DOING BUSINESS & WORKING

## Hyptique

17, impasse Truillot
75011 PARIS
Tel: 01 49 29 53 00
Fax: 01 49 29 53 19
Email: friends@hyptique.com
Web site: http://www.hyptique.com
Director: M. Pierre LAVOIE

## InterActive Bureau

*IAB is a Paris-based Web site development and content-driven design company with offices worldwide*
18, ave de l'Opéra
75001 PARIS
Tel: 01 42 60 86 86
Fax: 01 42 60 86 01
Email: rens@iabparis.com
Web site: http://www.iabparis.com
Director: Mme Martine WINTER

## Internet

9, villa Brune
75014 PARIS
Tel: 01 45 45 50 68
Fax: 01 45 41 72 74
Email: info@adi.fr
Web site: http://www.adi.fr

## Internet Partner

20, rue Pradier
75019 PARIS
Tel: 01 42 40 57 21
Fax: 01 40 40 79 44
Web site: http://www.inp.fr

## Le Lab

*Web creation*
67, rue Richelieu
75002 PARIS
Tel: 01 47 03 19 19
Fax: 01 49 26 04 18
Email: info@lelab.fr
Web site: http://www.lelab.fr
Contact: M. Vincent KNOBIL

## Le Pôle Multimédia

44-46, rue Saint-Maur
75011 PARIS
Tel: 01 47 00 39 18
Fax: 01 48 90 45 19
Email: chatelot@lpmstudio.com
Director: M. Pierre CHATELOT

## Mediaplay International

75, ave Niel
75017 PARIS
Tel: 01 47 54 05 65
Fax: 01 46 22 22 76
Web site: http://www.mediaplayintl.com
President: Mme Ferhan COOK

## Quartet Informatique

99-101, Chemin de Clères
76130 MONT SAINT AIGNAN
Tel: 02 35 98 29 08
Fax: 02 35 88 14 96
Email: quartet@mcom.mcom.fr
Sales Manager:
M. Emmanuel DA COSTA

## Rebus

*Web site design*
14, rue Saint Croix de la Bretonnerie
75004 PARIS
Tel: 01 42 77 20 49
Fax: 01 40 27 08 88
Email: rebus@iway.fr
Director: M. Robert HUNTER

## Solutions En Ligne

Solutions En Ligne

*Consulting, support, and turn-key systems solutions for data/tele-comms, finance, and small businesses*
13, rue Réaumur
75003 PARIS
Tel: 01 44 61 81 33
Fax: 01 44 61 81 34
Email: gbt@solutions.fr
Director: M. Geoffrey TOLCHIN

## Spinnaker Internet Services

*Advertising and communication agency on-line and off-line.*
96, ave du Géneral Leclerc
92100 BOULOGNE
Tel: 01 48 25 44 55
Email: silber@spinnaker.fr
Web site: http://www.spinnaker.fr
President: Mme Denise SILBER

## Unipower Systems Limited

32, rue Jacques Ibert
75858 PARIS Cedex 17
Tel: 01 40 89 59 96
Fax: 01 47 58 01 96
Email: laurent.prat@unipower.co.uk
Web site: http://www.unipower.co.uk
Consultant: M. Laurent PRAT

## Virtual Riviera

10, rue Sade
06600 ANTIBES
Tel: 04 92 90 60 83
Email: gw@bigfoot.com
Contact: M. Georges WAGNER

## Voicebook

94, Bd Flandrin
75116 PARIS
Tel: 01 45 53 73 23
Fax: 01 45 53 73 24
Email: voicebook@club-internet.fr
Web site: http://www.voicebook.com
Contact: M. Bertrand BEAUGONIN

## WebFrance International

3, les Grandes Bruyères
91470 BOULLAY LES TROUX
Tel: 01 60 12 05 65
Fax: 01 60 12 06 56
Email: info@wfi.fr
Web site: http://www.wfi.fr

## MULTIMEDIA-RELATED COMPANIES
## Autres services multimédia

## FormavisionFrance

87-89, rue des Rosiers
Le Mont Valérien
92500 RUEIL MALMAISON
Tel: 01 47 08 12 12
Fax: 01 47 08 01 58
Email: duncan@easynet.fr
Web site: http://www.wfi.fr/formavision
Contact: M. Bruce DUNCAN-SMITH

## Multimédia Investissement

42, rue de Bassano
75008 BRY SUR MARNE Cedex
Tel: 01 53 23 86 00
Fax: 01 53 23 86 09
Web site: http://www.2ni.com

## Numéro 6

*Audiovisual, broadcast production*
116, rue de Charenton
75012 PARIS
Tel: 01 42 42 36 36
Fax: 01 47 85 12 21
Email: pleonard@pratique.fr
Contacts: MM. Marcel LOSHOUARN
& Pascal LÉONARD

## VISA International

*Electronic commerce, cybermoney*
14, Bd Malesherbes
75008 PARIS
Tel: 01 53 30 87 49
Fax: 01 47 42 37 27
Email: hilt@visa.com
Web site: http://www.visa.com
Vice president: M. Jeff HILT

## NEWSGROUPS/ PARIS-RELATED WEB SITES
## Forums de discussion/ Sites web sur Paris

## AngloFiles

*To receive Paris community newsletter send email to:*
majordomo@iway.fr
or visit http://www.iway.fr/AngloFiles

## France Online

*For the French community in the United States*
http://www.france.com

## GAP Guide to Pubs & Bars

http://ourworld.compuserve.com/
homepages/Adams_page/

## Leeds Good Value Guide to Paris Restaurants

http://www.fi.fr/leeds

## Paris-Anglophone/ FrancoFile Club

http://www.paris-anglo.com

## Paris Pages

*Extensive collection of France-related cultural pages and links*
http://www.paris.org

## World Media

http://www.worldmedia.fr

DOING BUSINESS & WORKING

93

# LAWYERS/LAW FIRMS
## CABINETS D'AVOCATS

Although lawyers in France are regulated in the area of promotion, the presence of those who work with international clients need to be known, and thus PARIS-ANGLOPHONE has brought together an elaborate list of Paris-based lawyers handling both corporate and individual legal needs.

### Allen & Overy

1, ave Franklin Roosevelt
75008 PARIS
Tel: 01 49 53 06 37
Fax: 01 49 53 91 52
Email: helpdesk@allenovery.com
Web site: http://www.allenovery.com
Senior Partner:
M. David ST JOHN SUTTON

### Archibald Andersen Association d'Avocats

41, rue Ibry
92576 NEUILLY SUR SEINE
Tel: 01 55 61 10 10
Fax: 01 55 61 15 15

### Baker & McKenzie

32, ave Kléber
75116 PARIS
Tel: 01 44 17 53 00
Fax: 01 44 17 45 75
Senior Partner:
Mme Christine LAGARDE

### Barker-Davies

1, rue Lincoln
75008 PARIS
Tel: 01 45 62 10 61
Fax: 01 45 63 34 77
Senior Partner:
M. John Clive BARKER-DAVIES

### Bensoussan, Alain

29, rue du Colonel Pierre Avia
75015 PARIS
Tel: 01 41 33 35 35
Fax: 01 41 33 35 36
Email: 101510.113@compuserve.com

### Berlioz & Co.

68, Bd de Courcelles
75017 PARIS
Tel: 01 44 01 44 01
Fax: 01 42 67 04 43
Senior Partner: M. Georges BERLIOZ

### Bureau Francis Lefebvre

1-3, Villa Émile Bergerat
92522 NEUILLY SUR SEINE
Tel: 01 47 38 55 00
Fax: 01 47 38 55 55
Contact: M. Robert BACONNIER

### Cabinet Benoît

16, rue Etienne Marcel
75002 PARIS
Tel: 01 42 33 49 96
Fax: 01 42 33 49 97
Senior Partner: Me Marc-Luc BENOIT

### Cabinet Boquet

41, ave Bosquet
75007 PARIS
Tel: 01 47 05 48 64
Fax: 01 47 05 17 74

### Cabinet Catherine Kessedjian

72, Bd Saint Germain
75005 PARIS
Tel: 01 40 51 82 24
Fax: 01 44 07 20 51
Contact: Mme Catherine KESSEDJIAN

### Cabinet Gilles Khaïat

*General French European economic and international practice aviation law. General litigation, new technologies*

58, rue la Boétie
75008 PARIS
Tel: 01 45 63 06 20
Tel2: 06 60 47 85 59
Fax: 01 45 63 16 22
Email: gilles.khaiat@paris.barreau.fr

### Cabinet Jean Claude Richard

BP 67
13484 MARSEILLE Cedex 20
Tel: 04 91 54 01 23
Fax: 04 91 33 14 41
Email: jcr@easynet.fr

## Cahill Gordon & Reindel

19, rue François Ier
75008 PARIS
Tel: 01 47 20 10 50
Fax: 01 47 23 06 38
Senior Partner: Me Freddy DRESSEN

## Chaintrier & Associés

5, ave George V
75008 PARIS
Tel: 01 47 23 00 09
Fax: 01 47 23 68 79
Senior Partner: Me Philippe CHARHON

## Chance-Duzant, Patricia

6, ave Théophile Gautier
75016 PARIS
Tel: 01 42 88 08 22
Fax: 01 45 20 12 67

## CLEA

5, rue Beaujon
75008 PARIS
Tel: 01 53 81 53 00
Fax: 01 53 81 53 30

## Cleary, Gottlieb, Steen & Hamilton

41, ave de Friedland
75008 PARIS
Tel: 01 40 74 68 00
Fax: 01 45 63 35 09

## Clifford Chance

112, ave Kléber
BP 163 Trocadéro
75770 PARIS Cedex 16
Tel: 01 44 05 52 52
Fax: 01 44 05 52 00
Web site: http://www.cliffordchance.com
Contact: M. Brian CORDERY

## Coudert Frères

52, ave des Champs Élysées
75008 PARIS
Tel: 01 53 83 60 00
Fax: 01 53 83 60 60
Email: info@paris.coudert.com
Senior Partner: M. Jacques BUHART

## Curtis Mallet-Prévost Colt & Mosle

15, rue d'Astorg
75008 PARIS
Tel: 01 42 66 39 10
Fax: 01 42 66 39 62
Managing Partner: M. Peter WOLRICH

## Davis Polk & Wardwell

4, place de la Concorde
75008 PARIS
Tel: 01 40 17 36 00
Fax: 01 42 65 22 34

## Debevoise & Plimpton

21, ave George V
75008 PARIS
Tel: 01 40 73 12 12
Fax: 01 47 20 50 82
Contact: M. James KIERNAN

## Dechert Price & Rhoads

151, Bd Haussman
75008 PARIS
Tel: 01 53 83 84 70
Fax: 01 53 75 26 47
Contact: Mme Elizabeth MACEACHRAN

## Deloitte et Touche Juridique et Fiscal

185, ave Charles de Gaulle
92201 NEUILLY SUR SEINE Cedex
Tel: 01 40 88 28 00
Fax: 01 40 88 28 28
Contact: M. Hervé BARDON

## Deprez, Degroux, Brugère, De Pingon

83, Bd Haussmann
75008 PARIS
Tel: 01 42 65 70 81
Fax: 01 40 17 07 58
Partner: Me DELATTRE

## Donovan Leisure Newton & Irvine

130, rue du Fbg Saint Honoré
75008 PARIS
Tel: 01 42 25 47 10
Fax: 01 42 56 08 06
Senior Partner:
M. René de MONSEIGNAT

# LAWYERS/LAW FIRMS
## CABINETS D'AVOCATS

### FG Associés

50, ave Victor Hugo
75016 PARIS
Tel: 01 44 17 46 90
Fax: 01 44 17 97 30
Contact:
Mme Christiane FERAL-SCHUHL

### Fredenberger, John C.

109, ave Henri Martin
75116 PARIS
Tel: 01 45 04 10 10
Fax: 01 45 04 49 67

### Frere Cholmeley

42, ave du Président Wilson
75116 PARIS
Tel: 01 44 34 71 00
Fax: 01 44 34 71 11
Senior Partner: M. Richard MEESE

### Fried, Frank, Harris, Shriver & Jacobson

7, rue Royale
75008 PARIS
Tel: 01 40 17 04 04
Fax: 01 40 17 08 30
Contact: M. Éric CAFRITZ

### Hogan & Hartson

12, rue de la Paix
75002 PARIS
Tel: 01 42 61 57 71
Fax: 01 42 61 79 21

### HSD Juridique et Fiscal

Tour Manhattan
6, place de l'Iris
92095 PARIS LA DÉFENSE 2
Cedex 21
Tel: 01 46 93 60 00
Fax: 01 47 67 01 06
Contact: M. Pierre-Alain MOLINIER

### Hughes Hubbard & Reed

47, ave Georges Mandel
75116 PARIS
Tel: 01 44 05 80 00
Fax: 01 45 53 15 04
Email: baum@hugheshubbard.com
Managing Partner: M. Axel BAUM

### Itéanu & Associés

166, rue du Fbg Saint Honoré
75008 PARIS
Tel: 01 42 56 90 00
Fax: 01 42 56 90 02
Email: iteanu@calva.net
Web site: http://www.iteanu.com
Contact: Me Olivier ITEANU

### J.P. Karsenty & Associates

70, Bd de Courcelles
75017 PARIS
Tel: 01 47 63 74 75
Fax: 01 46 22 33 27
Contact: Me KARSENTY

### Jacob & Polier (Law Offices of)

*French, US & international law:
contract negotiations, creditors'
rights, litigation/arbitration, family*
4, rue de Marignan
75008 PARIS
Tel: 01 47 23 41 51
Fax: 01 47 23 37 93
Email: 100060.1724@compuserve.com
Web site:
http://ourworld.compuserve.com/
home pages/Paris_Law
Contact: M. Jonathon Wise POLIER

### Joan Squires-Lind Law Offices

6, rue du Foin
75003 PARIS
Tel: 01 44 59 82 57
Fax: 01 44 59 82 69
Email: 73411,226@compuserve.com

### Jones Day Reavis & Pogue

62, rue du Fbg Saint Honoré
75008 PARIS
Tel: 01 49 24 09 09
Fax: 01 49 24 04 71
Senior Partner: M. Wesley JOHNSON

### Joslove, Bradley

c/o Salès Vincent & Associés
43, rue du Fbg Saint Honoré
75008 PARIS
Tel: 01 42 66 50 31
Fax: 01 42 66 58 95

## Kahn & Associés

9, rue Anatole de la Forge
75017 PARIS
Tel: 01 42 67 03 20
Fax: 01 42 67 03 24
Email: dkahn@kahnlaw.com
Web site: http://www.kahnlaw.com
Contact: Me Daniel KAHN

## Kimbrough & Associés

72, Bd Saint Germain
75005 PARIS
Tel: 01 53 73 24 24
Fax: 01 43 29 98 38
Email: 100675,3454@compuserve.com
Senior Partner:
M. Philip R. KIMBROUGH

## KPMG Fidal Peat International

47, rue de Villiers
92200 NEUILLY SUR SEINE
Tel: 01 46 39 44 44
Fax: 01 47 59 71 38
Contact: M. STENOU

## KPMG Peat Marwick

53, ave Montaigne
75008 PARIS
Tel: 01 40 76 86 85
Fax: 01 45 61 69 25
Contact: Mme Kelly DONAWHO

## Laprès, Daniel

3, rue de l'Arrivée
75015 PARIS
Tel: 01 45 38 67 07
Fax: 01 45 38 69 89
Email: 100275.2144@compuserve.com
Web site: http://www.gyoza.com/lapres

## Lette, Lette & Associés

3, rue du Boccador
75008 PARIS
Tel: 01 40 73 16 00
Fax: 01 40 73 16 11
Email: 101621,3260@compuserve.com
Contact: Me Ph. LETTE

## Levine & Okoshken

*Income tax, wills and estate planning, corporate law, employment agreements, setting-up businesses, and obtaining French visas*

51, ave Montaigne
75008 PARIS
Tel: 01 44 13 69 50
Fax: 01 45 63 24 96
Email: 100537,2541@compuserve.com
Partner: M. Samuel OKOSHKEN

## Lichtlen, Dominique

9, rue Alfred de Vigny
75008 PARIS
Tel: 01 40 53 09 90
Fax: 01 40 53 09 08
Email: do.lichtlen@paris.barreau.fr

## Meade & Nabias

85, rue de Courcelles
75017 PARIS
Tel: 01 42 67 14 89
Fax: 01 42 67 06 08
Email:
cabinet@meadenabias.paris.barreau.fr
Contact: M. Richard MEADE

## Moquet, Borde, Dieux, Geens & Associés

30, ave de Messine
75008 PARIS
Tel: 01 42 99 04 50
Fax: 01 45 63 91 49
Partner: M. Dominique BORDE, Esq.

## Neuer, Jean-Jacques

22, rue de Longchamp
75116 PARIS
Tel: 01 47 04 39 21
Fax: 01 47 04 78 18

## Ngo, Miguères et Associés

45, ave Montaigne
75008 PARIS
Tel: 01 47 20 92 92
Fax: 01 47 23 53 21
Resident Partner:
Me Martine-Claire BOURRY D'ANTIN

# LAWYERS/LAW FIRMS
## CABINETS D'AVOCATS

## Osler Renault
4, rue Bayard
75008 PARIS
Tel: 01 42 89 00 54
Fax: 01 42 89 51 60
Partner: Me Serge GRAVEL

## Paul, Weiss, Rikfind, Wharton & Garrison
62, rue du Fbg Saint Honoré
75008 PARIS
Tel: 01 53 43 14 14
Fax: 01 53 43 00 23
Resident Partner:
M. Dominique FARGUE

## Pavie-Lucas Associés
22, ave de la Grande Armée
75017 PARIS
Tel: 01 44 09 98 98
Fax: 01 40 53 93 30
Contact: M. Philippe PAVIE

## Price Waterhouse Fiscal et Juridique
Tour AIG
34? place des Carolles
92908 PARIS LA DÉFENSE Cedex
Tel: 01 41 26 16 00
Fax: 01 41 26 16 16
Partner: M. Michel JAFFE

## Rogers & Wells
47, ave Hoche
75008 PARIS
Tel: 01 44 09 46 00
Fax: 01 44 09 46 01
Fax2: 01 42 67 50 81
Contact: Me MARQUARDT

## Rosman Leonard Law Offices
18, rue Bayard
75008 PARIS
Tel: 01 53 83 86 90
Fax: 01 53 83 86 91

## Sagot & Maintrieu
9, rue d'Anjou
75008 PARIS
Tel: 01 42 66 48 20
Fax: 01 42 68 02 50
Senior Partner:
Mme Valérie MAINTRIEU

## Salès Vincent & Associés
43, rue du Fbg Saint Honoré
75008 PARIS
Tel: 01 44 71 22 00
Fax: 01 42 66 58 95
Email: sva@worldnet.net

## SCP Barsi, Doumith et Associés
186, ave Victor Hugo
75116 PARIS
Tel: 01 45 03 16 26
Fax: 01 45 03 07 86

## SCP Bizet-Krassilchik
16, rue de Varenne
75007 PARIS
Tel: 01 45 44 23 93
Fax: 01 42 22 36 46
Senior Partners: MM. François &
Michel BIZET-KRASSILCHIK

## Serra Michaud & Associés
2, rue de la Baume
75008 PARIS
Tel: 01 44 21 97 97
Fax: 01 42 89 57 90
Email: sma@calvanet.calvacom.fr
Contact: M. James LEAVY

## Simenard (Cabinet)
16, ave George V
75008 PARIS
Tel: 01 53 23 94 20
Fax: 01 40 70 16 08
Contact: Stephanie SIMENARD

## Shearman & Sterling
14, ave des Champs Élysées
75008 PARIS
Tel: 01 53 89 70 00
Fax: 01 53 89 70 70
Contact: M. Hubertus SULKOWSKI

## Slaughter and May
112, ave Kléber
75116 PARIS
Tel: 01 44 05 60 00
Fax: 01 44 05 60 60
Senior Partner: M. Peter KETT

## Sullivan & Cromwell
8, place Vendôme
75001 PARIS
Tel: 01 44 50 60 00
Fax: 01 44 50 60 60
Contact: M. ASTHALTER

### Van Hagen
6, ave George V
75008 PARIS
Tel: 01 47 20 00 64
Fax: 01 47 20 25 09
Senior Partner:
M. Anthony VAN HAGEN

### Weissberg-Gaetjens-Ziegenfeuter
34, ave Marceau
75008 PARIS
Tel: 01 47 20 22 48
Fax: 01 47 20 21 59
Fax2: 01 47 20 21 64
Partner: M. Kenneth M. WEISSBERG

### White & Case
11, Bd de la Madeleine
75001 PARIS
Tel: 01 42 60 34 05
Fax: 01 42 60 82 46
Senior Partner: M. John H. RIGGS, Jr.

### Willkie Farr & Gallagher
21-23, rue de la Ville Évêque
75008 PARIS
Tel: 01 53 43 45 00
Fax: 01 40 06 96 06

*DOING BUSINESS & WORKING*

99

# MINITEL DIRECTORY
## SERVEURS MINITEL

These Minitel addresses have been selected for their usefulness in getting information that concerns commerce, professional services, legal issues, and financial reports on French companies.

**08 36 27 22 22***
*National database on bad checks*

**08 36 28 00 61**
*American Embassy, commercial services*

**08 36 29 00 57 DATA-PRESSE**
*Directory of journalists*

**3614 CADREMPLOI**
*Job listings for executive positions*

**3615 ABCJUSTICE**
*General information on legal matters, standard letters for official correspondence*

**3615 AFP**
*News bulletins dispatched by the Agence France Presse. Rubrique World News in English*

**3615 APNEWS**
*World news bulletins issued by Associated Press*

**3615 CEE**
*Legal and administrative facts concerning the European Economic Community*

**3615 CVCURSUS**
*Advice for writing résumés (in 5 languages). Free postal delivery within 48 hours*

**3615 DICO**
*Dictionaries of spelling, synonyms, conjugation (French & English), helps writing cover letters*

**3615 INPI**
*Guide issued by the Institut National de la Propriété Industrielle (INPI)*

**3615 INVESTIR**
*The stock market live*

**3615 LESECHOS**
*News of the Stock Exchange world*

**3615 LIBE**
*American and international news in English direct from Associated Press*

**3615 MONEY**
*Direct link to the Paris and New York stock markets*

**3616 AFNOR**
*French and European standards*

**3616 DINERSCLUB**
*Facilities extended to the members of Diner's Club International*

**3616 SALONS**
*International fairs and expos*

**3617 BIL**
*Legal information about the corporate world*

**3617 FISK**
*Assessment of income tax, Stock Exchange news*

**3617 INFOBREVET**
*French and European patents*

**3617 JANNONCE**
*More than 10000 classified ads (real estate, cars, employment)*

**3617 LES1000**
*Listing of the 1000 largest companies in France*

**3617 SALAIR**
*Salary assessment service, helps with resumés, labor laws...*

**3617 TASS**
*News from the Russian press agency Tass in French*

**3617 USA2**
*Stock Exchange data on foreign markets, Internet access*

**3617 VERIF**
*Information on the corporate world: turnover, staff, debt, profit, etc.*

**DOING BUSINESS & WORKING**

101

# ORGANIZATIONS/CLUBS
## ASSOCIATIONS/CLUBS

Professional organizations and clubs located in Paris have been assembled here for your convenience. These organizations deal with cross-cultural issues, international trade, and commerce. For other cultural, community, and service organizations and clubs, see the Living & Studying section of the directory.

### AABCC (Anglo-American Business and Culture Center)
20, rue Godot de Mauroy
75009 PARIS
Tel: 01 42 66 14 11
Fax: 01 42 66 31 89

### AFL-CIO
*European offices of the American Federation of Labour - Congress of Industrial Organizations*
23, rue de Rome
75008 PARIS
Tel: 01 43 87 74 57
Fax: 01 43 87 74 60
President: M. Lane KIRKLAND

### American Language in Context
2, rue des Gravilliers
75003 PARIS
Tel: 01 42 77 29 12
Contact: M. John DAVIDSON

### Association de la Presse Étrangère
*Foreign Press Association*
35, rue des Francs Bourgeois
75004 PARIS
Tel: 01 42 78 11 90
Fax: 01 42 78 08 78
Contact:
Mme Anne-Marie BOUCHAERT

### British Overseas Trade Board
British Embassy
35, rue du Fbg Saint Honoré
75008 PARIS
Tel: 01 44 51 31 00
Contact: M. Brian WEST

### Business and Industry Advisory Committee (BIAC)
13, chausée de la Muette
75016 PARIS
Tel: 01 42 30 09 60
Fax: 01 45 24 66 20

### ESL (European Strategy and Lobbying) Network
123, ave des Champs Élysées
75008 PARIS
Tel: 01 40 73 14 00
Fax: 01 40 73 14 01

### European Trading Union
22, Bd Gouvion Saint Cyr
75017 PARIS
Tel: 01 45 72 31 87

### Eurosynergy Network/ETRA (European Tire Recycling Association)
*Networking, developing links between towns or municipalities and small and medium-sized companies. Operates in conjunction with OCEAN*
7, rue Leroux
75016 PARIS
Tel: 01 45 00 37 77
Fax: 01 45 00 83 47
Contact: Mme Valerie SCHUMAN

### France-Amérique
*Fosters cultural and economic relations*
9, ave Franklin Roosevelt
75008 PARIS
Tel: 01 43 59 51 00
Fax: 01 40 75 00 97
President: M. André ROSS

## France Louisiane-Franco Américaine

*Develops cultural and economic relations between France and Louisiana*
28, Bd de Strasbourg
75010 PARIS
Tel: 01 42 40 68 78
Fax: 01 42 40 68 80

## International Business Service

120, ave des Champs Élysées
75008 PARIS
Tel: 01 43 59 12 07

## Software Publishers Association Europe

57, rue Pierre Charron
75008 PARIS
Tel: 01 53 77 63 77
Fax: 01 53 77 63 78
Email: info@spa-europe
Web site: http://www.spa-europe.org
Managing Director:
M. Gérard GABELLA

*DOING BUSINESS & WORKING*

103

# PRESS/MEDIA
## PRESSE/MÉDIAS

News agencies, English-language newspapers, journals, newsletters, magazines, radio and television correspondents and bureaus, and press associations concerning the English-speaking world have been listed here. PARIS-ANGLOPHONE has limited the list to those organizations that publish or broadcast in English, as well as those offering subscription and advertising opportunities for anglophone businesses. For an exhaustive listing of other press organs in France, consult *Media Sid*. Freelancers are encouraged to make themselves known for listing in a new category heading in the next edition.

### NEWS AGENCIES
### Agences de presse

### Agence France-Presse (AFP)
11-13-15, place de la Bourse
BP 20
75061 PARIS Cedex 02
Tel: 01 40 41 46 46
Fax: 01 40 41 47 43
President: M. Lionel FLEURY

### Agence Reuter
8, rue du Sentier
75081 PARIS Cedex 02
Tel: 01 42 21 50 00
Fax: 01 42 36 10 72
Web site:
http://www.session.rservices.com

### Associated Press (AP)
162, rue du Fbg Saint Honoré
75008 PARIS
Tel: 01 43 59 86 76
Fax: 01 40 74 00 45
Bureau Chief: M. Harry DUNPHY

### AP Dow Jones
162, rue du Fbg Saint Honoré
75008 PARIS
Tel: 01 42 56 09 72
Fax: 01 42 25 87 36
Bureau Chief: M. David PEARSON

### Baxter's Press Agency
*Photography news features*
Villa des Arts
15, rue Hegesippe Moreau
75018 PARIS
Tel: 01 42 93 34 19
Fax: 01 42 93 34 19
Contact: M. François BAXTER

### Bloomberg
*Financial news agency*
112, ave Kléber
75116 PARIS
Tel: 01 53 65 50 00
Fax: 01 53 65 51 10

### Gamma Press Photo Agency
70, rue Jean Bleuzen
92170 VANVES
Tel: 01 41 23 77 00
Fax: 01 41 23 77 77

### Knight-Ridder Financial News
115, rue Réaumur
75002 PARIS
Tel: 01 44 88 44 50
Fax: 01 40 13 05 40
Bureau Chief: M. Brian CHILDS

### Magnum Photos
5, passage Piver
75011 PARIS
Tel: 01 53 36 88 88
Fax: 01 53 36 88 89

### New York Times Syndication
3, rue Scribe
75009 PARIS
Tel: 01 47 42 17 11
Fax: 01 47 42 18 81

### Reporters sans Frontières
5, rue Geoffroy Marie
75009 PARIS
Tel: 01 44 83 84 84
Fax: 01 45 23 11 51

## Reuters

101, rue Réaumur
75080 PARIS Cedex 02
Tel: 01 42 21 50 00
Fax: 01 42 36 10 72

## Worldwide Television News

43, rue de Richelieu
75001 PARIS
Tel: 01 42 60 52 43
Fax: 01 42 60 49 44

## NEWSPAPERS
Journaux

## Asia Times

71 bis, rue du Cardinal Lemoine
75005 PARIS
Tel: 01 43 54 74 35
Fax: 01 43 54 73 40

## Daily Mail

36, rue du Sentier
75002 PARIS
Tel: 01 45 08 48 41
Fax: 01 45 08 48 43

## Daily Telegraph/Sunday Telegraph

242, rue de Rivoli
75001 PARIS
Tel: 01 42 60 38 85
Fax: 01 42 61 52 91
Correspondent:
Mme Suzanne LOWRY

## Evening Standard/Sunday Express

47, ave de Sorraines
78110 LE VÉSINET
Tel: 01 39 76 88 88
Correspondent:
M. Peter DEWHIRST

## Futurs World News

78, rue des Archives
75003 PARIS
Tel: 01 42 72 92 52
Fax: 01 40 27 83 00
Correspondent:
Mme Barbara CASASSUS

## International Herald Tribune

*Daily newspaper written and compiled by local staff with The New York Times and Washington Post*
181, ave Charles de Gaulle
92200 NEUILLY SUR SEINE Cedex
Tel: 01 41 43 93 96
Fax: 01 41 43 93 38 (editorial)
Web site: http://www.iht.com
Executive Editor: M. M. GETLER
Publisher: M. Richard McCLEAN

## Los Angeles Times

10, Bd Malesherbes
75008 PARIS
Tel: 01 49 24 96 65
Fax: 01 40 07 03 95
Bureau Chief: M. DAHLBURG

## The European

44, rue de la Bienfaisance
75008 PARIS
Tel: 01 45 63 03 62
Fax: 01 45 62 98 34
Correspondent:
Mme Anne-Elisabeth MOUTET

---

### The Financial Times

## FINANCIAL TIMES

*The Financial Times, renowned for its accurate, apolitical and on-the-spot reporting, is firmly established as one of the the world's leading English-language business newspapers*
*(See advertisement)*
40, rue de la Boétie
75008 PARIS
Tel: 01 53 76 82 50
Fax: 01 53 76 82 53
Email:
101746.1316@compuserve.com
Web site: http://www.ft.com
Bureau Chief: M. David BUCHAN
General Manager France:
M. Paul MARAVIGLIA

---

*DOING BUSINESS & WORKING*

105

# PRESS/MEDIA

## The Herald

39, rue Jean Jaurès
92300 LEVALLOIS PERRET
Tel: 01 45 74 28 17
Correspondent: M. Nicholas POWELL

## The Independent

155, ave du Fbg Saint Honoré
75008 PARIS
Tel: 01 45 63 03 22

## The New York Times

3, rue Scribe
75009 PARIS
Tel: 01 42 66 37 49
Fax: 01 47 42 88 21
Web site url: http://www.nytimes.com
Manager: Mme Daphné ANGLES

## The Times/ The Sunday Times

8, rue Halévy
75441 PARIS Cedex 09
Tel: 01 47 42 73 21
Fax: 01 47 42 72 96
Times Correspondent:
M. Charles BREMNER

## The Washington Post

181, ave Charles de Gaulle
92521 NEUILLY SUR SEINE Cedex
Tel: 01 41 43 92 22
Fax: 01 41 43 92 23
Correspondents:
Mme SWARSON & M. TRUEHART

## Trim International

94, rue Saint Lazare
75442 PARIS Cedex 09
Tel: 01 48 78 38 32
Fax: 01 45 26 07 00
President: M. Thierry AUMONIER

## USA Today International

17, rue Tronchet
75008 PARIS
Tel: 01 42 66 08 61
Fax: 01 42 66 08 74

## Wall Street Journal

3, rue du Fbg Saint Honoré
75008 PARIS
Tel: 01 47 42 08 06
Fax: 01 47 42 90 98
Bureau Chief: M. Thomas KAMM

## Ziff Davis France

14, place Marie-Jeanne Bassot
92593 LEVALLOIS PERRET Cedex
Tel: 01 46 39 55 00
Fax: 01 46 39 00 62
Minitel: 3615 PC EXPERT

## JOURNALS/ NEWSLETTERS
Revues/Périodiques

## Commerce in France

*Published by the American Chamber of Commerce*
c/o American Chamber of Commerce
21, ave George V
75008 PARIS
Tel: 01 40 73 89 90
Fax: 01 47 20 18 62
Editor: M. John DAVIDSON

## France-USA Contacts (FUSAC)

3, rue Larochelle
75014 PARIS
Tel: 01 45 38 56 57
Fax: 01 45 38 98 94
Editors: John & Lisa VAN DEN BOS

## Frank: An International Journal of Contemporary Writing & Art

# Frank

*Journal of fiction, poetry, literary interviews and contemporary art. Published since 1983*
32, rue Édouard Vaillant
93100 MONTREUIL SOUS BOIS
Tel: 01 49 59 66 58
Fax: 01 48 59 66 68
Email: david@paris-anglo.com
Web site:
http://www.paris-anglo.com/frank
Editor: M. David APPLEFIELD

106

## Paris Free Voice

*Arts, entertainment, commentary, and community news reaching 100000 readers every month. The magazine for English-speaking Parisians (See advertisement)*

American Church
65, quai d'Orsay
75007 PARIS
Tel: 01 40 62 05 07
Fax: 01 40 62 05 08
Email:
100574.3410@compuserve.com
Web site: http://www.paris-anglo.com
Editor/Publisher: M. Bob BISHOP
Commercial Dir. :
M. Stephen SOLOMONS

## Paris Transcontinental

Sorbonne Nouvelle
5, rue de l'Ecole de Médecine
75006 PARIS
Tel: 01 69 01 86 35
Publisher/Editor-in-Chief:
Mme Claire LARRIERE

## Raw Vision

*Periodical specialising in Art Brut and Primitive art*

37, rue de Gergovie
75015 PARIS
Tel: 01 43 87 55 08
Fax: 01 42 93 86 25
Paris Editor: M. Laurent DANCHIN

## MAGAZINES
Magazines

## Across the Board

16, rue Spontini
75116 PARIS
Tel: 01 45 53 36 32
Correspondent: M. Judson GOODING

## Boulevard Magazine

c/o Mediatime
68, rue des Archives
75003 PARIS
Tel: 01 44 78 82 82
Fax: 01 44 78 82 83
Email: boulevar@imaginet.fr
Web site:
http://www.parisfranceguide.imaginet.fr
Publisher: Mme Fiona LAZAREFF

## Christian Science Monitor

48, rue de la Clef
75005 PARIS
Tel: 01 43 31 22 90

## Citizen K. International

*Bilingual fashion magazine*

104, rue de la Folie Méricourt
75011 PARIS
Tel: 01 43 14 05 25
Fax: 01 43 14 05 87
Email: citizenk@imaginet.fr
Web site: http://www.ntt.fr/boutik/

## Fairchild Publications

9, rue Royale
75008 PARIS
Tel: 01 44 51 13 00
Fax: 01 42 68 16 41
Director: Mme Joëlle BONIFACE

## France Magazine

*If you like France you'll love FRANCE Magazine - the English-language quarterly review of "la vie française"*
*(See advertisement)*

58, ave de Wagram
75017 PARIS
Tel: 01 41 46 00 64
Fax: 01 39 08 06 35 (subs/ads)
Email: francemag@aol.fr
Contact: M. Martin RAWLINGS

## France - Why and Where

c/o Mediatime France
68, rue des Archives
75003 PARIS
Tel: 01 44 78 82 82
Fax: 01 44 78 82 83
Editor: Mme Christine HOHENADEL

## Hearst Publications

42, ave Montaigne
75008 PARIS
Tel: 01 47 23 63 44
Fax: 01 47 20 10 29
European Executive Editor:
Mme Jane CATTANI

## Life Magazine

14, rue de Marignan
75008 PARIS
Tel: 01 44 95 70 31
Fax: 01 45 63 01 10
Correspondent: Mme Tala SKARI

## Macmillan Magazines

3-5, rue Joseph Sansboeuf
75008 PARIS
Tel: 01 43 87 42 17
Fax: 01 43 87 42 15
Correspondent: M. SAVENAY

## New York Magazine

32, rue de Meudon
92100 BOULOGNE BILLANCOURT
Tel: 01 47 61 08 26

## Newsweek

162, rue du Fbg Saint Honoré
75008 PARIS
Tel: 01 53 83 76 10
Tel2: 01 42 25 97 05

## Nova Magazine

33, rue du Fbg Saint Antoine
75012 PARIS
Tel: 01 53 33 33 35
Fax: 01 53 33 33 28
Editor-in-Chief: M. Patrick ZERBIB

## Pariscope

*Entertainment weekly*
151, rue Anatole France
92534 LEVALLOIS PERRET Cedex
Tel: 01 41 34 73 47
Fax: 01 41 34 73 26

## Publisher's Weekly

BP 214
75264 PARIS Cedex 06
Tel: 01 43 21 77 82
Fax: 01 43 35 02 31
Correspondent Europe:
M. Herbert LOTTMAN

## The Economist

6, rue Paul Baudry
75008 PARIS
Tel: 01 53 93 66 13
Tel2: 01 53 93 66 00 (diffusion)
Fax: 01 53 93 66 03
Correspondent: M. Edward CARR

## Time Magazine

14, rue de Marignan
75008 PARIS
Tel: 01 44 95 00 30
Fax: 01 45 63 00 99

## Time Out Paris

*Selection of the city's best shows
and entertainment in English.
Published in Pariscope*
100, rue du Fbg Saint Antoine
75012 PARIS
Tel: 01 44 87 00 45
Fax: 01 44 73 90 60
Email: timeoutp@francenet.fr
Web site: http://www.timeout.co.uk
Managing Director:
Mme Karen ALBRECHT

## Time-Life International

67, ave de Wagram
75017 PARIS
Tel: 01 44 01 49 99
Fax: 01 44 01 49 29
President: M. Jeb SIDER

## Today in English

*Monthly news magazine devoted to
the anglophone world*
19, rue d'Orléans
92200 NEUILLY SUR SEINE
Tel: 01 41 43 48 86
Fax: 01 41 43 48 98
Email: 101372.2635@compuserve.com
Editor: Mme Barbara OUDIZ

## U.S. News & World Report

8, rue de Choiseul
75002 PARIS
Tel: 01 42 60 21 72
Fax: 01 42 60 37 42

## Vanity Fair Magazine

32, rue de Meudon
92100 BOULOGNE BILLANCOURT
Tel: 01 47 61 08 26

## Vintage International Magazine

140, rue de la Croix Nivert
75015 PARIS
Tel: 01 53 68 94 68
Fax: 01 53 68 94 60
Editor-in-Chief: M. Jacques SALLE

## Where Paris

6, rue de Ponthieu
75008 PARIS
Tel: 01 53 83 89 40
Fax: 01 53 83 89 50
Email: 100567.530@compuserve.com
Web site: http://www.wheremags.com
Publisher: Mme Kay ROLLAND

## RADIO - Radio

## British Broadcasting Corporation (BBC)

155, rue du Fbg Saint Honoré
75008 PARIS
Tel: 01 45 63 15 88
Fax: 01 45 63 67 12
Minitel: 3614 BBC
Correspondent: M. Kevin CONNOLLY

## Radio Canada CBC

17, ave Matignon
75008 PARIS
Tel: 01 44 21 15 15
Fax: 01 44 21 15 14

## Radio France Internationale (RFI)

*English and French language radio transmissions*
116, ave du Président Kennedy
75786 PARIS Cedex 16
Tel: 01 42 30 30 62
Fax: 01 42 30 40 37
Director: M. Arnaud LITTARDI
Editor-in-Chief English Service:
M. Simson NAJOVITS

## Riviera Radio

*English-language radio broadcast along the Riviera coast*
16, Bd Princesse Charlotte
98000 MONACO
Tel: 00 377 93 25 49 06
Fax: 00 377 93 30 42 45

## Trans World Radio

*Multilingual Christian radio network*
5, rue Louis Notari
PO Box 349
98007 MONTE CARLO
Tel: 00 377 92 16 56 00
Fax: 00 377 92 16 56 01
Manager: M. Dick OLSON

## TELEVISION - Télévision

## ABC News

3, rue de l'Arrivée
Immeuble CIT
75749 PARIS Cedex 15
Tel: 01 40 47 80 81
Fax: 01 40 47 66 58
Chief Bureau: M. B. SILVESTRE

## Cable News Network (CNN)

25, rue d'Artois
75008 PARIS
Tel: 01 42 25 41 68
Bureau Chief: M. Peter HUMI

## Canadian Broadcasting Corporation

17, ave Matignon
75008 PARIS
Tel: 01 44 21 15 15
Fax: 01 44 21 15 14

## CBS News

37, rue Marbeuf
75008 PARIS
Tel: 01 53 83 80 90
Fax: 01 45 61 49 76
Director: M. Bob ALBERTSON

## MTV Europe

19, rue Michel Le Comte
75003 PARIS
Tel: 01 44 54 51 30
Fax: 01 48 87 67 85

## Tokyo Broadcasting Systems
20, rue du Fbg Saint Honoré
75008 PARIS
Tel: 01 42 66 66 00
Fax: 01 42 66 66 01

## MISCELLANEOUS
Divers

## Anglo-American Press Association in Paris
4, rue Ruhmkorff
75017 PARIS
Tel: 01 44 09 76 47
Coordinator: Mme Elisa KITSON

## Association de la Presse Étrangère
*Foreign Press Association*
35, rue des Francs Bourgeois
75004 PARIS
Tel: 01 42 78 11 90
Fax: 01 42 78 08 78
Contact:
Mme Anne-Marie BOUCHAERT

## FIEJ (International Federation of Newspapers Publishers)
25, rue d'Astorg
75008 PARIS
Tel: 01 47 42 85 00
Fax: 01 47 42 49 48
Coordinator: Dr. Aralyn McMANE

## Johnston, Marsha
*Independent journalist specializing in technology*
5, passage d' Enfer
75014 PARIS
Tel: 01 40 47 03 18
Fax: 01 40 47 85 69
Email: johnston@club-internet.fr

## World Press Freedom Committee
*Defends and promotes independent media*
9, place du Président Mithouard
75007 PARIS
Tel: 01 47 83 39 88
Fax: 01 45 66 83 02
European Representative:
M. Ronald KOVEN

# PRINTING
## IMPRIMERIE

France has no shortage of printers and graphic designers. Here are a few places to get printing quotes, find desktop publishing (PAO) solutions, engage designers, contract film outputting services, etc. Be warned: although many non-anglophone printers and designers in France work in English, in some cases you should be prepared to make your requests in French. Independent and free lance English-speaking designers of all sorts are invited to make themselves known for future updates.

### PRINTING SERVICES
Imprimeurs

### 3M France
Bd de l'Oise
95006 CERGY PONTOISE Cedex
Tel: 01 30 31 61 61
Fax: 01 30 31 74 26
Contact: M. GRANDIN

### Carlton Cards France
184, ave Paul Vaillant-Couturier
93126 LA COURNEUVE
Tel: 01 48 38 10 05
Fax: 01 48 38 44 56
Sales Dir.: M. GREGOIRE

### Compo Rive Gauche
26, rue Monsieur le Prince
75006 PARIS
Tel: 01 43 25 33 43
Tel2: 01 44 10 71 35
Fax: 01 44 07 10 38
Director: Mme Monique LEPRINCE

### Fecomme Québecor
38, rue Gabriel Prolongée
77410 CLAYE SOUILLY
Tel: 01 60 26 67 00
Fax: 01 60 26 70 16
Director: M. BARNAY

### Graphics Group/France
*Visual aids, graphics, desktop publishing*
67, rue Croulebarbe
75013 PARIS
Tel: 01 43 36 79 00
Fax: 01 43 36 35 57
Email: 106246,652@compuserve.com
Director: M. Larry LARSON

### IMPC - Malia
*Discount photocopies and offset with a smile*
2, rue Robert Giraudineau
94300 VINCENNES
Tel: 01 43 28 63 81
Fax: 01 43 28 20 81
Contact: M. Michel CARAMANOS

### Imprimerie Bussière
23, rue Jean de Beauvais
75005 PARIS
Tel: 01 43 26 01 22
Fax: 01 46 34 58 87
Export Manager: M. Jean MALIAN

### Imprimerie Laballery
27, rue Etienne Marcel
75001 Paris
Tel: 01 42 33 29 51
Fax: 01 40 26 33 65
Contact: M. Claude BRIOT

### Moore France
Tour Kupka B
92906 PARIS LA DÉFENSE
Tel: 01 49 03 11 11
Fax: 01 49 03 11 15
President: M. POMPEÏ

### Prorata Services
27, rue Linné
75005 PARIS
Tel: 01 45 35 94 14
Fax: 01 45 35 19 13
Contact: M. David GRYNBAUM

# PRINTING
## IMPRIMERIE

### Astra Dessin
*Supplies for drawing and painting*
47, rue des Archives
75003 PARIS
Tel: 01 42 78 08 56
Fax: 01 42 71 81 48

### Brigitte Gleizes Design
42, rue Liancourt
75014 PARIS
Tel: 01 43 22 34 62
Fax: 01 43 22 63 18

### Callaghan
36, rue de Lévis
75017 PARIS
Tel: 01 55 65 13 10
Fax: 01 55 65 13 14
Contact: M. Rich ROBERTS

---

### Charlot, Christiane

*Graphic design, desktop publishing, hand-made bookbinding*
18, rue Robert Giraudineau
94300 VINCENNES
Tel: 01 48 08 12 87
Fax: 01 48 08 12 87
Email: chiao@micronet.fr

---

### Design Principals
60, ave du Général Leclerc
75014 PARIS
Tel: 01 45 40 54 02
Fax: 01 45 40 47 19
Contacts: Mmes Carole MOY & Karen SHECKLER-WILSON

### Graphics Group/France
*Visual aids, graphics, desktop publishing*
67, rue Croulebarbe
75013 PARIS
Tel: 01 43 36 79 00
Fax: 01 43 36 35 57
Email: 106246,652@compuserve.com
Director: M. Larry LARSON

### Graphigro Créa
157-159, rue Lecourbe
75015 PARIS
Tel: 01 42 50 45 49
Fax: 01 48 56 01 65
Contact: M. DUCLERC

### Graphiques Lafayette
10, rue Notre-Dame-de-Lorette
75009 PARIS
Tel: 01 42 80 32 23
Fax: 01 48 74 92 65
Contact: M. Nicolas PAGNIER

### Gyoza Media
*Interactive media design for screen & print*
9, rue aux Ours
75003 PARIS
Tel: 01 44 54 32 90
Fax: 01 44 54 32 99
Email: cory@gyoza.com
Web site: http://www.gyoza.com
Contact: M. Cory McCLOUD

### King, Peggy
79, rue Mouffetard
75005 PARIS
Tel: 01 43 37 13 19
Fax: 01 43 37 20 49
Email: 106160.1355@compuserve.com
Contact:
Mme Peggy FORD-FYFFE KING

### Legrand, Olivier
*Experienced graphic designer*
c/o Éditions Allia
16, rue Charlemagne
75004 PARIS
Tel: 01 42 72 77 25
Fax: 01 42 72 52 04

### Nadine Lennox
4, rue Eblé
75007 PARIS
Tel: 01 43 06 68 78
Fax: 01 44 18 31 62
Email: nlennox@aol.com

### Rebus
14, rue Saint Croix de la Bretonnerie
75004 PARIS
Tel: 01 42 77 20 49
Fax: 01 40 27 08 88
Email: rebus@iway.fr
Director: M. Robert HUNTER

### Rouyer, François-Charles
10, rue Véronèse
75013 PARIS
Tel: 01 43 36 63 46
Fax: 01 45 35 42 91
Email: fcrouyer@club-internet.fr

### Sharzad
48, rue Saint Placide
75006 PARIS
Tel: 01 45 48 86 65

### The Bridge

**EDITIONS & MULTIMEDIA**

*Tight deadlines-high quality-low cost!*
*Copywrite-Translate-Design in Paris*
*Print/Mail: Paris London NYC*
104, rue Bobillot
75013 PARIS
Tel: 01 53 62 15 33
Fax: 01 53 62 15 34
Email: westside@club-internet.fr
Contact: M. Victor VAL DERE

**DOING BUSINESS & WORKING**

113

# PUBLISHING
## ÉDITION

For a complete list of French publishers, consult the catalog from the French *Salon du Livre*, published by OIP. English-language publishers present or represented in France are listed here, as well as selected French addresses that are of service to anglophones, as well as, of course, literary agents and scouts.

### ABC France LTD
### Reed Travel Group
*Guides*
14, rue des Parisiens
92600 ASNIERES
Tel: 01 47 90 39 00
Fax: 01 47 90 06 43
Director: M. MASSON-LECOMTE

### Alastair Sawday Publishing
36, rue de Chabrol
75010 PARIS
Tel: 01 48 00 96 11
Fax: 01 48 00 96 11
Contact:
Mme Ann COOKE YARBOROUGH

### Alyscamps Press
*Publishes literary criticism, fiction, biography, poetry, translations*
35, rue de l'Espérance
75013 PARIS
Tel: 01 45 81 15 24
Fax: 01 45 81 15 24
Contact: M. Karl OREND

### Anglophone S.A

**anglophone s.a.**

*Publishes Paris-Anglophone and the www.paris-anglo.com web site (See advertisement)*
32, rue Édouard Vaillant
93100 MONTREUIL SOUS BOIS
Tel: 01 48 53 66 58
Fax: 01 48 59 66 68
email: info@paris-anglo.com
Web site: http://www.paris-anglo.com
Director: M. David APPLEFIELD

### Association Frank

# Frank

*Publishes Frank: International Journal of Contemporary Writing and Art*
32, rue Édouard Vaillant
93100 MONTREUIL SOUS BOIS
Tel: 01 48 59 66 58
Fax: 01 48 59 66 68
Email: david@paris-anglo.com
web site:
http://www.paris-anglo.com/frank
Editor: M. David APPLEFIELD

### Business News
3, rue de l'Arrivée
Tour CIT
75015 PARIS
Tel: 01 43 20 02 44
Fax: 01 43 20 02 00
Email: 100140,1452@compuserve.com
Contact: M. Jean-Michel HUMEAU

### Charles Letts & Co.
57, rue Dalayrac
94120 FONTENAY SOUS BOIS
Tel: 01 43 94 04 70
Fax: 01 48 77 69 28
Sales Manager: M. Marcel FRANCHI

### Culture Shock France
266, ave Daumesnil
75012 PARIS
Tel: 01 43 45 41 33
Fax: 01 43 43 01 42
Email: sallytaylo@aol.com
Web site:
http://www.bookwire.com/pw/Asia
Author: Mme Sally TAYLOR

## Data Research Publications

6, rue Mignard
75116 PARIS
Tel: 01 45 03 02 72
Fax: 01 45 03 02 96

## Dow Jones Publishing Company

42, rue Damrémont
75018 PARIS
Tel: 01 42 55 54 22
Fax: 01 42 23 96 13
Web site: http://www.wsj.com
Circulation Manager:
M. Stanley HERTZBERG

## Encyclopaedia Britannica

2, rue du Pont Colbert
78023 VERSAILLES Cedex
Tel: 01 39 24 45 45
Fax: 01 39 24 45 00
Contact: M. MAYORGA

## Entertainment Publications France

1 bis, rue Saint Augustin
75002 PARIS
Tel: 01 42 86 86 34
Fax: 01 42 86 86 30
Minitel: 3615 ENTERTAINMENT
Contact: M. Andrew WATKINS

## Europages

9, ave de Friedland
75008 PARIS
Tel: 01 53 77 54 00
Fax: 01 42 89 34 73
Web site: http://www.europages.com

## Handshake Editions

*Literary publishing (non commercial).
A kitchen-table folly - come for tea!*
83, rue de la Tombe-Issoire
Atelier A2
75014 PARIS
Tel: 01 43 27 17 67
Fax: 01 43 20 41 95
Email: jim-haynes@msn.com
Director: M. Jim HAYNES

## John Calder Publications

c/o Association Frank
Tel: 01 49 88 75 12

## Lonely Planet

71 bis, rue Cardinal Lemoine
75005 PARIS
Tel: 01 44 32 06 20
Fax: 01 46 34 72 55
Email: 100560.415@compuserve.com
Web site:
http://www.lonelyplanet.com.au

## Management Consulting France !

7, rue de la Verrerie
44100 NANTES
Tel: 02 40 69 70 54
Fax: 02 40 69 70 54
Email: mcfrance@IN-net.fr
Web site: http://www.mcfrance.IN-net.fr
Contact: M. Pierre ROUARCH

## McGraw Hill Publications

128, rue du Fbg Saint Honoré
75008 PARIS
Tel: 01 40 75 25 00
Fax: 01 42 89 04 00
Vice-President: M. Bruno HERMANN

## McGraw Hill Publications

15, rue Gabriel Péri
BP 32
94222 CHARENTON Cedex
Tel: 01 49 77 03 06
Fax: 01 43 76 74 29
Email: lequinio@club-internet.fr
Representative: M. Éric LE QUINIO

## National Geographic Magazine

90, ave des Champs Élysées
75008 PARIS
Tel: 01 43 59 25 06
Fax: 01 45 63 79 65
web site:
http://www.nationalgeographic.com
International Advertising Director:
M. Michel SIEGFRIED

# PUBLISHING
## ÉDITION

### Paris-Anglophone

*The complete directory of English-speaking Paris, published in book form and online on the World Wide Web*

32, rue Édouard Vaillant
93100 MONTREUIL SOUS BOIS
Tel: 01 48 59 66 58
Fax: 01 48 59 66 68
Email: david@paris-anglo.com
Web site: http://www.paris-anglo.com
Editor: M. David APPLEFIELD

### Reed Business Publishing

15 bis, rue Ernest Renan
92133 ISSY LES MOULINEAUX
Cedex
Tel: 01 46 29 46 29
Fax: 01 40 93 03 37
Director: M. Pierre MUSSARD

### Who's Top in European Commerce and Industry

10, rue de du Mont Dore
75017 PARIS
Tel: 01 43 87 04 93
Fax: 01 43 87 12 81

### OTHER PUBLISHERS/SERVICES
### Autres éditeurs/Services

### Assimil

*Foreign language methods: books, tapes, software, self-taught French method*

11, rue des Pyramides
75001 PARIS
Tel: 01 45 76 87 37 (Editorial)
Tel: 01 42 60 40 66 (Store)
Fax: 01 40 20 02 17
Web site: http://www.assimil.com
Contact: Mme Magdeleine GEFFROY

### CELF (Centre d'exportation du Livre Français)

9, rue de Toul
75012 PARIS
Tel: 01 44 67 83 83
Fax: 01 43 47 59 43
Email: celf@worldnet.net

### Dawson France

*Subscription agent and international bookseller*

Rue de la Prairie
91121 PALAISEAU Cedex
Tel: 01 69 10 47 00
Fax: 01 64 54 83 26
Web site: http://www.dawson.co.uk

### IDG Communications France

*Information technology publications*

Immeuble La Fayette
2, place des Vosges
92051 PARIS LA DÉFENSE 5
Tel: 01 49 04 79 00
Fax: 01 49 04 78 00
Web site: http://www.idg.fr
Director: Mme Patricia POUPAERT

### IMEC - Institut Mémoire de l'Édition Contemporaine

25, rue de Lille
75007 PARIS
Tel: 01 42 61 29 29
Fax: 01 49 27 03 15
Director: M. Olivier CORPET

### Média Sid

*Directory of press and multimedia companies*

19, rue de Constantine
75340 PARIS Cedex 7
Tel: 01 40 15 70 00
Info: 01 40 62 36 03
Fax: 01 48 39 56 01
Infopresse Chief Department:
Mme Sylvie PINCEMIN

116

### Show Business Guide
*40000 show business addresses*
24, rue Vieille du Temple
75004 PARIS
Tel: 01 48 87 34 34
Fax: 01 42 77 56 49
Minitel: 3617 GSB
Contact: Mme Béatrice BENOIT

## LITERARY AGENTS/SCOUTS
### Agents littéraires

### Agence Hoffman
77, Bd Saint Michel
75005 PARIS
Tel. 01 43 26 56 94
Fax: 01 43 26 34 07
Directors:
MM. Boris & Georges HOFFMAN

### Agence Littéraire Frédérique Porretta
70, rue d'Assas
75006 PARIS
Tel: 01 45 44 88 68
Fax: 01 45 44 69 36

### Agence Michelle Lapautre
*Children books*
6, rue Jean Carries
75007 PARIS
Tel: 01 47 34 82 41
Director: Mme Michelle LAPAUTRE

### Agence Michelle Lapautre
106, ave Denfert Rochereau
75014 PARIS
Tel: 01 42 79 03 48
Fax: 01 42 79 03 51
Director: Mme Catherine LAPAUTRE

### La Nouvelle Agence
7, rue Corneille
75006 PARIS
Tel: 01 43 25 85 60
Fax: 01 43 25 47 98
Director: Mme Mary KLING

### Lora Fountain Literary Agency
*Representing English-language agents and publishers to sell translation rights to French publishers*
7, rue de Belfort
75011 PARIS
Tel: 01 43 56 21 96
Fax: 01 43 48 22 72
Email: FountLit@aol.com
Director: Mme Lora FOUNTAIN

*DOING BUSINESS & WORKING*

117

# REAL ESTATE (COMMERCIAL)
## IMMOBILIER D'ENTERPRISE

In that most real estate agencies handle both commercial and residencial properties PARIS-ANGLOPHONE has included this subject heading in the Living & Studying section of the directory.

## See Living & Studying: Housing

# Would

you invest
$20 to find

## A JOB?
## A CAR?
## A FRIEND?
## A FLAT?

# PICS

## Paris
## International
## Classifieds

http://www.paris-anglo.com/pics
or 01 48 59 66 58

# RECRUITMENT
## RECRUTEMENT

If you are looking for a job or offering one, chances are solutions are to be found at the following addresses. Employment agencies and headhunters, short-term and long-term job placement possibilities, and more, have been assembled here. Also recommended is the Paris International Classifieds (PICS) on the http://www.paris-anglo.com Web site. (25% discount for FrancoFile Club members – owners of this book) - You!

## EMPLOYMENT AGENCIES
### Agences de placement

### Adecco International
4, place de La Défense
92090 PUTEAUX Cedex26
Tel: 01 49 01 94 94
Fax: 01 46 98 00 08

### Alpha Travail Temporaire
*Banks and finances*
60, rue de Londres
75008 PARIS
Tel: 01 53 42 53 60
Fax: 01 53 42 53 61

### Axel Assistance
59, rue des Mathurins
75008 PARIS
Tel: 01 42 66 50 51
Fax: 01 42 66 50 58

### BEPA
6, rue de Madrid
75008 PARIS
Tel: 01 43 87 48 13
Fax: 01 42 93 44 69

### Boyden Consulting
38, rue Vauthier
92744 BOULOGNE Cedex
Tel: 01 46 99 18 18
Fax: 01 46 99 18 19
Director: M. J.C. ROUSSOULIERE

### Britt International Consultants
32, rue Tronchet
75009 PARIS
Tel: 01 47 42 06 12
Fax: 01 47 42 18 66
Director: Mme COHEN

### Conviction Right France
*Outplacement*
152, ave Malakoff
75116 PARIS
Tel: 01 44 17 18 88
Fax: 01 45 02 12 34
Director: M. J.P. LECLERCQ

### Euro-Pair Services
13, rue Vavin
75006 PARIS
Tel: 01 43 29 80 01
Fax: 01 43 29 80 37
Contact: Mme DAVAY

### GR Intérim Services
*GR Interim is recruiting temporary and permanent positions for international companies in Paris*
12, rue de la Paix
75002 PARIS
Tel: 01 42 61 82 11
Fax: 01 47 03 40 49
Contact: Mme Brigitte JOLLY

### Grey Consulting
47, Bd du Montparnasse
75006 PARIS
Tel: 01 42 22 33 35
Fax: 01 42 22 86 51
Email: grey@easynet.fr
Contact: Mme Jane GREY

### Kelly Services
73, Bd Haussmann
75008 PARIS
Tel: 01 44 94 64 64
Fax: 01 44 94 64 65
Director: M. TOMASINI

## Kelly Services

130 bis, ave Charles de Gaulle
92200 NEUILLY SUR SEINE
Tel: 01 47 47 41 18
Fax: 01 47 47 19 20
Web site: http://www.kellyservices.fr
Director: Mme Martine LEININGER

## Kelly Services

106 bis, rue Saint Lazare
75008 PARIS
Tel: 01 42 93 26 82
Director: Mme Virginie BAKOUCHE

## Kelly Services

Tour Maine Montparnasse
33, ave du Maine
75015 PARIS
Tel: 01 45 38 52 03
Fax: 01 43 21 29 30
Director: Mme Sybille TARD

## Kelly Services

37, ave d'Italie
75013 PARIS
Tel: 01 45 84 32 10
Director: Mme Claudine COCHET

## Kelly Services

258, Bd Voltaire
75011 PARIS
Tel: 01 43 67 18 18
Fax: 01 43 67 18 14
Director: Mme Annie PAOLINI

## LTD International

47, rue de Ponthieu
75008 PARIS
Tel: 01 45 63 51 67
Fax: 01 45 63 51 58

## Magnitude

90, ave des Champs Élysées
75008 PARIS
Tel: 01 53 76 11 76

## Manpower France

7-9, rue Jacques Bingen
BP 53
75825 PARIS Cedex 17
Tel: 01 44 15 40 40
Fax: 01 42 67 76 66
Director: M. Michael GRUNELIUS

## Marketing Search

61, ave Marceau
75116 PARIS
Tel: 01 40 70 10 70
Fax: 01 40 70 99 66
Director: Mme Camille VOLKER

## Metropolitan Models

7, Bd des Capucines
75002 PARIS
Tel: 01 42 66 52 85
Fax: 01 42 66 48 75
Contact: M. Michel LEVATON

## Minerve Intérim

422, rue Saint Honoré
Angle rue Royale
75008 PARIS
Tel: 01 42 61 76 76
Fax: 01 42 60 22 62
Director: Mme DE LABEAU

## PCM Europe

26, rue de Berri
75008 PARIS
Tel: 01 45 62 20 00
Fax: 01 45 62 30 04
Web site:
http://www.groupecourtaud.com
Contact: M. Michel HARMANT

## Personnel Research

3, Bd de Sébastopol
75001 PARIS
Tel: 01 42 36 22 69
Fax: 01 42 36 04 46
Contact: Mme Guylaine MOREAU

## Plus International

60, rue de l'Arcade
75008 PARIS
Tel: 01 40 08 40 00
Fax: 01 45 22 49 53
Contact: Mme Maria CORREIA

## Selective Executive Assistants

91, rue du Fbg Saint Honoré
75008 PARIS
Tel: 01 44 71 35 16
Fax: 01 42 66 15 60
Director: Mme Sibyl VIDAL

## Selpro

43, rue Lafayette
75009 PARIS
Tel: 01 42 80 92 12
Fax: 01 42 80 90 99

## Sheila Burgess International

*The bilingual secretarial/PA Specialists in Paris, also Brussels and Frankfurt*

62, rue Saint Lazare
75009 PARIS
Tel: 01 44 63 02 57
Fax: 01 44 63 02 59
Director: Mme Sheila BURGESS

## Sintel Interim

*Bilingual secretaries*

32, rue de la Boétie
75008 PARIS
Tel: 01 42 89 08 01
Fax: 01 42 89 06 92

## Spencer Stuart & Associates

39, ave Franklin Roosevelt
75008 PARIS
Tel: 01 53 76 81 23
Fax: 01 53 76 81 00
President: M. Jean-Jacques PIC

## SRS International

26, rue Lafayette
75009 PARIS
Tel: 01 42 46 11 33
Tel2: 01 42 46 70 10

## Synerval

11, rue Tronchet
75008 PARIS
Tel: 01 47 42 73 43
Fax: 01 47 42 05 07
Contact: M. VALENSI

## TM International

*Recruitment of bilingual secretaries and executive assistants*

36-38, rue des Mathurins
75008 PARIS
Tel: 01 47 42 71 00
Fax: 01 47 42 18 87
Managing Director:
Mme Tanya IRELAND

### HEAD HUNTERS
Cabinets de recrutement

## Antoinette Lefèvre

3, rue de Duras
75008 PARIS
Tel: 01 42 66 26 26

## Berndtson Paul Ray

73, ave des Champs Élysées
75008 PARIS
Tel: 01 53 77 22 00
Fax: 01 53 77 22 09

## Cabinet Joublin McCann

*Bilingual recruitment consultants*

62, ave de Wagram
75017 PARIS
Tel: 01 47 63 09 25
Fax: 01 47 63 09 18
Contact: M. Patrick McCANN

## Capic

18, rue Volney
75002 PARIS
Tel: 01 42 61 03 27
Fax: 01 42 61 36 29

## Coopers & Lybrand

32, rue Guersant
75017 PARIS
Tel: 01 45 72 80 00
Fax: 01 45 72 22 19
President: M. P.B. ANGLADE

## Daniel Braga Consulting

100, Bd Masséna
75013 PARIS
Tel: 01 45 84 64 30
Fax: 01 45 84 64 22
Email: BragaD@aol.com
Director: M. Daniel BRAGA

*DOING BUSINESS & WORKING*

121

# RECRUITMENT

## DBM France

17, rue du Fbg Saint Honoré
75008 PARIS
Tel: 01 44 51 52 80
Fax: 01 44 51 52 82
Director: M. J. ELIARD

## Egon Zehnder International

12, ave George V
75008 PARIS
Tel: 01 44 31 81 00
Fax: 01 47 20 39 82
Web site:
http://www.egonzehnder.com/zehnder/
Contact: M. J.L. PETITBON

## Forgeot Weeks

*Career consultants*

128, rue Fbg Saint Honoré
75008 PARIS
Tel: 01 45 63 35 15
Fax: 01 45 63 35 18
Director: M. Alain FORGEOT

## Hay Management Consultant

Tour Kupka B
La Défense 7
92906 PARIS LA DÉFENSE
Tel: 01 46 53 71 71
Fax: 01 46 53 71 50

## Heidrick and Struggles

112, ave Kléber
75116 PARIS
Tel: 01 44 34 17 00
Fax: 01 44 34 17 17
Director: M. Gérard CLERY-MELIN

## I.B.D. Algoe

Tour Gamma A
BP 410
75560 PARIS Cedex 12
Tel: 01 53 02 26 86
Fax: 01 53 02 26 80
Director: Mme Carole DE CHILLY

## John Stork International

10, rue des Saussaies
75008 PARIS
Tel: 01 42 65 26 13
Fax: 01 42 68 13 23
Director: M. F. GRANDCLAUDE

## Josiane Agard Développement

67, ave Georges Mandel
75116 PARIS
Tel: 01 45 04 69 56
Fax: 01 45 04 68 57

## Korn/Ferry Carré/Orban International

166, rue du Fbg Saint Honoré
75008 PARIS
Tel: 01 45 61 66 60
Fax: 01 45 63 56 67
Managing Partner:
M. Charles AMAGLIOT

## Leroy Consultants

32, rue d'Armaille
75017 PARIS`
Tel: 01 40 68 38 38
Fax: 01 40 55 95 12

## PA Consulting Group

114, ave Charles de Gaulle
92200 NEUILLY SUR SEINE
Tel: 01 40 88 79 79
Fax: 01 47 45 48 65

## Profile International

43, rue de Châteaudun
75009 PARIS
Tel: 01 44 53 49 12
Fax: 01 44 53 49 21
Email: profile@wanadoo.fr
Web site: http://www.profile-int.co.uk
Consultant: Mme. Fiona LEGROS

## TASA International

6, ave Marceau
75008 PARIS
Tel: 01 47 23 53 31
Fax: 01 47 20 59 19
Managing Director:
M. Pierre AUSSURE

# RELOCATION SERVICES
## BIENVENUE EN FRANCE

Companies and professionals relocating to France or exploring the possibilities of settling in France for professional reasons need a helping hand in finding housing, schooling, insurance, legal and administrative assistance, and general orientation to a new culture. Here are some great leads.

## A.B.M. Rent a Flat

ABM RENT A FLAT

*Furnished apartment rentals from studio to 5 rooms in the best areas of Paris. Phone line, dishes, TV...*
12, rue Valentin Haüy
75015 PARIS
Tel: 01 45 67 04 04
Fax: 01 45 67 90 15
Email: abm@abmrentaflat.com
Web site:
http://www.abmrentaflat.paris
Director: M. Laurent MARIONNEAU

## At Home Abroad
28, rue Basfroi
75011 PARIS
Tel: 01 40 09 08 37
Fax: 01 40 09 98 16
Director: Mme Susan ORSONI

## Brunet Accueil International
104, Bd Camelinat
92240 MALAKOFF
Tel: 01 40 84 92 51
Fax: 01 40 84 04 88
Email: cjbrunet@worldnet.fr
Director: Mme Claudette BRUNET

## Corporate Relocations France
15, rue Croix Castel
78600 MAISONS LAFFITTE
Tel: 01 39 12 00 60
Fax: 01 39 12 36 00
Email:
annabelgreen@corporaterelo-france.com
Managing Director:
Mme Annabel GREEN

## Cosmopolitan Services Unlimited (CSU)

*Specialists in Relocation*
*SINCE 1978*

Specialists in relocation since 1978, CSU offers complete & flexible relocation programs including orientation, homefinding & immigration assistance
*(See advertisement)*
113, Bd Pereire
75017 PARIS
Tel: 01 55 65 11 65
Fax: 01 55 65 11 69
Email: csu@easynet.fr
Web site: http://www.paris-anglo.com/housing/csu
Director: Mme Joy CHEZAUD

## Entrée into Paris - E.I.P.
184, ave Charles de Gaullle
92200 NEUILLY SUR SEINE
Tel: 01 40 88 39 40
Fax: 01 46 37 22 09
Contact:
Mme Sylvie BORNICHE-ROUANET

## Executive Relocations France

**EXECUTIVE RELOCATIONS**
- PARIS -

*City introduction/orientation, homefinding, settling-in, French language lessons, work + residence permits, school enrolments, cross-cultural counseling*

3, rue Berryer
75008 PARIS
Tel: 01 40 74 00 02
Fax: 01 42 56 19 29
Email: judy@executive-france.com
Web site:
http://www.executive-france.com
Managing Director:
Mme Judy BRAHAM

## France Welcome

Chemin du Radium
91190 GIF SUR YVETTE
Tel: 01 69 41 28 79
President: Mme LAPEYRE

## I.M.S. Relocaliser

8, rue de Berri
75008 PARIS
Tel: 01 53 77 21 40
Fax: 01 53 77 21 44
Web site:
http://www.groupecourtaud.com
Contact: M. Jean-Marc SELLES

## International Relocation Assistance

116 bis, ave des Champs Élysées
75008 PARIS
Tel: 01 45 63 43 00
Fax: 01 45 63 03 42
Director:
Mme Marie-Christine BAUCHE

## NDH Conseil

17, rue Auguste Gervais
92445 ISSY LES MOULINEAUX
Tel: 01 46 45 78 00
Fax: 01 46 45 99 03

## Paris Welcome Service

*Help for your arrival in France, housing-schooling..., English-French-Spanish & Japanese*

16, Rue Vézelay
75008 PARIS
Tel: 01 43 59 70 40
Fax: 01 43 59 70 39
Director: Mme Marie-Anne LENCLUD

## Relocation Service

57, rue Pierre Charron
75008 PARIS
Tel: 01 42 89 09 15

## Riviera Relocation

*Since 1990, RR has been helping foreign nationals – both companies' executives & private individuals – to integrate in the South of France*

17, rue du Presbytère
06560 VALBONNE
Tel: 04 93 12 97 01
Tel2: 06 08 61 09 70
Fax: 04 93 12 97 03
Email: CathieH@msn.com
Manager: Mme Catherine HUBERT

## Settler International

1, promenade de la Bonnette
92633 GENNEVILLIERS Cedex
Tel: 01 41 85 85 00
Fax: 01 41 85 85 01
Email: 101361.1411@compuserve.com
Director: M. Thibaut MANTOUX

# SHIPPING
## TRANSPORTEURS

PARIS-ANGLOPHONE offers a list of professionals who specialize in shipping cargo, freight, and excess baggage. For international and domestic movers, you are invited to go to the Movers category in Living & Studying.

### SHIPPERS
### Agents maritimes

### Air Express International France
*International air freight forwarder*
1, rue du Pré
BP 10406
95707 ROISSY CDG
Tel: 01 49 19 68 68
Fax: 01 49 62 73 42
Assistant of the President:
Mme COUVREUR

### Daher America
Zone de Fret 4
Rue du Chapelier
95707 ROISSY CDG Cedex
Tel: 01 48 62 74 44
Fax: 01 48 62 55 58
Director: M. Gerald WHITE
Commercial Contact: M. GEMEVEY

### Excess Baggage Company
Batiment 3456 B
17, rue de la Belle Borne
BP 10077
95723 ROISSY CDG Cedex
Tel: 01 48 62 73 05
Fax: 01 48 62 73 01
Contact: Mme Isabelle LE

### French Freight Professionals
10, rue des Deux Cèdres
95700 ROISSY EN FRANCE
Tel: 01 48 62 49 65

### Hedleys Humpers
6, Bd de la Libération
93284 SAINT DENIS Cedex
Tel: 01 48 13 01 02
Tel NY: (212) 219 28 77
Fax: 01 48 13 07 08
Fax NY: (212) 219 28 26

### Heppner Paris International
ZI de Coudray
5-7, ave Armand-Esders
BP 27
93152 LE BLANC MESNIL
Tel: 01 49 39 39 39
Fax: 01 49 39 39 77
Sales manager: M. JUNG

### Johnson Henry Sons
*Customs and shipping agent*
5, rue Jacques Kable
75018 PARIS
Tel: 01 46 07 94 39
Fax: 01 46 07 52 83
Commercial Director: M. GILLES

### Jules Roy S.A. Groupe Schenker
BP 10216
95703 ROISSY CDG
Tel: 01 48 62 34 44
Fax: 01 48 62 33 10
Commercial Director:
M. Alexandre CUVELIER

### Lloyd's Register of Shipping
32, rue Caumartin
75009 PARIS
Tel: 01 47 42 60 30
Fax: 01 47 42 10 58
Fax2: 01 42 66 99 10
Director: M. J.P. PAGE

### Logistic Air/Sea France
*Specialize in excess baggage*
BP 10351
95706 ROISSY CDG
Tel: 01 48 62 80 42
Fax: 01 48 62 80 44

### Sagatrans
8-10, Route des Deux Cèdres
BP 10404
95707 ROISSY CDG
Tel: 01 49 19 23 54
Fax: 01 49 19 25 25
Email: palamede@imaginet.fr
Contact: M. Greg KONESKY

### Urschel International Ltd

Orly Fret 747
94398 ORLY AÉROGARE Cedex
Tel: 01 48 52 75 75
Fax: 01 46 86 00 45
Commercial Director:
M. Alain PENSEC

### World Freight

4, Chemin Dime
95700 ROISSY EN FRANCE
Tel: 01 34 29 00 44
Fax: 01 34 29 92 44

### MOVERS
Déménageurs

See Living & Studying:
Movers

# SPECIAL SERVICES
## SERVICES DIVERS

Here you're just going to have to read down the page, because PARIS-ANGLOPHONE presents a truly eclectic list of great services in Paris with highly useful professional and commercial applications. Find others in the Living & Studying section. Feel free to submit your own choices for the next edition.

### ABC Secrétariat
51, rue Dutot
75015 PARIS
Tel: 01 43 06 08 11
Fax: 01 45 66 83 12
Free-Lance: Mme Danielle DEVILLE

### Appeltel Telephone Answering Services

*Transfer your calls to reliable a bilingual secretary. Never miss a potential client, contract or appointment*
215, rue Jean-Jacques Rousseau
92136 ISSY LES MOULINEAUX Cedex
Tel: 01 41 46 00 60
Fax: 01 41 46 00 90
Email: appeltel@pepiniere.com
Web site:
http://www.entreprises.fr/appeltel
Director:
Mme Catherine BRONGNIART

### Atal
*Office planning workspace*
7, rue Mariotte
75017 PARIS
Tel: 01 53 04 22 00
Chairman: M. DOMINIONI

### Bella Voce International

*𝓑𝓥*

*Improve your speaking voice! Dev. vocal quality, health, expressivity. Gain confidence both professionally and personally. Call for free introduction*
10, place de la Bastille
75011 PARIS
Tel: 01 43 41 36 80
Director:
Mme Marie-Christine ALLEN

### Canon France
ZI Coudray
7, ave Albert Einstein
93154 BLANC MESNIL Cedex
Tel: 01 49 39 25 25
Fax: 01 49 39 30 90
Minitel: 3615 CANON
Web site: http://www.canon.fr

### Cha-cha-cha
*Fashion show video production*
25, Bd Saint Germain
75005 PARIS
Tel: 01 43 29 36 81
Fax: 01 43 29 36 81
Email: info@cha-cha-cha.com
web site: http://www.cha-cha-cha.com

### Culture Crossings Ltd
*Cultural adaptation seminars directed by the author of "French or foe?" Bestseller on everything you need to know of the French. Lots of laughs and insights. US price:$14.95*
51, rue de Bellechasse
75007 PARIS
Tel: 01 45 56 04 62
Fax: 01 45 55 91 86
Email: platt@club-internet.fr
For USA orders:
Email: distribooks@mepnet.com
Director: Mme Polly PLATT

# SPECIAL SERVICES
## SERVICES DIVERS

### Dernis Organisation
*Office and secretarial service*
23, ave de Wagram
75017 PARIS
Tel: 01 45 72 91 11
Fax: 01 45 72 91 12
Director: M. Jean-Philippe DERNIS

### Dudley W.A.
*Anglophone business and political events photographer*
85, rue Saint Dominique
75007 PARIS
Tel: 01 47 05 54 05
Fax: 01 45 51 27 16
Email: paris-dudley@magic.fr

### Esmerk Information
*Customized information service for executives*
38, rue d'Hauteville
75010 PARIS
Tel: 01 44 83 64 83
Fax: 01 44 83 90 44
Email: 100431.1417@compuserve.com
Web site: http://www.esmerk.com
Contact: Mme Lynn LINDSTROM

---

### Harry's New York Bar

Established in 1911 at Sank Roo Doe Noo. Remains today a great meeting place for adopted anglophile Parisians. Cocktail service for businesses
5, rue Daunou
75002 PARIS
Tel: 01 42 61 71 14
Fax: 01 42 61 58 99

---

### Haworth International
*Office furnishings*
7, terrasse des Reflets
92081 PARIS LA DÉFENSE Cedex 2
Tel: 01 41 97 41 00
Fax: 01 41 97 41 97
Director: M. Christian ROOXEL

### Hermann Miller & Cie
*Setting up offices*
37, ave Pierre 1er de Serbie
75008 PARIS
Tel: 01 40 69 62 62
Fax: 01 40 70 15 15

### Intea
*Designs all types of packaging (aluminium, cardboard, plastic)*
37, ave Junot
75018 PARIS
Tel: 01 46 06 68 01
Fax: 01 46 06 35 36
Manager: Mme Corinne LELARGE

### Iter International
*Mail service for businesses*
33, ave Philippe Auguste
75011 PARIS
Tel: 01 44 64 89 00
Fax: 01 43 71 93 60
Minitel: 3615 ITER
Contact: Mme Mireille HARREAU

### Mailboxes Etc.
*Office supplies, copy service, international shipping...*
208, rue de la Convention
75015 PARIS
Tel: 01 44 19 60 20
Fax: 01 44 19 60 29

### MP Bureau Business
*Mail service for businesses settling in France*
92, rue de Lévis
75017 PARIS
Tel: 01 43 80 40 41
Fax: 01 43 80 26 25

### Nissen, Liselott
*Reporter and business photographer*
7, rue de Thorigny
75003 PARIS
Tel: 01 42 77 76 89

### Numéro 6
*Audiovisual, broadcast production*
116, rue de Charenton
75012 PARIS
Tel: 01 42 42 36 36
Fax: 01 47 85 12 21
Email: pleonard@pratique.fr
Contacts: MM. Marcel LOSHOUARN
& Pascal LÉONARD

# PARIS VISITE

## La solution transport
## à tous vos déplacements dans la capitale

PARIS VISITE est un forfait transport valable 1, 2, 3 ou 5 jours pour découvrir Paris et sa région
en bus, métro, RER et trains SNCF d'Ile-de-France jusqu'au parc Disneyland® Paris, Versailles,
Fontainebleau et aux aéroports de Roissy - Charles-de-Gaulle et Orly.
PARIS VISITE vous permet également de bénéficier d'avantages exclusifs
sur l'entrée de nombreux sites touristiques de la capitale.

PARIS VISITE existe en version demi-tarif pour les enfants de moins de 12 ans.

PARIS VISITE est en vente dans les principales stations de métro et gares RER, dans
les gares SNCF Ile-de-France, dans les aéroports internationaux parisiens
et dans les bureaux de l'Office de Tourisme de Paris.

**La RATP vous souhaite un agréable séjour à Paris.**

## The best way to travel around the capital

PARIS VISITE is a travel card valid for 1, 2, 3 or 5 days for exploring Paris and the Paris area
by bus, metro, RER or Ile de France SNCF train including journeys
to Disneyland® Paris, Versailles and the Roissy - Charles-de-Gaulle or Orly airports.
A PARIS VISITE card also entitles you to exclusive benefits on admission
to many of the capital's tourist attractions.

There is also a half-price PARIS VISITE card for children under 12.

PARIS VISITE is on sale at the principal metro stations, RER stations
and Ile de France SNCF (main line) stations, at Paris's international airports
and at branches of the Office de Tourisme in Paris.

**RATP hopes you enjoy your stay in Paris.**

*LA MEILLEURE FAÇON D'AVANCER*

# We all have a favourite image of France...

whether it's the long straight stretches of tree-lined country roads, the street cafés, the rustic backwaters, the wind-blown granite cliffs of Brittany, the endless sandy beaches of the Aquitaine coast, the elegant spa towns, the volcanic splendour of the Auvergne, the half-timbered charm of Normandy, the cosmopolitan clamour of Paris or the indelible memory of long relaxed flavoursome meals served with panache ... Whatever your favourite image, if you like France you'll love *FRANCE* magazine — the quarterly English-language review of *la vie française*.

## FULL REFUND IF NOT ENTIRELY DELIGHTED

*A 1-year subscription to FRANCE costs just £16.50 to UK addresses (or £19.50 to any address outside UK), and if you are not entirely happy with your first copy, you will receive a full 'no-quibble' refund.*

Return the coupon (below) today (or a photocopy) along with your cheque (or card details) to:

**FRANCE Magazine (PA97),
58 av de Wagram, 75017 Paris**
Tel: **(01) 41 46 00 64**
Fax: **(01) 39 08 06 35**

*FRANCE also makes an ideal gift for a Francophile, sent to any address in the world on your behalf at no extra cost.*

PAYING IN FRANCS? 195ff

Please enter me for a 1-year subscription to FRANCE on the understanding that I can request a full refund within 30 days of receiving my first copy if not entirely delighted.

Name ........................................

Address ........................................

........................................

Cheques payable to FRANCE, or please charge my card no: ........................................

Expiry: ........................................

Signed: ........................................

PA97

# Développez vos activités
## grâce à Internet

**Diffusez** votre proposition commerciale sur Internet grâce au réseau des Chambres de Commerce et d'Industrie, **IBCC-NET** :
• achat ou vente de produits/services,
• recherche de partenaires,
• joint venture,
• représentation,
• coopération technique,
• licence…

**et profitez** de la notoriété des Chambres de Commerce et d'Industrie pour augmenter **la votre** (publicité électronique).

**http : www.worldchambers.com**

**Contact :**

e-mail : telexport@ccip.fr - Tél. : 01 55 65 65 20

CHAMBRE DE COMMERCE ET D'INDUSTRIE DE PARIS

## Otis
*24h service for elevator installations*
4, place Victor Hugo
92400 COURBEVOIE
Tel: 01 46 91 60 00
Toll-Free: 0 800 24 24 07
Fax: 01 47 68 95 97

## Rank Xerox
*Office equipment*
7, rue Touzet
93586 SAINT OUEN Cedex
Tel: 01 49 48 47 46
Fax: 01 49 48 43 21
President: M. J.M. MACHON

## ReCreate Your Career in France
*Find challenging, enjoyable work that fits your values. Develop step-by-step strategy. Practical results oriented*
4, impasse de la Gaîté
75014 PARIS
Tel: 01 43 21 36 99
Fax: 01 43 20 09 46
Email: soul-works@compuserve.com
Contact: Mme Libby ROBINSON

## Rischard et Newman
*Architectural firm for companies*
18, cité Malesherbes
75009 PARIS
Tel: 01 42 80 53 80
Fax: 01 42 80 85 18
Contact: Mme Rebecca NEWMAN

## Spectrum Hotel Group
*Sells and buys hotels*
63, Bd du Commandant Charcot
92 200 NEUILLY SUR SEINE
Tel: 01 46 40 06 53
Fax: 01 46 40 06 53
Email: 101731.1501@compuserve.com
Broker: Mme Patricia LINN

## World Trade Center Paris
Palais des Congrès
2, place de la Porte Maillot
BP 18
75853 PARIS Cedex 17
Tel: 01 40 68 14 95
Fax: 01 40 68 14 21
Email: wtcpa@wtcpa.geis.com
Contact: Mme Geneviève FOURNIER

**DOING BUSINESS & WORKING**

129

# TELECOMMUNICATIONS
## TÉLÉCOMMUNICATIONS

An exploding field, the telecommunications industry is soon to be deregulated in France and all the major players are positioning themselves for the change. Here's how to find many of them. For the time being, if you just need a telephone line installed call your local France Telecom office by dialing 14.

### AT&T France

*The AT&T International Call Plan. This new call-back service is simply the ideal way to get exclusively low rates on international calls from home, office or mobile phone (See advertisement)*

Tour Horizon
52, quai de Dion-Bouton
92806 PUTEAUX Cedex
Tel: 01 47 67 47 67
Free call: 0 800 90 82 93
Fax: 01 47 67 47 71
Director: M. François MAIRE

### AXS Telecom

*Discount call-back service*
19, rue Auguste Chabrières
75015 PARIS
Tel: 01 45 57 54 40
Fax: 01 45 57 54 45

### Bouygues Télécom

51, ave de l'Europe
78944 VÉLIZY Cedex
Tel: 01 39 26 60 00
Toll-Free: 0 801 630 330

### British Telecom France

Immeuble Jean Monnet
92061 PARIS LA DÉFENSE Cedex 56
Tel: 01 46 67 25 00
Fax: 01 47 68 95 76
Marketing Manager: M. Richard VIEL

### Cable & Wireless France

Les Collines de l'Arche
Bâtiment Madeleine
92057 PARIS LA DÉFENSE
Tel: 01 46 92 91 00
Fax: 01 49 01 01 09
Director: M. Robert TREHIN

### Canal France International

*Satellite TV network*
59, Bd Exelmans
75016 PARIS
Tel: 01 40 71 11 71
Fax: 01 40 71 11 72

### Central Call International

*Call back routing*
192, ave du Général de Gaulle
92140 CLAMART
Tel: 01 46 31 80 90
Fax: 01 46 30 76 20
Email: sauzeau@hol.fr
Contact: M. SAUZEAU

### DD Electronics

*Bringing English-language channels to your existing TV*
4, rue de Calais
75009 PARIS
Tel: 01 42 82 13 65
Fax: 01 42 82 95 55

### Dynatech Communications France

Bâtiment GAIA
9, Parc Ariane
78284 GUYANCOURT Cedex
Tel: 01 30 48 83 00
Fax: 01 30 48 83 10
Director: M. Christopher JACKSON

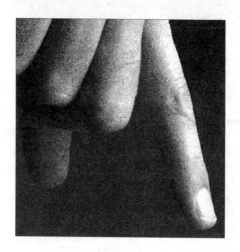

# Now, there's a callback service with just the right touch.

**The New AT&T International Call Plan**

Get all the savings of a callback service with the added touch of quality connections and dependability only AT&T can offer. To find out more, just ask your local operator to place a collect call to AT&T on **0800 90 82 93**.

Not available in all countries.
©1997 AT&T

**AT&T**

## Eicon Technology

1-3, rue Eugène Varlin
BP 82
92243 MALAKOFF Cedex
Tel: 01 46 57 05 05
Fax: 01 46 57 40 76
Director: M. Robert CLARKE

## Ellinas Phone Rentals

*Supplies portable phones in France*
Roissypole
Le Dôme 2
2, rue de la Haye
10901 ROISSY CDG Cedex
Tel: 01 48 16 10 99
Fax: 01 49 19 49 28

## Espace SFR Techno Cellular

*Specializes in servicing companies
and individuals in mobile cellular
communication (mobile phones, car
kit installation, transmission of fax &
data...)*
1, rue Jacques Daguerre
92500 RUEIL MALMAISON
Tel: 01 47 49 89 89
Fax: 01 47 49 88 11
Contact: Mme Tyla HAMBURG

## France Télécom Direction des Réseaux et Services Internationaux

*Worldwide networks and services*
37-39, ave Ledru Rollin
75012 PARIS
Tel: 01 43 42 68 55
Fax: 01 43 42 61 42
Communications & Marketing Director:
Mme Constance CAPDENAT
Public Relations Director:
Mme Sylvaine ROUSSEAU

## Hutchison Telecom

131, ave Charles de Gaulle
92200 NEUILLY SUR SEINE
Tel: 01 46 41 91 00
Fax: 01 46 41 91 53
Contact: Mme Laetitia GEORGES

## Matra Communication

Rue Jean-Pierre Timbaud
BP 26
78392 BOIS D'ARCY Cedex
Tel: 01 34 60 70 00
Fax: 01 34 60 74 16

## MCI International France

*International telecommunications
services*
125, ave des Champ Élysées
75008 PARIS
Tel: 01 47 20 50 80
Fax: 01 47 20 49 51
Director: M. Alexandre DEMIDOFF

## Nortel Europe

12 bis, rue Jean Jaurès
92807 PUTEAUX Cedex
Tel: 01 46 96 17 17
Fax: 01 46 96 15 00
President: M. Jacques BERUBE

## Northern Telecom France

NT Meridian
Parc Léonard de Vinci
15, ave Alexandre Bell
77607 BUSSY SAINT GEORGES Cedex
Tel: 01 64 76 76 76
Fax: 01 64 76 76 00

## Rent a Cell

*Cellular phone rental*
116 bis, ave des Champs Élysées
75008 PARIS
Tel: 01 53 93 78 00
Fax: 01 53 93 78 09
Contact: M. Michael DANA

## Sprint International France

*Telecommunications networks and
services*
164 bis, ave Charles de Gaulle
92526 NEUILLY SUR SEINE
Tel: 01 46 43 34 00
Fax: 01 46 43 34 34
President: M. Paolo COLOMBI

## Telecash Distribution B.V.

*Interactive cable TV networks*
145, rue Jean-Jacques Rousseau
92130 ISSY LES MOULINEAUX
Tel: 01 41 08 33 33
Fax: 01 41 08 33 30

## Teleconom/Interworld

*Cheap telephone rates*
1, rue de l'Université
75007 PARIS
Tel: 01 40 15 06 82
Fax: 01 40 15 07 17
Contact: M. Pierre BÈS DE BERC

## Telegroup Global Access France

13, rue Témara
BP 5234
78175 SAINT GERMAIN EN LAYE
Tel: 01 30 87 99 00
Fax: 01 30 87 99 02
Email: telegrup@dialup.francenet.fr
Contact: M. Georges APPLE

## Télétam

*Provides a strictly personal phone number to those without their own telephone, including a voice mailbox for messages*
Tel: 01 46 44 40 00
Contact: M. Bruno LECLERC

*DOING BUSINESS & WORKING*

133

# TRADE SHOWS
## SALONS

France is loaded with an exhuberant schedule of trade shows, professional exhibitions, and commercial and cultural fairs. The *Chambre de Commerce et d'Industrie de Paris* web site publishes a complete schedule which can be accessed via link at http://www.paris-anglo.com/data/rubriques/chamb.html

### CNIT - Centre des Nouvelles Technologies et Industries
2-4, place de la Défense
92053 PARIS LA DÉFENSE
Tel: 01 46 92 12 12
Fax: 01 46 92 24 49

### Collectives Réseaux
*For professionals only*
Reed OIP
11, rue du Colonel Pierre Avia
BP 571
75726 PARIS Cedex 15
Tel: 01 41 90 47 47
Fax: 01 41 90 47 00
Web site: http://www.salon.reed-oip.fr

### Comité des Expositions de Paris
55, quai Alphonse Le Gallo
92107 BOULOGNE
Tel: 01 49 09 61 13
Fax: 01 49 09 60 03
Director: Mme Silvana MARTINO

### Deauville Festival
*American film festival*
Le Public Système
36, rue Pierret
92000 NEUILLY SUR SEINE
Tel: 01 46 40 55 00
Fax: 01 47 38 10 10
President: M. CHOUCHAN

### Dietexpo
*For professionals only*
Reed OIP
11, rue du Colonel Pierre Avia
BP 571
75726 PARIS Cedex 15
Tel: 01 41 90 47 47
Fax: 01 41 90 47 00
Web site: http://www.salon.reed-oip.fr

### Expo Concept Développement
*Stands for trade shows*
8, rue Paul Langevin
78373 PLAISIR Cedex
Tel: 01 30 54 60 57
Fax: 01 30 55 12 86
Web site:
http://www.expoconcept.integra.fr
Contact: Stéphanie

### Expolangues
OIP
62, rue de Miromesnil
75008 PARIS
Tel: 01 41 90 47 47
Fax: 01 41 90 48 78

### FIAC
*Contemporary Art Trade Show*
Reed OIP
11, rue du Colonel Pierre Avia
BP 571
75726 PARIS Cedex 15
Tel: 01 41 90 47 47
Fax: 01 41 90 47 00
Web site: http://www.salon.reed-oip.fr

### Forum de la Geide
*For professionals only*
Reed OIP
11, rue du Colonel Pierre Avia
BP 571
75726 PARIS Cedex 15
Tel: 01 41 90 47 47
Fax: 01 41 90 47 00
Web site: http://www.salon.reed-oip.fr

### Reed Midem Organisation
11, rue du Colonel Pierre Avia
75015 PARIS
Tel: 01 41 90 47 60
Fax: 01 41 90 47 69
Chief Executive: M. Xavier ROY

## Reed OIP

*Organizes trade fairs*
11-13, rue du Colonel Pierre Avia
75015 PARIS
Tel: 01 41 90 47 60
Fax: 01 41 90 47 09
Contact: Mme Christine FRICHET

## Salon de la Musique

Reed OIP
11, rue du Colonel Pierre Avia
BP 571
75726 PARIS Cedex 15
Tel: 01 41 90 47 47
Fax: 01 41 90 47 00
Web site: http://www.salon.reed-oip.fr

## Salon de la Piscine

Reed OIP
11, rue du Colonel Pierre Avia
BP 571
75726 PARIS Cedex 15
Tel: 01 41 90 47 47
Fax: 01 41 90 47 00
Web site: http://www.salon.reed-oip.fr

## Salon de la Revue

*Annual journal publishing fair within the book fair*
Reed OIP
11, rue du Colonel Pierre Avia
75726 PARIS Cedex 15
Tel: 01 41 90 44 00
Fax: 01 41 90 47 00
Email: livre@reed-oip.fr
Web site: http://www.salon.reed-oip.fr
Contact: Marie-Hélène PASDELOUP

## Salon de la vidéo

Reed OIP
11, rue du Colonel Pierre Avia
BP 571
75726 PARIS Cedex 15
Tel: 01 41 90 44 00
Fax: 01 41 90 47 00
Web site: http://www.salon.reed-oip.fr

## Salon des Métiers du Livre

Reed OIP
11, rue du Colonel Pierre Avia
BP 571
75726 PARIS Cedex 15
Tel: 01 41 90 44 00
Fax: 01 41 90 47 00
Web site: http://www.salon.reed-oip.fr

## Salon du Livre

*Annual book/publishing fair*
Reed OIP
11, rue du Colonel Pierre Avia
BP 571
75726 PARIS Cedex 15
Tel: 01 41 90 44 00
Fax: 01 41 90 47 00
Email: livre@reed-oip.fr
Web site: http://www.salon.reed-oip.fr

## Salon du Livre de Jeunesse

Reed OIP
11, rue du Colonel Pierre Avia
BP 571
75726 PARIS Cedex 15
Tel: 01 41 90 47 47
Fax: 01 41 90 47 00
Web site: http://www.salon.reed-oip.fr

## Salon du Lycéen et de l'Étudiant

Reed OIP
11, rue du Colonel Pierre Avia
BP 571
75726 PARIS Cedex 15
Tel: 01 41 90 47 47
Fax: 01 41 90 47 00
Web site: http://www.salon.reed-oip.fr

## Salon du Multimédia et de l'Édition Electronique

Reed OIP
11, rue du Colonel Pierre Avia
BP 571
75726 PARIS Cedex 15
Tel: 01 41 90 47 47
Fax: 01 41 90 47 00
Web site: http://www.salon.reed-oip.fr

## Salon du Théâtre

*For professionals only*
Reed OIP
11, rue du Colonel Pierre Avia
BP 571
75726 PARIS Cedex 15
Tel: 01 41 90 47 47
Fax: 01 41 90 47 00
Web site: http://www.salon.reed-oip.fr

135

### Salon Nautique de Paris

Reed OIP
11, rue du Colonel Pierre Avia
BP 571
75726 PARIS Cedex 15
Tel: 01 41 90 47 47
Fax: 01 41 90 47 00
Web site: http://www.salon.reed-oip.fr

### Salon Professionnel de la Papeterie

*For professionals only*
Reed OIP
11, rue du Colonel Pierre Avia
BP 571
75726 PARIS Cedex 15
Tel: 01 41 90 47 47
Fax: 01 41 90 47 00
Web site: http://www.salon.reed-oip.fr

136

From English to French and back, your documents, letters, annual reports, brochures, manuscripts, etc. need professional translation skills. Business meetings, conferences, courses... interpreters are required. Here are some competent choices.

## A'BTI - Agence Bilis Traduction Interprètes

*Translation, interpreting, visa legalisations*
24, rue Laffitte
75009 PARIS
Tel: 01 47 70 50 80
Fax: 01 42 46 37 43
Director: M. Jean D'ANTHONAY

## AC3 Formation/Conseils

38, rue du Temple
75004 PARIS
Tel: 01 40 29 97 40
Fax: 01 40 29 97 47

## Ad Litteram - Translators

1, rue Chrétien de Troyes
78540 VERNOUILLET
Tel: 01 39 71 16 71
Tel2: 06 80 13 81 37
Fax: 01 39 28 07 91
Email: 100761.1746@compuserve.com
Contact: Mme Barbara JORIO

## Agence Translantic

170, rue du Fbg Saint Antoine
75012 PARIS
Tel: 01 40 09 89 62
Fax: 01 40 09 92 66
Email: translantic@compuserve.com
Web site:
http://ourworld.compuserve.com/
home pages/translantic

## Agence Volker Marek

361, rue Lecourbe
75015 PARIS
Tel: 01 45 57 16 76
Fax: 01 45 57 49 45
Managing Director: M. Volker MAREK

## Alinter

28, rue Théodore Ducos
33000 BORDEAUX
Tel: 05 56 99 42 42
Fax: 05 56 99 00 46
Email: traduction@alinter.alienor.fr
Web site: http://www.alienor.fr/alinter
Contact: M. Patrick SERRANO

## Astradul

BP 225 07
75327 PARIS Cedex 07
Tel: 01 39 83 66 63
Tel2: 01 39 84 23 30

## Berlitz Traduction

63, rue Aristide Briand
92300 LEVALLOIS PERRET
Tel: 01 47 57 71 71
Fax: 01 47 57 29 92
Email: btzparis@iway.fr
Director: Mme Aurélie LOGIEZ

## Business Editing

89, rue du Fbg Saint Martin
75010 PARIS
Tel: 01 42 06 66 15
Fax: 01 42 06 69 02
Email: 101444,3226@compuserve.com

## Cabinet de la Hanse

40, rue La Boétie
75008 PARIS
Tel: 01 45 63 81 18
Fax: 01 42 25 45 26
Director: M. Cornelis DE PREST

## CG Traduction

8, rue Rameau
BP 235
78002 VERSAILLES Cedex
Tel: 01 39 24 88 55
Fax: 01 39 02 00 64
Director: Mme Catherine GRANELL

## Communications Européennes

8, rue de Surène
75008 PARIS
Tel: 01 42 66 43 30
Fax: 01 42 66 28 20

# TRANSLATION
## TRADUCTION

### Courcoulas, Nelly

*Freelance translator English-French working experience in international institutions: United Nations Geneva, World Bank Washington, Olympic Games Atlanta*

23, rue Louis-Willaume
92270 BOIS COLOMBES
Tel: 01 42 42 66 29
Tel2: 06 09 03 23 84
Fax: 01 41 19 04 90
Email: 103650.473@compuserve.com

### Delille-Gomory, Julia

*Bilingual Conference Interpreter (AIIC)*

31, rue Franklin
91704 SAINTE GENEVIEVE
DES BOIS
Tel: 01 60 16 08 88
Fax: 01 69 51 01 93
Email: jd2512@mail.cl.b-internet.fr

### Depreiter & Clarke

320, rue Saint Honoré
75001 PARIS
Tel: 01 47 04 71 81
Fax: 01 47 04 71 82
Email: 101534,1433@compuserve.com

### Drogman

*English/French translators (Harvard & Sorbonne) + All language service. Advanced computer software*

14, rue des Fossés Saint Jacques
75005 PARIS
Tel: 01 46 34 25 32
Fax: 01 43 54 51 53
Email: 100556.1525@compuserve.com
Production Manager:
M. Jordan ARZOGLOU

### Effitrad

7, ave des Ternes
75017 PARIS
Tel: 01 44 09 02 03
Fax: 01 44 09 02 03
Director:
M. Stéphane RONSIN-EDWARDS

### Europublica

21, rue Saint Fiacre
75002 PARIS
Tel: 01 40 26 44 77
Fax: 01 45 08 44 25

### EuroTexte

73, Bd de Sébastopol
75001 PARIS
Tel: 01 42 21 14 00
Fax: 01 42 21 14 17
Email: eurotexte@easynet.fr
Web site: http://www.eurotexte.com
Director: Mme Lori THICKE

### Extratext

19, rue Le Brun
75013 PARIS
Tel: 01 43 31 93 92
Fax: 01 43 31 96 33
Director: M. Kevin HARRIGAN

### GTI Communication

206, Bd Jean Jaurès
92100 BOULOGNE
Tel: 01 46 20 25 09
Fax: 01 46 20 25 29
Email: GTI.Paris@wanadoo.fr
Contact: M. Kenneth YOUNG

### Harder, Peter Jeremy

97, Bd Jean Behra
06100 NICE
Email: pjharder@webstore.fr

### International Corporate Communication

3, rue des Batignolles
75017 PARIS
Tel: 01 43 87 29 29
Fax: 01 45 22 49 13
Email: 100497,1676@compuserve.com
Contact: M. Gordon GOLDING

### Kane Traduction

10, rue Paul Vaillant Couturier
92300 LEVALLOIS PERRET
Tel: 01 40 89 08 16
Email: 100555.52@compuserve.com
Director: M. Franklin KANE

### Leslie, Tanya

*Translating and interpreting services in French, English, Italian and Spanish (advertising, fiction, travel, film)*

29, rue au Maire
75003 PARIS
Tel: 01 42 77 39 44

## Linguacom International

83, rue Michel Ange
75016 PARIS
Tel: 01 46 51 29 77
Fax: 01 47 43 18 94
Director: M. Asamanja GHOSE

## McElhearn - Benini

91, rue de la Mésangerie
37540 SAINT CYR SUR LOIRE
Tel: 02 47 49 24 54
Fax: 02 47 42 67 15
Email: kirk@lenet.fr

## Nagpal International Translation

*General, medical and scientific translations*
65, rue Pascal
75013 PARIS
Tel: 01 47 07 55 28
Fax: 01 43 37 11 46
Director: M. D.C. NAGPAL

## Nataf, Florence

8, impasse de la Mare
95110 SANNOIS
Tel: 01 34 10 95 94
Fax: 01 34 10 95 94

## Paschall, Tony Frank

*Translation for broadcast & print media*
19, allée Marc Chagall
75013 PARIS
Tel: 01 45 86 03 28
Fax: 01 45 86 05 24
Email: cxp@compuserve.com

## Petch, Sandra

261, Bd Voltaire
75011 PARIS
Tel: 01 43 71 07 12
Fax: 01 43 72 58 97
Email: SPetch@aol.com

## Savdié, Eileen Osmond

4, rue Descombes
75017 PARIS
Tel: 01 43 80 80 75
Fax: on request
Email: on request

## Sirett, David

153, rue Championnet
75018 PARIS
Tel: 01 42 58 49 14
Fax: 01 42 58 49 14
Email: 100720.2165@compuserve.com

## Société Française des Traducteurs

*National union of professional translators*
22, rue des Martyrs
75009 PARIS
Tel: 01 48 78 43 32
Fax: 01 60 36 05 81

## Tectrad

1, Villa Montcalm
75018 PARIS
Tel: 01 44 92 93 11
Fax: 01 44 92 93 10

## The Bridge

EDITIONS & MULTIMEDIA

*Tight deadlines-high quality-low cost !*
*Copywrite-Translate-Design in Paris*
*Print/Mail: Paris London NYC*
104, rue Bobillot
75013 PARIS
Tel: 01 53 62 15 33
Fax: 01 53 62 15 34
Email: westside@club-internet.fr
Contact: M. Victor VAL DERE

## Titra-Film

*French subtitles for foreign films*
1, quai Gabriel Péri
94340 JOINVILLE LE PONT
Tel: 01 48 89 19 89
Fax: 01 48 86 41 70

# TRANSLATION
## TRADUCTION

### Traductor

120, ave des Champs Élysées
75008 PARIS
Tel: 01 45 62 50 41
Fax: 01 42 25 03 74
Director: Mme Marie-France THUREL

### Ursula Grüber
### Communication Internationale

*Copywriting, adaptation of
advertising texts*

83, rue Saint Honoré
75001 PARIS
Tel: 01 42 33 57 61
Fax: 01 42 21 41 14
President: Mme Ursula GRUBER

### Varlet, Bernard

24, rue de la Libération
77230 DAMMARTIN EN GOELE
Tel: 01 60 54 96 30
Fax: 01 60 54 96 30

### Voices

10 bis, ave Jean Jaurès
92240 MALAKOFF
Tel: 01 47 35 19 19
Fax: 01 47 35 44 46
Contact: Mme Michèle MARSHALL

### WordPower

12, rue Roger Bacon
75017 PARIS
Tel: 01 45 72 37 27
Fax: 01 40 68 74 89
Email: 100666.301compuserve.com
Contact: Mme Gina DOGGETT

# FRENCH-AMERICAN CHAMBERS OF COMMERCE
## (F.A.C.C.) - Chapters in the USA

### Atlanta
999 Peachtree Street, N.E.
Suite 2095
Atlanta, GA 30309
(404) 874-2602
(404) 875-9452
Co-Executive Directors:
Hilary Bumm &
Valérie Polevoy

### Chicago
The Merchandise Mart
Suite 940
Chicago, IL 60654
(312) 595-9524
(312)595-9529
Managing Director:
Michel Gilbert

### Dallas-Ft. Worth
4835 LBJ Freeway
Suite 455
Dallas, TX 75244
(972) 991-4888
(972) 991-4887
Executive Director:
Erin Petit

### Houston
1776 St. James Place
Suite 425
Houston, TX 77056
(713) 960-0575
(713) 960-0495
Executive Director:
Kendall Knaus

### Louisiana
2938 World Trade Center
2 Canal Street
New Orleans, LA 70130
(504) 524-2042
(504) 529-1691
Executive Director:
Valérie Guillet

### Miami/Fort Lauder-dale
New World Tower
31th Floor100
North Biscayne Bvd
Miami, FL 33132-2306
(305) 373-93333
(305) 373-8315

### Michigan
c/o Schmaltz & Co., P.C.
/Nexia International
27777 Franklin Road
Suite 1200
Southfield, MI 48034
(810) 358-1861
(810) 358-4766
Executive Director:
Darcy Mellen-Sullivan

### Minneapolis/St. Paul
Foshay Tower,
Suite 904
821 Marquette Avenue
Minneapolis, MN 55402
(612) 338-7750
(612) 338-7750
Executive Director:
N. Christine Heinerscheid

### National Chamber
520 Madison Ave.
37th flor
New York, NY 10022
Tel: (212) 715-4444
Fax: (212) 715-4441
President:
Serge BELLANGER

### New England
31 St. James Avenue
Suite 775
Boston, MA 02116
(617) 542-7071
(617) 542-7002
Executive Director:
Mary Rinaldi

### New York
1350 Avenue of the
Americas
New York, NY 10019
(212) 765-4460
(212) 765-4650
Managing Director:
Lenir Drake

### Northern Ohio
3300 BP America Building
200 Public Square
Cleveland, OH 44114
(216) 621-0150
(216) 241-2824
Deputy Executive Director:
Sonja M. Lechowick

### Pacific Northwest
2101 Fourth Avenue
Suite 2030
Seattle, WA 98121-2317
(206) 443-4703
(206) 448-4218
Executive Director:
Jack A. Cowan

### Philadelphia
4000 Bell Atlantic Tower
1717 Arch Street
Philadelphia, PA 19103
(215) 994-5373
(215) 994-5366
Executive Director:
Judith L. Ujobai

### Pittsburgh
c/o Reed, Smith, Shaw &
McClay
435 Sixth Avenue
Pittsburgh, PA 15219
(412) 288-4174
(412) 288-3063
Executive Director:
Janet B. Stiehler

### San Francisco
425 Bush Street
Suite 401
San Francisco, CA 94108
(415) 398-2449
(415) 398-8912
Executive Director:
Jean Jacote

### Southern California
6380 Wilshire Boulevard
Suite 1608
Los Angeles, CA 90048
(213) 651-4741
(213) 651-2547
Executive Director:
Barbara Hearn

### Washington, D.C.
1730 Rhode Island Avenue,
N.W.
Suite 711
Washington, D.C. 20036
(202) 775-0256
(202) 785-4604
Executive Director:
Susan Shillinglaw

# LIVING & STUDYING

If you're not a tourist and you're not doing in business in France, you probably live here already or are thinking of moving to Paris. Anglophones living in France, including students spending one or more semesters, are a special hybrid of "Parisian." You're both part of the scene and apart from it. The Editors of PARIS-ANGLOPHONE know the world of the expat very well.

One thing is for sure: you're not alone. Anglophones since Benjamin Franklin and Thomas Jefferson have been coming to Paris and setting-up home or shop. Why? Well, you know already: you each have your own reply.

## THE NUMBERS

Some estimates today state that there are nearly 200 000 permanent Anglo-American residents in France. Official numbers are considerably lower (the US Embassy has some 30 000 American citizens on its books, but few people ever officially register at their embassy). In any case, collectively there is a real niche, a community with a common linguistic culture and both diverse and converging needs and interests. PARIS-ANGLOPHONE attempts here to respond to the nature and character of the community by assembling 40 major headings and 47 sub-headings relating to daily life in the French capital. Aside from the services and contacts assembled in the Travel & Tourism and Doing Business & Working sections of this directory, collected on the following pages are the addresses you'll need to live in Paris in a more comfortable and culturally-enriched manner. The numerous areas of overlap between the working and living sections are marked with notes that send you to the appropriate section and heading.

You know Paris already, and have established your own habits, private preferences, favorite venue, little tricks and great secrets, but knowing and engaging with a city requires constant updating and renewing of key addresses and inside contacts. Here's a good start. Be sure to write to PARIS-ANGLOPHONE with your own choice of useful services and preferred places in this glorious adopted city.

# ART GALLERIES
## GALERIES D'ART

Although the Paris art market has dropped off, the Paris art scene is vibrant. And not only is gallery-hopping a favorite activity of anglophone Parisians, a number of them maintain their own establishments.

### Art Service International

30, rue du Château d'Eau
75010 PARIS
Tel: 01 42 39 14 00
Fax: 01 42 39 14 02
Director: Mme Bénédicte PESLE

### Christie's

6, rue Paul Baudry
75008 PARIS
Tel: 01 42 56 17 66
Fax: 01 42 56 26 01
Web site: http://www.christies.com

### Claude Elisabeth Fillet

109, rue du Cherche Midi
75006 PARIS
Tel: 01 45 48 87 83

### Darthea Speyer

6, rue Jacques Callot
75006 PARIS
Tel: 01 43 54 78 41
Fax: 01 43 29 62 36

### Espace Cannibal Pierce

7, rue Samson
BP 224
93200 SAINT DENIS
Tel: 01 48 09 94 59
Directors: Ken SHEPHERD &
June SHENFIELD

### Galerie Pierre Boogaerts

44, rue Vieille du Temple
75004 PARIS
Tel: 01 42 74 44 68
Fax: 01 42 08 59 78
Director: M. Pierre BOOGAERTS

### Gilbert Brownstone et Cie

26, rue Saint Gilles
75003 PARIS
Tel: 01 42 78 43 21
Fax: 01 42 74 04 00
Director: M. Gilbert BROWNSTONE

### Palladio

27, rue des Saints-Pères
75006 PARIS
Tel: 01 01 40 15 09 15
Fax: 01 40 15 09 55

### Sotheby's

3, rue Miromesnil
75008 PARIS
Tel: 01 53 05 53 05
Fax: 01 47 42 22 32
Web site: http://www.sothebys.com

### Zabriskie

37, rue Quincampoix
75004 PARIS
Tel: 01 42 72 35 47
Fax: 01 40 27 99 66
Director: M. Thierry MARLAT

# BANKING
## BANQUES

(See Doing Business & Working: Banking)

146

# BEAUTY
## BEAUTÉ

Need your hair cut, your nails done, your body tanned *à l'américaine*? Here are some suggested places to go. And of course you'll find here the name-brand beauty services that make France so famous...massages, facials, make-up, etc.

## BEAUTY SALONS
## Salons de beauté

### American Style Beauté
*Acrylic or natural nails, hair cuts and perms, reasonable prices, your place or mine*
29, rue au Maire
75003 PARIS
Tel: 01 42 72 83 55
Contact: Mme Kathleen SAINT CLARE

### Carlota
*Manicure and pedicure home visits, massage*
15, rue Sablonville
92200 NEUILLY SUR SEINE
Tel: 01 47 47 12 12

### Clarins
4, rue Berteaux Dumas
92200 NEUILLY SUR SEINE
Tel: 01 46 24 01 81
Director: M. Christian Jacques
COURTIN-CLARINS

### Courcelles
115, rue de Courcelles
75017 PARIS
Tel: 01 47 66 73 60

### Estée Lauder
17-21, rue du Fbg Saint Honoré
75008 PARIS
Tel: 01 40 06 89 00
Fax: 01 40 66 64 55
President: M. MAICENT

### Iéna Top International Dames
4, ave Pierre 1er de Serbie
75016 PARIS
Tel: 01 47 20 53 54
Fax: 01 47 20 93 46

### Iéna Top International Messieurs
2, ave Pierre 1er de Serbie
75016 PARIS
Tel: 01 47 23 61 19
Fax: 01 47 20 93 46

### Jeanne Piaubert Institut
27, rue Jean Goujon
75008 PARIS
Tel: 01 53 77 55 31

### Lancôme Institut
29, rue du Fbg Saint Honoré
75008 PARIS
Tel: 01 42 65 30 74
Fax: 01 42 65 31 42

### Lucie Saint-Clair
29, rue de Marignan
75008 PARIS
Tel: 01 42 25 10 01

### Maria Galland Institut
7, ave Marceau
75016 PARIS
Tel: 01 47 20 14 77

### Orlane

163, ave Victor Hugo
75116 PARIS
Tel: 01 47 04 65 00

### Revlon France/E.P.B.
Charles of the Ritz
23, rue Boissière
75116 PARIS
Tel: 01 44 05 55 55
fax: 01 47 04 75 71
Director: M. GOULARD

# BEAUTY
BEAUTÉ

## Salon Montparnasse

20, ave du Maine
75015 PARIS
Tel: 01 45 48 00 40

## Soleil Plus

*Sun-tanning center*
5, rue Brey
75017 PARIS
Tel: 01 45 72 46 48

## Sothys

128, rue du Fbg Saint Honoré
75008 PARIS
Tel: 01 53 93 91 53 (Reservations)
Fax: 01 42 56 40 61

---

### USA Health & Beauty

*Skin and nail care at home salon.
Tips manicure, pedicure, facials,
waxing, make-up and more*
18-20, Bd Saint Denis
75010 PARIS
Tel: 01 48 01 08 71
Fax: 01 48 01 08 71
Contact: Mme Jenneine WILSON

---

## HAIRDRESSERS
Salons de coiffure

## A.C.S. Dean Coiffure Studio

235, rue Saint Honoré
75001 PARIS
Tel: 01 47 03 46 64

## Alengrin, Marc

29, ave Duquesne
75007 PARIS
Tel: 01 47 05 17 63

## Alexandre de Paris

3, ave Matignon
75008 PARIS
Tel: 01 43 59 40 09
Fax: 01 42 56 66 12

## Alexandre Zouari

1, ave du Président Wilson
75016 PARIS
Tel: 01 47 23 79 00
Fax: 01 40 70 07 30

## Claude Maxime Mondiale

27, ave George V
75008 PARIS
Tel: 01 53 23 03 03
Fax: 01 47 23 39 40

## Coiffure d'Art José et Ruby Soto Arias

33, ave George V
75008 PARIS
Tel: 01 47 20 37 50

## Desfossé

19, ave Matignon
75008 PARIS
Tel: 01 43 59 95 13
Fax: 01 43 59 07 93
Contact: M. Guillaume SÉNÉCHAL

## Elida Institut Capillaire

114, ave des Champs Élysées
75008 PARIS
Tel: 01 44 13 65 60
Fax: 01 45 63 31 62

## Franck Provost

61, ave Franklin Roosevelt
75008 PARIS
Tel: 01 43 59 97 05
Fax: 01 42 89 58 74

## Françoise Raoult

8, rue Saint Paul
75004 PARIS
Tel: 01 42 77 45 97

## Georges Bejjani

40, rue de Richelieu
75001 PARIS
Tel: 01 42 96 23 90

## Harlow

70, rue du Ranelagh
75016 PARIS
Tel: 01 45 24 04 54
Fax: 01 42 88 37 87

## Jacques Moisant

93, rue de Seine
75006 PARIS
Tel: 01 46 33 51 21
Fax: 01 43 25 67 72

## James Coiffure

51, rue Jouffroy
75017 PARIS
Tel: 01 42 27 13 84

## Jean Louis David Training Center

5, rue Cambon
75001 PARIS
Tel: 01 42 97 51 71
Tel2: 01 49 26 02 67

## Jean-Claude Gallon

3, rue Paul Louis Courrier
75007 PARIS
Tel: 01 42 22 04 36

## Jean-Louis David International

*Many locations in Paris*
47, rue Pierre-Charron
75008 PARIS
Tel: 01 43 59 82 08
Fax: 01 43 59 80 08

## Judith Sutherland

56, rue Jean-Jacques Rousseau
75001 PARIS
Tel: 01 42 21 10 31

## Look Lemon

10, rue Richepanse
75008 PARIS
Tel: 01 42 60 77 29
Contact: Alex

## Maniatis

18, rue Marbeuf
75008 PARIS
Tel: 01 47 23 30 14
Fax: 01 47 23 66 13

## Marc Delacre

17, ave George V
75008 PARIS
Tel: 01 40 70 99 70
Fax: 01 40 70 92 33

## Maurice Franck

26-28, ave Marceau
75008 PARIS
Tel: 01 47 20 11 45
Fax: 01 40 70 90 36

## Michel Brosseau

122, rue du Fbg Saint Honoré
75008 PARIS
Tel: 01 45 62 75 06
Fax: 01 43 59 79 07

## Michèle & Heinz Coiffeurs

4, rue de la Trémoille
75008 PARIS
Tel: 01 47 23 75 55
Contact: Mme Susan TOURSEL

## Mod's Hair

114, ave Champs Élysées
75008 PARIS
Tel: 01 42 25 14 29
Fax: 01 42 25 04 54

## Nicole Thomas Haute Coiffure

34, rue Bassano
75008 PARIS
Tel: 01 47 20 25 03

## Patrick Ales

37, ave Franklin Roosevelt
75008 PARIS
Tel: 01 43 59 33 96
Tel2: 01 53 93 99 01

## René Furterer Institut

15, place de la Madeleine
75008 PARIS
Tel: 01 42 65 30 60
Fax: 01 42 65 00 14

## S'Trim

130, ave de Suffren
75015 PARIS
Tel: 01 47 83 24 74
Fax: 01 53 17 61 32

## Tiffy's Hair Design

21, rue Neuve Saint Pierre
75004 PARIS
Tel: 01 42 77 61 04

*LIVING & STUDYING*

149

# BEAUTY
## BEAUTÉ

### Yves Saint Laurent Institut
32, rue du Fbg Saint Honoré
75008 PARIS
Tel: 01 49 24 99 66
Director: Mme Céline COURANT

### MISCELLANEOUS
### Divers

### Coty Group Worldwide
20, rue Troyon
92316 SÈVRES Cedex
Tel: 01 41 14 13 21
Fax: 01 41 14 13 25
Contact: Mme FENELON

### Natura-Diet
*Health food store*
15, rue Rambuteau
75004 PARIS
Tel: 01 42 71 08 13
Owner: Mme VIDET

### Naturalia
*Natural and organic food products*
52, rue Saint Antoine
75004 PARIS
Tel: 01 48 87 87 50
Fax: 01 42 86 85 84

### Naturalia
16, ave du Général Leclerc
75014 PARIS
Tel: 01 42 61 74 14
Fax: 01 42 86 85 84

### Rendez-Vous de la Nature
*Health products*
96, rue Mouffetard
75005 PARIS
Tel: 01 43 36 59 34

### Vita Santé
*Distributor of Herbalife*
12, rue Champfleury
91410 DOURDAN
Tel: 01 64 59 60 66
Fax: 01 60 81 04 09
Contact: M. David SIDDALL

### USA Health & Beauty

*Skin and nail care at home salon.
Tips manicure, pedicure, facials,
waxing, make-up and more*
18-20, Bd Saint Denis
75010 PARIS
Tel: 01 48 01 08 71
Fax: 01 48 01 08 71
Contact: Mme Jenneine WILSON

### Weight Watchers Food
89, rue La Boétie
75008 PARIS
Tel: 01 53 77 17 17
Fax: 01 53 77 17 18

# BOOKSTORES
## LIBRAIRIES

Paris' English-language bookshops not only keep you connected to your language and culture, they contribute vibrantly to the cultural life of the city by organizing readings, signings, launchings, and literary promotions for local and visiting authors. Get yourself on the mailing lists of some of these stores. Also find here the major Parisian bookstores with English-language and specialized sections.

## ENGLISH-LANGUAGE BOOKSTORES
Librairies anglophones

### Abbey Bookshop/ La Librairie Canadienne
29, rue de la Parcheminerie
75005 PARIS
Tel: 01 46 33 16 24
Fax: 01 46 33 03 33
President: M. Brian SPENCE

### Albion
13, rue Charles V
75004 PARIS
Tel: 01 42 72 50 71
Fax: 01 42 72 85 27

### Album
*Comics, strip cartoons, US imports*
6, rue Dante
75005 PARIS
Tel: 01 43 54 67 09
Fax: 01 43 25 82 70
Contact: M. Olivier JALABERT

### American University of Paris Bookstore
American Church
65, quai d'Orsay
75007 PARIS
Tel: 01 40 62 05 92
Fax: 01 45 56 06 00
Email: 104472.3303@compuserve.com
Web site: http://www.aup.fr
Manager: Mme Julia FITZGERALD

### Attica Bookshop
64, rue de la Folie Méricourt
75011 PARIS
Tel: 01 48 06 17 00
English section: 01 48 06 49 80
Fax: 01 48 06 47 85

### Australian Bookshop
33, quai des Grands Augustins
75006 PARIS
Tel: 01 43 29 08 65
Fax: 01 43 29 01 78
Email: 106325.3040@compuserve.com
Contact: Mme Elaine LEWIS

### Bookmaster
21, rue du Bos
60240 DELINCOURT
Tel: 03 44 49 22 44
Fax: 03 44 49 21 61
Director: M. HASTINGS

### Bookshop Distribution
5, rue Rainssant
51100 REIMS
Tel: 03 26 47 57 00
Fax: 03 26 47 57 35
Minitel: 3615 BOOKSHOP

### Brentano's
*Anglo-American literature, art books, magazines and newspapers. Book signings and events*
37, ave de l'Opéra
75002 PARIS
Tel: 01 42 61 52 50
Fax: 01 42 61 07 61
Director: M. Maurice DARBELLAY
Contact: Mme Sherri ALDIS

### Espace Cannibal Pierce
*Australian bookshop and art gallery*
7, rue Samson
BP 224
93200 SAINT DENIS
Tel: 01 48 09 94 59
Directors: Ken SHEPHERD & June SHENFIELD

# BOOKSTORES
LIBRAIRIES

## Foot-Note

*English business and management books, retail and mail order*

Bd de Constance
77305 FONTAINEBEAU Cedex
Tel: 01 60 72 42 61
Fax: 01 60 72 43 42
Email: footnote@insead.fr
Director: Mme Chana WEINSTEIN

## Galignani

*Fine arts, Anglo-American literature, guidebooks, newspapers and magazines. Tthe oldest English bookstore on the continent*

224, rue de Rivoli
75001 PARIS
Tel: 01 42 60 76 07
Fax: 01 42 86 09 31
Director: Mme Marie PACCARD

## Neal, Michael

*Collector of rare books*

6, rue des Bas Jardins Feugères
91650 SAINT YON
Tel: 01 64 58 40 64

## Nouveau Quartier Latin

78, Bd Saint Michel
75006 PARIS
Tel: 01 43 26 42 70
Fax: 01 40 51 74 09
General Manager: Mme Anne WARTER

## Shakespeare & Company

*The Rag & Bone Shop of the Heart. Open daily from noon until midnight*

37, rue de la Bûcherie
75005 PARIS
No Telephone
Web site: http://www.gyoza.com
Owner: M. George WHITMAN

## Tea and Tattered Pages

*Secondhand books, small tea room at the back. Open every day 11h00-19h00*

24, rue Mayet
75006 PARIS
Tel: 01 40 65 94 35
Fax: 01 39 50 33 76
Owner: Mme Kristi CHAVANE

## Tridias Bookshop

19, place du Marché
78110 LE VÉSINET
Tel: 01 39 76 11 13
Fax: 01 39 76 60 70
Director: M. JUDD

## Village Voice Bookshop

# Village Voice
Bookshop

*High-quality literary bookstore and reading series. Vast collection in modern and contemporary fiction, poetry and translations as well as works in the social and political sciences, philosophy, literary criticism, etc. (See advertisement)*

6, rue Princesse
75006 PARIS
Tel: 01 46 33 36 47
Fax: 01 46 33 27 48
Minitel: 3615 VILLAGE VOICE
Email: yhellier@worldnet.fr
Web site: http://www.paris-anglo.com
Director: Mme Odile HELLIER

## W.H. Smith

# WH SMITH

*The only British-owned bookstore in Paris. Literature, guides, magazines and a good teaching resources section upstairs (See advertisement)*

248, rue de Rivoli
75001 PARIS
Tel: 01 44 77 88 99
Fax: 01 42 96 83 71
Minitel: 3615 SMITH
Web site: http://www.paris-anglo.com
Manager: M. Stuart WALKER

## Wildman Press

31, rue Louis Rolland
92120 MONTROUGE
Tel: 01 40 84 03
Fax: 01 40 84 09 44
Email: 100645.2160@compuserve.com
Director: M. Elliot KLEIN

## OTHER BOOKSTORES
## Autres librairies

### Au Fil du Temps
*Specialized in cinema,
English-language magazines*
8, rue Saint Martin
75004 PARIS
Tel: 01 42 71 93 48
Fax: 01 42 71 94 84

### Boutique Michelin, Maps and Guides

32, ave de l'Opéra
75002 PARIS
Tel: 01 42 68 05 20
Web site: http://www.michelin.fr
Contact: M. Philippe DUMONCEAU

### FNAC Étoile
26-30, ave des Ternes
75017 PARIS
Tel: 01 44 09 18 00
Fax: 01 44 09 18 20
Web site: http://www.fnac.fr
Contact: Mme Catherine BAILLY

### FNAC Forum
1, rue Pierre Lescot
Porte Lescot, Niveau -3
75001 PARIS
Tel: 01 40 41 40 00
Fax: 01 40 41 40 86
Web site: http://www.fnac.fr

### FNAC Montparnasse
136, rue de Rennes
75006 PARIS
Tel: 01 49 54 30 00
Fax: 01 49 54 31 11
Web site: http://www.fnac.fr
Contact: Mme Maryse DIALL

### Gibert Jeune
10, place Saint Michel
75006 PARIS
Tel: 01 43 25 91 19
Fax: 01 40 51 77 72
Contact: Mme NGUYEN

### Gibert Joseph
26-30-32, Bd Saint Michel
75006 PARIS
Tel: 01 44 41 88 88
Fax: 01 40 46 83 62
Contact: M. AGOB

### Librairie de l'UNESCO
7, place de Fontenoy
75007 PARIS
Tel: 01 45 68 22 22
Fax: 01 45 68 57 41

### Librairie Gaël
19, rue du Cardinal Lemoine
75005 PARIS
Tel: 01 46 34 60 82
Fax: 01 46 34 61 01
Contacts: MM. DONIOL & SOLTI

### Librairie Gilda
36, rue des Bourdonnais
75001 PARIS
Tel: 42 33 60 00
Contact: Bud

### Librairie Tekhné
7, rue des Carmes
75005 PARIS
Tel: 01 43 54 70 84
Fax: 01 44 07 07 39
Contact: Mme Caroline de PEYSTER

### Virgin Megastore

52-60, ave des Champs Élysées
75008 PARIS
Tel: 01 49 53 50 00
Fax: 01 49 53 50 40
Email: postmaster@virgin.fr
Web site: http://www.virgin.fr
Contact: Mme Patricia SUIGNARD

*LIVING & STUDYING*

153

**The largest English Bookshop in France with
more than 70,000 titles to choose from, including :**

---

- English & American Fiction • Management,
Computer and Reference Books • Children's Books
- English Language Teaching Material
- Magazines - Stationery • Audio/Video Cassettes
- Films Video in VO • Mail Order CD-ROM

---

**W.H. SMITH**
248 rue de Rivoli
75001 PARIS
Tél. 01 44 77 88 99
Fax : 01 42 96 83 71
Minitel : 3615 Smith (2,23 F/mn)
Métro : Concorde
*Open Monday to Saturday from 9:30 to 19:00*
*Sunday from 13:00 to 18:00*

# CAR DEALERS
## CONCESSIONAIRES AUTOMOBILES

Need a car, new or used? Here are some suggestions. Need info on car insurance, registration and French drivers licences, consult insurance companies. Legally, you can only drive in France with a US drivers license for one year. To buy and sell, consult PICS at http://www.paris-anglo.com

### British Motors
56-58, rue de La Fontaine
75016 PARIS
Tel: 01 42 88 05 34
Fax: 01 45 27 23 83
Director: M. URBAN

### Cadillac Jean Charles
50, ave de New York
75116 PARIS
Tel: 01 47 20 00 40
Fax: 01 47 20 59 42

### Chrysler
44, rue de la Convention
75015 PARIS
Tel: 01 45 79 30 30

### Citroën Direction vente/export
19 bis, rue Friant
75014 PARIS
Tel: 01 45 40 30 30
Fax: 01 45 39 10 07

### Concession Potache
*Rover dealership*
56-58, rue Fondary
75015 PARIS
Tel: 01 45 79 81 51
Fax: 01 45 79 44 95

### Dixie Driver's Association
5, rue Drouhin
93150 BLANC MESNIL
Tel: 01 48 67 33 24
Fax: 01 48 67 46 57
President: M. Michel LAMOURANNE

### Ford Priod
52-58, ave Lénine
BP 307
92200 NANTERRE
Tel: 01 41 20 25 25
Fax: 01 47 25 73 69

### Franco Britannic Automobiles
48, ave Kléber
75116 PARIS
Tel: 01 53 70 97 97
Fax: 01 53 70 99 00

### Garage Wilson
*Jaguar dealership*
116, rue du Président Wilson
92300 LEVALLOIS PERRET
Tel: 01 47 39 92 50
Fax: 01 47 39 50 31

### Harley-Davidson
48, rue de la Chapelle
75018 PARIS
Tel: 01 46 07 81 31
Fax: 01 42 05 96 49

### Luchard Automobiles Groupe Bernier
*Peugeot dealership*
39, rue Saint Didier
75116 PARIS
Tel: 01 45 05 13 53
Fax: 01 47 27 18 72

### Mercedes-Benz
80, rue de Longchamp
75116 PARIS
Tel: 01 44 05 78 00
Fax: 01 44 05 78 02

### Renault Rive Gauche
29, quai de Grenelle
75015 PARIS
Tel: 01 44 37 20 20
Fax: 01 44 37 20 10

# CAR DEALERS
## CONCESSIONAIRES AUTOMOBILES

### René Petit Automobile

*General Motors, Buick, Pontiac, Cadillac and Chevrolet dealership*

98, ave Jean Lolive
93500 PANTIN
Tel: 01 48 45 92 00
Fax: 01 49 42 17 55

### SAAB

60, Bd de Reuilly
75012 PARIS
Tel: 01 40 02 02 77
Fax: 01 40 02 08 62

# CHILDREN
## ENFANTS

Living in Paris with kids can be a veritable delight when you know where to go and what to do. There are lots of resources for children in Paris and here is a list of everything from babysitters to good places to buy children's clothing. The service organizations listed under Organizations are also a great source of information concerning children and family activities in Paris. Note that pediatricians are listed under Health Professionals.

## NANNIES/BABYSITTERS
## Gardes d'enfant

### Ababa
8, ave du Maine
75015 PARIS
Tel: 01 45 49 46 46

### ABC Puériculture
9, rue la Fontaine
75016 PARIS
Tel: 01 40 50 13 64
Fax: 01 45 27 11 54
Email: 106354,212@compuserve.com

### Alliance Française
101, Bd Raspail
75006 PARIS
Tel: 01 45 44 38 28
Fax: 01 45 44 89 42
Email: info@paris.alliancefrancaise.fr
Web site:
http://www.paris.alliancefrancaise.fr

### Alpha Baby
75, rue de Fontenay
94300 VINCENNES
Tel: 01 43 65 58 58

### Baby Sitting Service
18, rue Tronchet
75008 PARIS
Tel: 01 46 37 51 24
Fax: 01 42 66 52 45

### Good Morning Europe
38, rue Traversière
75012 PARIS
Tel: 01 44 87 01 22
Fax: 01 44 87 01 42

### Home Service
2, rue Pierre Semard
75009 PARIS
Tel: 01 42 82 05 04
Fax: 01 42 85 27 77

### International Nannies
14, ave de Villars
75007 PARIS
Tel: 01 47 05 41 33
Fax: 01 47 05 41 43

### Kid Services
75, Bd Pereire
75017 PARIS
Tel: 01 47 66 00 52
Fax: 01 42 67 76 88
Director: Mme Anne MANSOURET

### Nannies Incorporated
8, rue du Dobropol
75017 PARIS
Tel: 01 45 74 62 74
Tel: 0 171 437 1312 (UK)
Fax: 01 45 74 69 71

### Nurse Au Pair Placement
*Nannies, mothers helpers, maternity nurses, and au pairs for a professional, serious, and friendly service*
32, rue des Renauds
75017 PARIS
Tel: 01 47 64 46 87
Fax: 01 47 64 48 20
Contact: Mme Carolina GONCALVES

### Soames International
BP 28
16, rue du Château
77302 FONTAINEBLEAU
Tel: 01 64 22 99 26
Fax: 01 64 22 03 08

# CHILDREN
## ENFANTS

## CLOTHING
Habillement

### Agnès B
2, rue du Jour
75001 PARIS
Tel: 01 40 39 96 88

### Boutique Clayeux
80, ave Victor Hugo
75116 PARIS
Tel: 01 47 55 15 24

### Chattawak
125, rue Saint Dominique
75007 PARIS
Tel: 01 45 55 76 85

### Coup de Coeur
2, ave des Ternes
75017 PARIS
Tel: 01 43 80 59 40
Manager: Mme Laure APELBAUM

### Du Pareil au Même Kids
14, rue Saint Placide
75006 PARIS
Tel: 01 45 44 04 40
Fax: 01 45 44 80 36
Contact: Mme GAUTIER

### Du Pareil au Même Teens
7, rue Saint Placide
75006 PARIS
Tel: 01 40 09 00 33
Fax: 01 45 44 12 43

### LC Waikiki
339, rue Saint Martin
75002 PARIS
Tel: 01 42 72 01 01
Fax: 01 42 72 03 04
Contact: M. Georges AMOUYAL

### Natalys
92, ave des Champs Élysées
75008 PARIS
Tel: 01 43 59 17 65

### Petit Bateau
81, rue de Sèvres
75006 PARIS
Tel: 01 45 49 48 38
Fax: 01 45 49 48 38
Contact: Mme BOYER CHAMMARD

### Repetto
*Dance and gym clothes*
22, rue de la Paix
75002 PARIS
Tel: 01 44 71 83 00
Fax: 01 44 71 83 01

### Tartine et Chocolat
266, Bd Saint Germain
75007 PARIS
Tel: 01 45 56 10 45
Fax: 01 45 56 11 23

## MISCELLANEOUS
Divers

### A la Poupée Merveilleuse
*Party novelties, masks, fancy dress, tricks, fireworks*
9, rue du Temple
75004 PARIS
Tel: 01 42 72 63 46
Fax: 01 44 59 85 87
Contact: Mme BAROUHIEL

### Au Café Chantant
*Theater for kids*
36, rue Bichat
75010 PARIS
Tél: 01 42 08 83 33

### Bebel le Magicien
*Magician for children's parties*
17, rue André Antoine
75018 PARIS
Tel: 01 42 55 10 69
Fax: 01 42 55 10 69**

### Bête Curieuse
2, rue des Fossés Saint Jacques
75005 PARIS
Tel: 01 46 34 76 91
Fax: 01 46 34 76 91
Contacts: Mmes Marie VANASSE & Carole LUSSIER

### C'est ma Chambre
*A large choice of charming bedroom furniture and accessories for babies and children*
45, rue des Archives
75003 PARIS
Tel: 01 48 87 26 67
Manager: Mme DESORMEAUX

158

## Chantelivre

*An excellent address for books, games, tapes and videos for kids*

13, rue de Sèvres
75006 PARIS
Tel: 01 45 48 87 90
Fax: 01 45 48 97 69
Contact: Mme MÉQUILLET

## Children's Academy on Tour

*A children's organization for cultural awareness*

66, ave des Champs Élysées n° 74
75008 PARIS
Tel: 01 44 95 14 31
Fax: 01 42 89 87 37
Contact: Mme Sabrina SCOTT

## Children's Parties

*Magicians, puppets and games for birthday parties, Halloween, Christmas...*

108, rue Lourmel
75015 PARIS
Tel: 01 40 60 03 60
Contact: Mme Christine SERIE

## Cité des Sciences et de l'Industrie

*The world of Science and Technology presented in an original manner with many interactive video games*

Parc de la Villette
30, ave Corentin Cariou
75019 PARIS
Tel: 01 40 05 70 00
Res: 01 40 05 12 12
Minitel: 3615 VILLETTE

## Disneyland Paris

*Disney theme park*

BP 100
77777 MARNE LA VALLÉE
Info: 01 60 30 60 30
Res: 01 64 74 60 65
Minitel: 3615 EURO DISNEY
Director: M. Philippe BOURGUIGNON

## English Juniors' Club

*English and computer courses for children aged 3 to 12*

16, rue de la Liberté
75019 PARIS
Tel: 01 42 03 66 87
Contact: Mme Monique IFERGAN

## Eurobaby

*Baby equipment rental*

18, rue de la Chapelle
Magny Saint Loup
77470 BOUTIGNY
Tel: 01 60 61 81 79
Contact: Mme Adèle GOODMAN

## Hoppmann

*Shows for kids (mime, clown, following)*

10, rue Carnot
93100 MONTREUIL SOUS BOIS
Fax: 01 48 59 80 00

## La Belle Étoile

92, rue du Cherche Midi
75006 PARIS
Tel: 01 45 44 02 50
Fax: 01 45 49 94 12

## La Pelucherie

*Plush toys*

84, ave des Champs Élysées
75008 PARIS
Tel: 01 43 59 49 05
Fax: 01 43 59 49 05
Contact: Mme Catherine VILLAIN

## Le Funambule

53, rue des Saules
75018 PARIS
Tel: 01 42 23 88 83
Fax: 01 46 06 31 97

## Le Paris des Tout Petits

*A children's guide to Paris in French*

Editions d'Annabelle
8, rue d'Anjou
75008 PARIS
Tel: 01 47 42 01 61
Fax: 01 47 42 42 14
Director: Mme ROLLAND

## Little Dragons

*Kindergarten*

2, rue Jacquemont
75017 PARIS
Tel: 01 42 28 56 17
Fax: 01 47 00 53 39

**LIVING & STUDYING**

159

# CHILDREN
## ENFANTS

### Mille Fêtes
*The shop for birthday and every party: invitations, balloons, garlands, novelties, prizes, face paint, toys*
60, rue du Cherche Midi
75006 PARIS
Tel: 01 42 22 09 43
Fax: 01 42 22 60 26
Contact: Mme Véronique HORNUSS

### Musée de la Curiosité et de la Magie
11, rue Saint Paul
75004 PARIS
Tel: 01 42 72 13 26

### Musée en Herbe
*Children's museum*
Jardin d'Acclimatation
Bois de Boulogne
Tel: 01 40 67 97 66
Fax: 01 40 67 97 13

### Stepping Stones
*Activities for anglophone children 3-5 years old*
1, route du Grand Pont
78110 LE VÉSINET
Tel: 01 30 53 14 73
Director: Mme S. TAYLOR

### Théo Théâtre
20, rue Théodore Deck
75015 PARIS
Tel: 01 45 57 92 74

### Toys-R-Us
Centre Commercial "Les Quatre Temps"
92092 PARIS LA DÉFENSE
Tel: 01 47 76 29 78
Admin: 01 60 76 83 00

### Toys-R-Us
Forum des Halles
Porte Lescot
Niveau - 1
75001 PARIS
Tel: 01 53 00 93 33

# COMPUTERS
## INFORMATIQUE

(See Doing Business & Working: Computers)

To/*A*:

ANGLOPHONE SA
32, rue Edouard Vaillant
93100 MONTREUIL
France

From/*De*: _____

_____

_____

RUSH:
# FF Membership

# OUI, I own a copy of PARIS-ANGLOPHONE 5th Edition and therefore am a Member of the FrancoFile Club, entitling me to lots of benefits & reductions in Paris and online.

Please send me my personalized FF NUMBER and list of FF BENEFITS. I understand that beyond the purchase of the PARIS-ANGLOPHONE directory and the completion of this card, I have no obligations or costs and that being a FF Member is absolutely <u>FREE</u>.

Family Name: _____

FirstName: _____

Title/Positions: _____

Company/Organization: _____

Street Address: _____

City: _____

Postal Code: _____

Country: _____

Tel: _____

Fax: _____

Email: _____

## A Few Friendly Questions

1) Where did you pick-up your copy of Paris-Anglophone? _____

2) What's the nature of your trips to France? (one or more)
___ pleasure ___ work/business ___ studying ___ other

3) What kind of additional information/contacts would be useful to you? _____

4) How would you describe your French?
___ fluent ___ not bad ___ dreadful ___ non-existant!

5) Who was the President of your country when you were born? _____
(we just want to know your age!)

To what extent do you use the World Wide Web?
___ not at all ___ once in a while ___ everyday

Mention the types of activities/sports/cultural events/etc. you'd like to participate in when in France _____

David Applefield, Publisher

*Merci.* Thanks. Your FF Number & List of Benefits will be sent to you shortly.

# The Pantry
## 01 39 65 82 24

**American & British Foods At Your Door**

Email:
thepantry@compuserve.com

# COUNSELING/SUPPORT
## ASSOCIATIONS D'AIDE

Life in any large city requires support services, and Paris' English-speaking community includes a remarkably complete and indepth network of such groups, ranging from specialized medicine, therapists, and substance-abuse hotlines to cancer support groups and elderly care.

### Alcoholics Anonymous
c/o American Church
65, quai d'Orsay
75007 PARIS
Tel: 01 46 34 59 65
Tel2: 01 45 31 67 71
Contact: Jane

### Alliance Conseils
*Relations counseling*
32, rue Etienne Marcel
75002 PARIS
Tel: 01 42 36 27 07
Fax: 01 42 21 40 59
Contact: Mme Anne WAGNER

### American Aid Society
*Helps U.S. citizens who encounter problems in France*
US Consulate
2, rue Saint Florentin
75001 PARIS
Tel: 01 43 12 47 90
President: Mme Adèle ANIS

### Bio Art/ Voice Dialogue
*Life enhancement skills*
66, rue du Château des Rentiers
75013 PARIS
Tel: 01 45 85 03 38
Fax: 01 44 23 71 60
Email: IN% "Diana_l1@verifone.com
Contact: Mme Diana SMITH

### Bourdais, Jill
*Psychotherapist, couple counselor, PAIRS teacher*
19, quai aux Fleurs
75004 PARIS
Tel: 01 43 54 79 25
Fax: 01 43 54 79 25
Email: 101446.2060@compuserve.com
Web site: http://www.pairs.com

### Counseling Center American Cathedral
23, ave George V
75008 PARIS
Tel: 01 47 23 61 13

### F.A.C.T.S
### (Free AIDS Counseling Treatment and Support)
*HIV services for anglophones*
190, Bd de Charonne
75020 PARIS
Tel: 01 44 93 16 32
AIDS Counseling evening line:
01 44 93 16 79
Fax: 01 44 93 16 60
Email: 100614.1041@compuserve.com
Director: M. Chris WHITNEY

### Feld, Elizabeth Leafy

*Adventures in creativity and recovery. Creative arts therapy worshops. Individuals, couples sessions for personal, professional development*
32, rue Damrémont
75018 PARIS
Tel: 01 42 62 04 66
Fax: 01 42 62 04 66
Email: leafy@easynet.fr

### Flanagan, Brendan
*Singles/Couples NLP Hypnotherapy*
36, rue de Chabrol
75010 PARIS
Tel: 01 48 00 07 48
Fax: 01 48 00 96 11

## Focus on the Family

St. Michael's Anglican Church
5, rue d'Aguesseau
75008 PARIS
Tel: 01 47 42 70 88
Fax: 01 47 42 70 11
Contact:
Mme ALENA-WOARBURTON

## Inter Service Parents

*Telephone counseling on childcare, education, law, schooling, leisure activities and family relationships*

5, impasse du Bon Secours
75011 PARIS
Tel: 01 44 93 44 93
Fax: 01 44 93 44 65
Contact: Mme Martine GRUÈRE

## International Counseling Service

*Individual, couple and family therapy*

65, quai d'Orsay
75007 PARIS
Tel: 01 45 50 26 49
Co-Presidents: Mmes Marie-Anne BRUN
& Jane PLIMSOLL

## MESSAGE Mother Support Group

18, rue Michel Ange
91250 SAINT GERMAIN
LÉS CORBEIL
Tel: 01 69 89 94 75
Contact: Mme Sally BURLET

## Parenting Plus

791, ave du Général Leclerc
92100 BOULOGNE
Tel: 01 46 21 64 29
Fax: 01 47 61 19 69
Email: julied@easynet.fr
Contact: Mme Julie DAVIS

## Paris Therapy Center

*Individual, couple and group therapy*

27, rue Daubenton
75005 PARIS
Tel: 01 47 07 74 14
Director: M. GRILL, Ph.D.

---

PAIRS

**(Practical Application of Intimate Relationship Skills)**

*A comprehensive, hands-on seminar which teaches concrete skills for improving close relationships*

10, rue Saint Louis en l'Ile
75004 PARIS
Tel: 01 43 54 79 25
Fax: 01 43 54 79 25
Email:
101446.2060@compuserve.com
Web site: http://www.pairs.com
Contact: Mmes Jill BOURDAIS &
Judith COLLIGNON

## Presence

*Cancer support group in English & French*

American Hospital of Paris
63, Bd Victor Hugo
92200 NEUILLY SUR SEINE
Tel: 01 41 46 17 66
Fax: 01 30 54 94 67
Contact:
Mme Élisabeth DE VULPILLIERES

## ReCreate Your Career in France

*Find challenging, enjoyable work that fits your values. Develop step-by-step strategy. Practical results oriented*

4, impasse de la Gaîté
75014 PARIS
Tel: 01 43 21 36 99
Fax: 01 43 20 09 46
Email: soul-work@compuserve.com
Contact: Mme Libby ROBINSON

## Sacks, Susan

*Psychotherapist*

46, rue de la Clef
75005 PARIS
Tel: 01 43 31 78 81

*LIVING & STUDYING*

163

## COUNSELING/SUPPORT
### ASSOCIATIONS D'AIDE

### SOS Help! Crisis Line
*A friendly listener daily 15h00-23h00*
BP 239-16
75765 PARIS Cedex 16
Tel: 01 47 23 80 80

### Sprint Parents' Action Network (SPAN)
*Special needs children*
30, ave de l'Alliance
95600 EAUBONNE
Tel: 01 39 59 10 64
President: Mme Rosemary LAUNAY

### The British Charitable Fund
*For British citizens in need or hardship*
12, rue Barbès
92300 LEVALLOIS PERRET
Tel: 01 47 59 07 69
Fax: 01 47 59 07 69

### The Victoria Home
*Home for elderly British people*
1, rue des Dardanelles
75017 PARIS
Tel: 01 30 53 21 33
Contact: Mme LONGLEY

### Weight Watchers France
4, allée de la Fresnerie
Immeuble Le Florilège
BP 64
78330 FONTENAY LES FLEURI
Tel: 01 45 22 78 76
Fax: 01 30 23 06 00
Minitel: 3615 WW
Director: M. BASTIEN

## COURIER SERVICES
### COURSIERS INTERNATIONAUX

(See Doing Business/ Working: Courier Services)

## CREDIT CARDS

### CARTES DE CRÉDIT

(See Living & Studying: Useful Numbers)

# CULTURAL CENTERS
## CENTRES CULTURELS

The famed American Center tragically closed its doors in 1996, less than a year after opening its $51 million Frank Gehry building in the Bercy area of Paris. Fortunately, Paris enjoys a host of other cultural centers each with a lively program of literary, social, musical and otherwise educational events.

### Alliance Française

101, Bd Raspail
75006 PARIS
Tel: 01 45 44 38 28
Fax: 01 45 44 25 95
Email: info@paris.alliancefrancaise.fr
Web site:
http://www.paris.alliancefrancaise.fr
Deputy Director: M. BAILLY

### British Council

9-11, rue de Constantine
75007 PARIS
Tel: 01 49 55 73 00
Fax: 01 47 05 77 02
Minitel: 3615 BRITISH
Public Relations:
M. Duncan JACKMAN

### Centre Culturel Canadien

5, rue de Constantine
75007 PARIS
Tel: 01 44 43 21 90
Minitel: 3614 CANADA
Cultural Attaché: M. Emile MARTEL

### Centre Culturel Indo-Français

12, rue Notre-Dame-de-Nazareth
75003 PARIS
Tel: 01 42 78 80 53

### Collège des Irlandais

*Cultural and residential exchanges between Ireland and France*
5, rue des Irlandais
75005 PARIS
Tel: 01 45 35 59 79 (College)
Tel: 01 45 35 32 07 (Cultural Center)
Fax: 01 45 35 72 09
Administrator: Mme Roisin DOCKERY

### Délégation Générale du Québec

Cultural Service
66, rue Pergolèse
75116 PARIS
Tel: 01 40 67 85 70

### Franco-Australian Cultural Association

11, ave de Lattre de Tassigny
92100 BOULOGNE
Tel: 01 46 03 01 92
Fax: 01 46 03 48 16
President: M. Jean-Paul DELAMOTTE

### Maison de la Poésie

*20th-century poetry (exhibitions, conferences, theater, library)*
Théâtre Molière
161, rue Saint Martin
75003 PARIS
Tel: 01 42 36 27 53
Fax: 01 42 36 27 54
Director: Mme Michelle CHAIZE

### Théâtre de la Cité Internationale

21, Bd Jourdan
75014 PARIS
Tel: 01 45 89 38 69

Although only 1% of French households are "wired," Paris enjoys a flourishing public web scene. The list changes rather frequently so be sure to check before heading out to "surf." You'll find a good list at www.quelm.fr./CSphere/Cafes.html.

### Bistro Internet
Galeries Lafayette
40, Bd Haussmann
75009 PARIS
Tel: 01 42 82 30 33
Web site: http://www.bistrotinternet.fr

### Bonjour Tout Le Monde
15, rue Pérignon
75007 PARIS
Tel: 01 45 66 65 35
Web site: http://www.micronet.fr/~roulez

### Café Cox
15, rue des Archives
75004 PARIS
Tel: 01 42 72 08 00

### Café Orbital Quartier Latin
13, rue de Médicis
75006 PARIS
Tel: 01 43 25 76 77
Web site: http://www.orbital.fr

### Cyber Espace Fnac CNIT
2, place de la Défense
92062 PARIS LA DÉFENSE
Tel: 01 46 92 29 00
Web site: http://www.fnac.fr

### Cyberia
Centre Georges Pompidou
75004 PARIS
Tel: 01 44 54 53 49
Web site: http://www.cyberia.fr

### Cyberport
Forum des Halles
75001 PARIS
Tel: 01 44 76 62 00
Web site: http://www.vdp.fr

### Extrapole
2, parvis de la Défense
92800 PUTEAUX
Tel: 01 41 02 99 00

### Gaumont Parnasse
3, rue d'Odessa
75014 PARIS
Tel: 01 40 64 72 64

### High Tech Café
66, Bd Montparnasse
75014 PARIS
Tel: 01 45 38 67 61
Web site: http://www.htc.fr

### Laboscope
1, rue Le Goff
75005 PARIS
Tel: 01 44 32 03 32

### Médiathèque
33, rue du Gouverneur Éboué
91130 ISSY LES MOULINEAUX
Tel: 01 45 29 34 00

### Micro Université
13, rue Champollion
75005 PARIS
Tel: 01 43 54 42 25

### Planet Cyber Café
173, rue de Vaugirard
75015 PARIS
Tel: 01 45 67 71 14
Web site:
http://www.starnet.fr/planet-cybercafé

### Travel Café
2, rue d'Alleroy
75015 PARIS
Tel: 01 42 50 11 10
Web site: http://www.abcvoyage.com

### UGC WorldNet Café
Forum des Halles
75001 PARIS
Tel: 01 40 26 40 45

LIVING & STUDYING

167

## Virgin Megastore
52, ave des Champs Élysées
75008 PARIS
Tel: 01 49 53 50 00
Web site: http://www.virgin.fr

## Web Bar
32, rue de Picardie
75003 PARIS
Tel: 01 42 72 66 55
Fax: 01 42 72 66 75
Email: webbar@webbar.fr
Web site: http://www.webbar.fr

## Zowezo
37, rue Fontaine
75009 PARIS
Tel: 01 40 23 00 71

# DOCTORS
## MÉDECINS

(See Living & Studying: Health/Professionals)

# EMPLOYMENT
## EMPLOI

(See Doing Business & Working: Recruitment)

# ENTERTAINMENT
## LOISIRS

For weekly entertainment information and schedules consult *l'Officiel des Spectacles*, *Nova* or *Pariscope*. However, for your anglophone-specific entertainment needs, PARIS-ANGLOPHONE presents particularly useful addresses including English-language video rentals, bowling alleys, and other venues for keeping yourself amused.

### VIDEO RENTAL
### Location de vidéos

### Album
7, rue Dante
75005 PARIS
Tel: 01 43 54 67 09
Fax: 01 43 25 82 70

### Locatel Rentals
86, Bd Saint Marcel
75005 PARIS
Tel: 01 47 07 77 99

### Playtime
44, ave Bosquet
75007 PARIS
Tel: 01 45 55 43 36

### Playtime
36, ave d'Eylau
75116 PARIS
Tel: 01 47 27 56 22

### Prime Time Video
24, rue Mayet
75006 PARIS
Tel: 01 40 56 33 44
Fax: 01 40 56 33 99
Contact: M. Ian WILSON

### Prime Time Video
12, rue Léonce Reynaud
75116 PARIS
Tel: 01 47 20 50 01
Fax: 01 47 20 50 01
Contact: M. Ian WILSON

### Reels on Wheels
*English-language films in V.O*
12, villa de la Croix Nivert
75015 PARIS
Tel: 01 45 67 64 99
Fax: 01 45 67 69 51

### Reuilly Video
73, rue de Reuilly
75012 PARIS
Tel: 01 43 45 16 62

### V.O. Only
*Video laser V.O. (PAL & NTSC)*
25, Bd de la Somme
75017 PARIS
Tel: 01 43 80 70 60
Fax: 01 42 27 04 90

### Warner Home Video
BP 656
75826 PARIS Cedex 17
Tel: 01 44 01 49 99
Fax: 01 40 54 71 79

### BOWLING
### Bowling

### Bowling de Paris
Jardin d'Acclimatation
Bois de Boulogne
75116 PARIS
Tel: 01 40 67 94 00
Fax: 01 40 67 10 92

### Bowling Montparnasse
*Bowling, billiards, games room*
25-27, rue du Commandant Mouchotte
75014 PARIS
Tel: 01 43 21 61 32
Fax: 01 42 79 84 51

### Bowling Mouffetard
*Bowling, billiards, snack-bar*
13, rue Gracieuse
75005 PARIS
Tel: 01 43 31 09 35
Fax: 01 45 35 91 49

## CLUBS
### Discothèques

### Les Bains
*Once Turkish baths, hip place to be seen. House, techno*
7, rue du Bourg L'Abbé
75003 PARIS
Tel: 01 48 87 01 80

### Le Balajo
*Rock, cuban, techno during the week and Bal Musette Sunday afternoons*
9, rue de Lappe
75011 PARIS
Tel: 01 47 00 07 87

### Le Gibus
*Trance, techno, jungle*
18, rue du fbg du Temple
75011 PARIS
Tel: 01 47 00 78 88

### La Java
*World music*
105, rue du Fbg du Temple
75011 PARIS
Tel: 01 42 02 20 52

### La Locomotive
*Three-story club*
90, Bd de Clichy
75018 PARIS
Tel: 01 53 41 88 88

### Le Queen
*The hippest in Paris. Gay club - Hetero Night on Wednesdays*
102, ave des Champs Elysées
75008 PARIS
Tel: 01 53 89 08 90

### Rex Club
*House - Techno*
5, Bd Poissonière
75002 PARIS
Tel: 01 42 36 83 98

## MISCELLANOUS
### Divers

### Chèque Théâtre
*Advance ticket booking with delivery service for all expos, opera, theater, and concerts*
Tel: 01 42 46 72 40
Fax: 01 48 00 93 93

### La Main Jaune
*Indoor roller skating rink and dance hall*
Place de la Porte de Champerret
75017 PARIS
Tel: 01 47 63 26 47
Fax: 01 47 63 15 03

### Mont Blanc Helicopters
43, rue Boissière
75116 PARIS
Tel: 01 47 27 54 10
Fax: 01 47 27 54 11
Email: info@mont-blanc.helicopteres.fr
Web site:
http://www.mont-blanc.helicopteres.fr
Contact: M. Frank ARRESTIER

### Patinoire Édouard Pailleron
*Skating rink with bar*
30, rue Édouard Pailleron
75019 PARIS
Tel: 01 42 39 86 10

*LIVING & STUDYING*

171

# FINANCIAL SERVICES
## ÉTABLISSEMENTS FINANCIERS

See Doing Business & Working: Financial Services

# FRENCH ADMINISTRATION
## ADMINISTRATION FRANÇAISE

See Doing Business & Working: French Administration

# FOOD/GROCERY STORES/CATERERS
## ÉPICERIES/TRAITEURS/ALIMENTATION

With Paris's numerous open-air markets and abundance of food shops, restaurants, and supermarkets, there is no excuse not to eat well and shop well in the French capital. However, for those culinary homesick moments, those special holiday needs, and those pangs for ribs or jello here is where you go. Also included are caterers, mail order services, and other addresses for anglo-american groceries and culinary contacts.

## GROCERY STORES
Épiceries

### Authentic American Donut
53, rue Sainte Anne
75002 PARIS
Tel: 01 48 71 38 80
Fax: 01 48 71 43 91
Contact: Mme Nathalie DUCLERC

### Bread and Best
*High-quality English sandwich and salad restaurant (also home/office delivery)*
10, rue Saint Marc
75002 PARIS
Tel: 01 40 26 56 66
Fax: 01 40 26 58 06
Email: 73631.1672@compuserve.com
Contact: M. Alistair WHATMORE

### British Meat
114, rue La Boétie
75008 PARIS
Tel: 01 49 53 96 86

### Comptoir Irlandais
*Irish food and drink, gifts, clothing*
153, Bd Voltaire
75011 PARIS
Tel: 01 43 71 25 81

### Food From Britain
134, rue du Fbg Saint Honoré
75016 PARIS
Tel: 01 42 25 01 86
Fax: 01 42 25 01 85
Contact: D. MINE

### Grande Épicerie de Paris
142, rue du Bac
75007 PARIS
Tel: 01 44 39 81 00

### L'Épicerie du Monde
30, rue François Miron
75004 PARIS
Tel: 01 42 72 66 23
Manager: M. Patrick ELOUARGHI

### La Mixteca
*Mexican specialties*
59, rue de Mouzaia
75019 PARIS
Tel: 01 42 41 23 80

### Mexi & Co.
10, rue Dante
75005 PARIS
Tel: 01 46 34 14 12
Fax: 01 40 61 77 17
Director: Mme Claudia ORREGO

### Pickwicks
*Pickwicks true foods from Britain and Ireland. Baked beans at 4FF, Cadburys chocolate: 4FF, HP sauce: 9FF & more*
8, rue Mandar
75002 PARIS
Tel: 01 40 26 06 58
Fax: 01 40 20 98 72
Contact: M. R.WILSON

### Saumon Fumé d'Irlande
*Irish smoked salmon*
13, rue Eugène Varlin
75010 PARIS
Tel: 01 42 09 63 73
Tel2: 01 39 55 94 30

### Saveurs d'Irlande
*Irish products*
5, cité Vauxhall
75010 PARIS
Tel: 01 42 00 36 20
Fax: 01 42 00 33 12

# FOOD/GROCERY STORES/CATERERS
## ÉPICERIES/TRAITEURS/ALIMENTATION

### Saveurs des AmÉriques
*North & South American specialties*
39, rue Letellier
75015 PARIS
Tel: 01 45 71 05 49

### SDV - Le Marché des Amériques
*Sells Mexican and American food and beverages to restaurants and industries. No private sales*
20, rue Jean Daudin
75015 PARIS
Tel: 01 53 69 63 50
Fax: 01 53 69 63 51
Contact: Jacques

### Thanksgiving
*American groceries and restaurant + catering*
20, rue Saint Paul
75004 PARIS
Tel: 01 42 77 68 29
fax: 01 42 77 70 83
Contacts: Judith et Frédéric BLUYSEN

### The General Store
*American groceries and wines*
82, rue de Grenelle
75007 PARIS
Tel: 01 45 48 63 16

### The General Store
30, rue de Longchamp
75116 PARIS
Tel: 01 47 55 41 14

### The Pantry

**THE PANTRY**

*US & Brit. food products mail order ex. : cranberry juice, cake mixes & frostings, mac & cheese, PB cups, Hersheys much more!*
13, rue Charles D'Orléans
78540 VERNOUILLET
Tel: 01 39 65 82 24
Fax: 01 39 65 82 24
Email: thepantry@compuserve.com
Contacts: Mmes Marla ESTES & Claire GACHES

### The Real McCoy
*American groceries*
194, rue de Grenelle
75007 PARIS
Tel: 01 45 56 98 82
Fax: 01 45 56 98 82

## CATERERS
## Traiteurs

### À la Carte
*Lunch/Dinner delivered to your home or office*
20, rue Lesueur
75116 PARIS
Tel: 01 45 00 12 12
Fax: 01 45 00 12 28
Manager:
M. Stéphane DE MAINTENANT

### Chavy
90, ave Charles de Gaulle
92200 NEUILLY SUR SEINE
Tel: 01 47 47 27 70

### Cross-Channel Catering Company
116, rue de Maubeuge
75010 PARIS
Tel: 01 44 53 75 55
Fax: 01 42 85 49 44

### Dalloyau
99-100, rue du Fbg Saint Honoré
75008 PARIS
Tel: 01 42 99 90 00
Fax: 01 45 63 82 92

### In Your Home Catering
41, rue des Bartoux
92150 SURESNES
Tel: 01 46 97 07 87
Contact: Mme Susan KUTNER

### Maison Fauchon
7, rue Vignon
75008 PARIS
Tel: 01 47 42 60 11
Fax: 01 47 42 83 75
Communications Director:
Mlle LE SOUDER

174

## WINES AND SPIRITS
## Vins et spiritueux

### Champagne Moët et Chandon
*Supplies the public as well as the catering industry*
20, ave de Champagne
51200 EPERNAY
Tel: 03 26 51 20 00
Fax: 03 26 54 84 23
President: M. LETZELTER

### Champagne Perrier-Jouet
24-28, ave de Champagne
BP 31
51201 EPERNAY Cedex
Tel: 03 26 53 38 00
Fax: 03 26 54 27 29
Fax2: 03 26 54 54 55
President: M. Pierre ERNST

### Champagne Taittinger
9, place Saint Nicaise
51100 REIMS
Tel: 03 26 85 45 35
Fax: 03 26 85 44 39
Export Director: Mme SCHILLIGER

### Cointreau
*Spirits production*
152, ave des Champs Élysées
75008 PARIS
Tel: 01 44 13 44 13
Fax: 01 45 62 82 52
Chairman: M. Pierre COINTREAU

### Daniel Chotard

*Daniel Chotard*
*Vigneron*

*Producer of fine Sancerre wines. Sells direct to the public and to restaurants*
Reigny
18300 CREZANCY EN SANCERRE
Tel: 02 48 79 08 12
Fax: 02 48 79 09 21
Web site: http://www.paris-anglo.com
Director: M. Daniel CHOTARD

### Découverte du Vin
*Information center on wine*
30, rue de la Sablière
75014 PARIS
Tel: 01 45 45 44 20
Fax: 01 45 42 78 20

### GH Mumm
*Spirits & juices*
Vinicole de Champagne
17-19, ave Montaigne
75008 PARIS
Tel: 01 44 43 15 00
Fax: 01 44 43 15 01

### Lusina I.S.G.

*Bilingual site about South West France: tourism information and emphasis on Cognac, Pineau des Charentes, Armagnac (market, prices, gossips, and results of our bi-weekly tastings). Purchase on our site with secured payment!*
7, route de Coucoussac
17160 MATHA
Tel: 05 46 26 67 01
Fax: 05 46 26 67 50
Email: cognac@msn.com
Web site: http://www.swfrance.com
Contact: M. Mac ANDREW

### Maison de la Vigne et du Vin de France
*Wine tasting, documentation, boutique*
21, rue François Ier
75008 PARIS
Tel: 01 47 20 20 76
Fax: 01 47 23 07 21
Director: M. de CATHELINEAU

# FOOD/GROCERY STORES/CATERERS
## ÉPICERIES/TRAITEURS/ALIMENTATION

### Moët-Hennessy
*Cognac, Champagne*
30, ave Hoche
75008 PARIS
Tel: 01 44 13 22 22
Fax: 01 44 13 22 23

### Nectar des Bourbons Fine Wines
37, rue de Turenne
75003 PARIS
Tel: 01 40 27 99 12
Fax: 01 40 27 99 12
Manager: M. Alain DECHY

### Remy Martin & Cie
*Cognacs*
20, rue de la Société Vinicole
BP 37
16102 COGNAC Cedex
Tel: 01 45 35 16 16
Export Service: M. PELOUX

### Seagram France Distribution
*Distributor of fine wines, whiskies and spirits: Four Roses, Absolut Vodka, Chivas Regal, Glen Grant, Crown Royal, Seagram's VO...*
Tour Gamma A
193-197, rue de Bercy
75582 PARIS Cedex 12
Tel: 01 40 04 46 00
Fax: 01 40 04 45 50

### Vignerons de France
*French wine-making cooperative*
108, rue du Chemin Vert
75011 PARIS
Tel: 01 48 05 28 85

176

## MISCELLANEOUS
## Divers

### Atlanta Bar & Grill
229, rue Saint Honoré
75001 PARIS
Tel: 01 42 96 10 60
Fax: 01 42 96 23 26
Email: atlantav@easynet.fr

### Australian Import Center (A.I.C.)
103, rue Blomet
75015 PARIS
Tel: 01 53 68 95 59
Fax: 01 45 30 00 63

### Baskin Robbins Ice Cream
1, rue du Four
75006 PARIS
Tel: 01 43 25 10 63
Contact: M. GALLET

### Baskin Robbins
88, rue du Dôme
92100 BOULOGNE BILLANCOURT
Tel: 01 47 61 88 40
Fax: 01 47 61 88 41
Director: M. Stéphane KLEIN

### Boulangerie de l'Ancienne Comédie
*24-hour bakery*
10, rue de l'Ancienne Comédie
75006 PARIS
Tel: 01 43 26 89 72
Fax: 01 43 29 07 40
Director: M. Jean-Michel GALEK

### Celestial Seasonings
*Herbal teas*
23, rue du Sergent Bauchat
75012 PARIS
Tel: 01 44 75 34 71
Fax: 01 49 28 92 88
Sales Director:
Mme Helen MARSHALL

### Colorado Cookie Company
*American bakery*
4, rue Becquerel
EAE de la Tuilerie
77645 CHELLES Cedex
Tel: 01 64 72 00 55
Fax: 01 64 72 10 30
Contact: Mme Heather McEVOY

### Cookie Connexion
160, ave Ledru Rollin
75011 PARIS
Tel: 01 43 79 16 79

## Cookie Délice

26, ave Jean Moulin
75014 PARIS
Tel: 01 45 45 41 02

## Cynthia Bread & Chocolate Bakery

31 rue Pétion
75011 PARIS
Tel: 01 43 48 06 84

## David's Western Cookies

*American bakery products for professionals*

253, ave Président Wilson
93214 LA PLAINE SAINT DENIS
Tel: 01 48 20 30 00
Fax: 01 48 20 50 00
Contact: M. David FRIEDMAN

## Godiva

*Chocolates*

237, rue Saint Honoré
75001 PARIS
Tel: 01 42 60 61 31
Fax: 01 42 60 61 33
Regional director: M. D. GERALD

## Häagen-Daz

*Many locations in Paris*

144, Bd Saint Germain
75006 PARIS
Tel: 01 43 26 96 97
Fax: 01 43 26 57 47

## Laura Todd Cookies

2, rue Pierre Lescot
75001 PARIS
Tel: 01 42 36 15 87
Contact: M. Thierry HONORE

## Mille Break-First

*Breakfast home delivery*

7-9, passage Abel Leblanc
75012 PARIS
Tel: 01 43 45 76 53
Fax: 01 43 07 59 71
Contact: Valérie

## Reels on Wheels

*Home delivery*

12, Villa Croix Nivert
75015 PARIS
Tel: 01 45 67 64 99
Fax: 01 45 67 69 51

## San Francisco Muffin Company

*American bakery - retail and wholesale*

35, rue du Dragon
75006 PARIS
Tel: 01 45 79 09 09
Fax: 01 45 79 03 50
Director: Mme Lisa KOBLENTZ

## San Francisco Muffin Company

41, rue Linois
75015 PARIS
Tel: 01 45 79 09 09
Fax: 01 45 79 03 50
Director: Mme Lisa KOBLENTZ

## The Bagel Place

6, place Sainte Opportune
75001 PARIS
Tel: 01 40 28 96 40
Fax: 01 40 28 97 94
Email: BagelPlace@aol.com
Contact: M. Barry WILKINSON

## The Original Cookie Company

Centre Commercial Galaxie
30, ave d'Italie
75013 PARIS
Tel: 01 45 88 86 92

## The World's Finest Flavored Coffees

49, rue Burgaud-Desmarets
17100 SAINTES
Tel: 05 46 74 44 94
Fax: 05 46 92 16 49

LIVING & STUDYING

177

# HEALTH
## SANTÉ

The anglophone community in Paris enjoys several well-equipped hospitals and many English-speaking doctors, dentists, and other health providers.

## HOSPITALS
### Hôpitaux

### American Hospital of Paris
63, Bd Victor Hugo
BP 109
92202 NEUILLY SUR SEINE
Tel: 01 46 41 25 25
Fax: 01 46 24 49 38 (Welcome Service)
Director: M. Hal VAUGHAN

### Hertford British Hospital
*General medicine, surgery*
3, rue Barbès
92300 LEVALLOIS PERRET
Tel: 01 46 39 22 22
Fax: 01 46 39 22 26

## PROFESSIONALS
### Médecins

## GENERAL PRACTITIONERS
### Généralistes

### Dr. Gamon, Hubert
*General practitioner/allergist*
20, rue Cler
75007 PARIS
Tel: 01 45 55 79 91

### Dr. Guichard, Claude
37, rue du Départ
75014 PARIS
Tel: 01 43 22 22 96
Fax: 01 43 20 78 46

### Dr. Lancry, Gilbert
63, Bd Victor Hugo
92202 NEUILLY SUR SEINE
Tel: 01 46 41 25 25

### Dr. Salzman, Nancy
36, rue du Colisée
75008 PARIS
Tel: 01 45 63 18 43
Email:
nancy.salzman@paris01.X400.gc.ca

### Dr. Wilson, Stephen
54, rue des Archives
75004 PARIS
Tel: 01 48 87 21 10
Email: docsteve@club-internet.fr

## SPECIALISTS
### Spécialistes

### Dr. Abitbol, Yvan
*Opthalmologist*
63, Bd Victor Hugo
92202 NEUILLY SUR SEINE
Tel: 01 46 41 25 25

### Dr. Adra, Denis
*Dentist*
69-71, ave Raymond Poincaré
75116 PARIS
Tel: 01 47 04 39 09
Fax: 01 44 05 94 49

### Dr. Aron, Jean-Jacques
*Opthalmologist*
63, Bd Victor Hugo
92202 NEUILLY SUR SEINE
Tel: 01 46 41 25 25

### Dr. Bismuth, Céline
*Dentist*
7, rue Bernard de Clairvaux
75003 PARIS
Tel: 01 48 87 61 61

## Dr. Bitoun, Pierre
*Pediatrician*
6, rue Jarente
75004 PARIS
Tel: 01 42 77 74 37

## Dr. Bordarier, Cécile
*Pediatrician*
30, rue Racine
75006 PARIS
Tel: 01 40 51 70 55

## Dr. Bouffette, Patrick
*Blood disease specialist*
American Hospital
63, Bd Victor Hugo
BP 109
92202 NEUILLY SUR SEINE
Tel: 01 46 41 27 32
Fax: 01 46 37 32 29

## Dr. Bourgoin, Gilles et Dr. Mareuil, Philippe
*Orthodontists*
29, ave Poincaré
75116 PARIS
Tel: 01 47 04 79 97
Fax: 01 47 04 58 40

## Dr. Bretton, Rosine
*Dermatologist and hair specialist*
63, Bd Victor Hugo
92202 NEUILLY SUR SEINE
Tel: 01 46 41 27 60
Fax: 01 46 41 27 00

## Cabinet Médical
*Ophthalmologist*
41, ave Bosquet
75007 PARIS
Tel: 01 45 55 65 45
Fax: 01 45 55 91 20
Dr Linda ABITBOL

## Dr. Clot, Jean-Paul
*General surgeon*
63, Bd Victor Hugo
92202 NEUILLY SUR SEINE
Tel: 01 46 41 25 25

## Dr. Cohen, Edouard
*Dentist*
20, rue de la Paix
75002 PARIS
Tel: 01 42 61 65 64
Fax: 01 42 61 20 81

## Dr. Derycke, R.
*Dental surgeon*
66, ave Victor Hugo
75016 PARIS
Tel: 01 45 01 88 02
Fax: 01 45 00 10 45

## Dr. Desgrez, Jean-Pierre
*Urologist*
63, Bd Victor Hugo
92202 NEUILLY SUR SEINE
Tel: 01 46 41 25 25

## Dr. Ducellier, Joyce
*Pediatrician*
38, rue des Sablons
75116 PARIS
Tel: 01 44 05 01 50
Fax: 01 44 05 06 63

## Dr. Ficat, Christian
*Orthopedist*
63, Bd Victor Hugo
92202 NEUILLY SUR SEINE
Tel: 01 46 41 25 25

## Dr. Fitterer, Richard
*Opthalmologist*
9, ave Bosquet
75007 PARIS
Tel: 01 47 05 52 43

## Dr. Frajder, Henri
*Dentist*
35, Bd Malesherbes
75008 PARIS
Tel: 01 42 66 25 44

## Dr. Gauthier
*Dentist (Master of Science)*
47, ave Hoche
75008 PARIS
Tel: 01 47 66 33 25

## Dr. Gittins, N.R.
*British veterinarian*
47, rue Saint Charles
75015 PARIS
Tel: 01 40 59 04 76

## Dr. Hewes, Thomas
*Gastroenterology*
63, Bd Victor Hugo
92202 NEUILLY SUR SEINE
Tel: 01 46 41 25 25

*LIVING & STUDYING*

179

# HEALTH
SANTÉ

### Dr. Homareau, Sylvie
*Dermatologist*
63, Bd Victor Hugo
92202 NEUILLY SUR SEINE
Tel: 01 46 41 27 24

### Dr. Huard, Claude
*Orthopedics - no consultation*
63, Bd Victor Hugo
92202 NEUILLY SUR SEINE
Tel: 01 46 41 25 25

### Dr. Krygie,r Georges
*Dental surgeon*
63, ave Franklin Roosevelt
75008 PARIS
Tel: 01 43 59 47 67

### Dr. Le Buisson, Dan
*Ophthalmologist, ocular surgery*
63, Bd Victor Hugo
92202 NEUILLY SUR SEINE
Tel: 01 46 41 25 25
Fax: 01 40 99 98 49

### Dr. Lemoine, Claude
*Dentist*
16, ave du Président Wilson
75016 PARIS
Tel: 01 47 23 06 63
Fax: 01 47 23 74 18

### Dr. Lisfranc, Regis
*Orthopedist*
63, Bd Victor Hugo
92202 NEUILLY SUR SEINE
Tel: 01 46 41 25 25

### Dr. Manière, Francis
*Sports medicine*
64, rue de Rennes
75006 PARIS
Tel: 01 45 44 03 21
Fax: 01 45 49 19 96

### Dr. Marchal
*Dermatologist*
40, ave Bosquet
75007 PARIS
Tel: 01 45 51 04 40

180

### Dr. Marois, Pierre
*Dentist*
32, Bd Haussmann
75009 PARIS
Tel: 01 47 70 81 81
Fax: 01 47 70 39 39

### Dr. Natali, Robert
*Ear, Nose, Throat*
63, Bd Victor Hugo
92202 NEUILLY SUR SEINE
Tel: 01 46 41 25 25

### Dr. Netter, Laurence
*Dermatologist, wrinkle treatment, laser*
29, ave Franklin Roosevelt
75008 PARIS
Tel: 01 43 59 88 17

### Dr. Nys, Alain, M.D.
*Orthopedic medicine - Rehabilitation*
63, Bd Victor Hugo
92202 NEUILLY SUR SEINE
Tel: 01 46 41 25 25
Fax: 01 46 41 29 96

### Dr. Oppenheim, Tatiane
*Gynecologist*
17, Bd du Temple
75003 PARIS
Tel: 01 48 87 22 63
Fax: 01 42 77 11 12

### Osteopathic Clinic
66, rue René Boulanger
75010 PARIS
Tel: 01 42 39 33 11
Fax: 01 42 38 03 21
Contact: M. Gregory DAY

### Dr. Pruvost, Jean-Luc
*Orthodontist for adults & children*
98, ave Kléber
75016 PARIS
Tel: 01 45 53 84 84
Fax: 01 45 53 24 60
Email: 102313,0742@compuserve.com

### Dr. Rachinel, Jean
*Ear, Nose, Throat*
63, Bd Victor Hugo
92202 NEUILLY SUR SEINE
Tel: 01 46 41 25 25

## Dr. Raygot, Pierre
*Dentist*
32, Bd Haussmann
75009 PARIS
Tel: 01 47 70 81 81
Fax: 01 47 70 39 39

## Radiology Center - Dr. Lebar Philippe
*X-rays, ultra sounds, dopplers, MRI, encephaloscan. Emergency appointments accepted, English spoken*
199, rue de Grenelle
75007 PARIS
Tel: 01 45 55 08 09
Fax: 01 44 18 32 17
Owner/Radiologist: M. Philippe LEBAR

## Dr. Relland, John, M.D., F.A.C.S.
*General and cardiovascular surgery*
63, Bd Victor Hugo
92202 NEUILLY SUR SEINE
Tel: 01 46 41 27 07
Fax: 01 46 41 27 00

## Dr. Richet, Anne-Isabelle
*English-speaking gynecologist*
109, rue de l'Université
75007 PARIS
Tel: 01 45 51 82 32
Fax: 01 45 51 00 27

## Dr. Rignault, Daniel
*General and laparoscopic surgery*
63, Bd Victor Hugo
92202 NEUILLY SUR SEINE
Tel: 01 46 41 25 25
Tel: 01 43 50 14 13 (Direct Line)
Fax: 01 43 50 14 47 (Hospital)

## Dr. Rolet, François
*Gynecologist*
63, Bd Victor Hugo
92202 NEUILLY SUR SEINE
Tel: 01 46 41 25 25

## Dr. Sarrot, Gilbert
*Gynecologist*
6, ave Sully-Prudhomme
75007 PARIS
Tel: 01 45 56 03 30
Fax: 01 45 51 15 88

## Dr. Sauvan, Caroline
*Allergist*
92, rue Saint Antoine
75004 PARIS
Tel: 01 40 27 81 51
Fax: 01 42 72 04 07

## Dr. Specter, Michael
*Cardiologist*
63, Bd Victor Hugo
92202 NEUILLY SUR SEINE
Tel: 01 46 41 25 25

## Dr. Steinmetzer, Robert, M.D., F.A.C.S.
*Internal medicine*
63, Bd Victor Hugo
92202 NEUILLY SUR SEINE Cedex
Tel: 01 46 41 27 04
Fax: 01 46 41 27 00

## Dr. Tecucianu, Jean-François
*Dental surgeon*
174, rue de Courcelles
75017 PARIS
Tel: 01 46 22 40 82
Fax: 01 47 66 54 60

## Dr. Torkia, Joseph
*British-trained generalist*
54, rue de Paris
93100 MONTREUIL
Tel: 01 48 59 66 60

## Dr. Veroli, Aldo
*English-speaking dental surgeon*
2, rue des Halles
75001 PARIS
Tel: 01 42 36 09 70
Fax: 01 42 36 09 70

## Dr. Vialatte, Philippe
*Urologist*
63, Bd Victor Hugo
92202 NEUILLY SUR SEINE
Tel: 01 46 41 25 25

## Dr. Viterbo, Guy
*Pediatrician for the American Hospital*
6, rue Champfleury
75007 PARIS
Tel: 01 47 34 68 09

*LIVING & STUDYING*

181

### Dr. Winaver, Diane
*English-speaking gynecologist*
109, rue de l'Université
75007 PARIS
Tel: 01 45 51 82 32
Fax: 01 45 51 00 27

## PSYCHOLOGISTS/ PSYCHIATRISTS
Psychologues/Psychiatres

### Ansart, Emmanuelle, M.D.
*Psychiatrist*
43, rue La Bruyère
75009 PARIS
Tel: 01 48 78 04 60
Fax: 01 42 85 42 11

### Berg, Debra
*Psychotherapist*
4, rue Ledru Rollin
92240 MALAKOFF
Tel: 01 46 55 96 96

### Cox, Barbara
*British and US trained psychotherapist. Interpersonal relations, personal growth, adaptation to loss and changes*
115, rue du Théâtre
75015 PARIS
Tel: 01 45 75 74 61

### Dobbs, Hugh
*Psychologist*
2, allée des Rosiers
92230 GENNEVILLIERS
Tel: 01 47 90 33 40

### Feld, Elizabeth Leafy

*Adventures in creativity and recovery. Creative arts therapy worshops. Individuals, couples sessions for personal, professional development*
32, rue Damrémont
75018 PARIS
Tel: 01 42 62 04 66
Fax: 01 42 62 04 66
Email: leafy@easynet.fr

### Mathijsen, Claire
*Psychotherapist*
11, rue de Sèvres
75006 PARIS
Tel: 01 42 22 06 23

### Dr Nagpal, H.R.S.
*Psychoanalysis, psychiatry, group therapy with a special interest in problems of displacement, bilingualism and cultural difference. Reimbursed by French social security & private insurance schemes*
65, rue Pascal
75013 PARIS
Tel: 01 47 07 55 28
Fax: 01 43 37 11 46
Email: nagpal@magic.fr
Secretary: Mme Julliet BLAIR

### Oberman, Marjorie
*Psychotherapist*
32, rue de la Paroisse
78000 VERSAILLES
Tel: 01 39 51 98 99

### Pedevilla, Sandra
*British person centred psychotherapist and counsellor (British Association of Counseling accredited). Also music therapy children/adults*
22, rue Marcel Allegot
Bellevue Village
92190 MEUDON
Tel: 01 45 07 29 75

### Sadowsky, Nancy
*Clinical psychologist, psychotherapist*
12, rue Marie Stuart
75002 PARIS
Tel: 01 42 33 10 07

### Safier, David
*Psychotherapist*
36, ave de Suffren
75015 PARIS
Tel: 01 40 65 96 10

## OTHER HEALTH PROFESSIONALS - AUTRES

### American Chiropractic Center
119 rue de l'Université
75007 PARIS
Tel: 01 45 51 38 38
Fax: 01 47 05 58 97
Contact: Dr CHIAPINELLI

### Boulay, Patricia
*Relaxation therapist: Alexander Technique*
32, rue Remond du Temple
94300 VINCENNES
Tel: 01 41 74 01 65

### Cabinet Chiropractic Étoile
15, rue Villaret de Joyeuse
75017 PARIS
Tel: 01 44 09 91 92
Fax: 01 44 09 91 92
Contact: Dr Bruno FAŸ

### Cabinet Chiropractique Précloux
*USA licensed Doctor of Chiropractic*
43, rue de Richelieu
75001 PARIS
Tel: 01 42 60 42 36
Fax: 01 42 60 47 88

### Centre Heliotrope
*Relaxation*
43 rue de Richelieu
75001 PARIS
Tel: 01 42 60 42 36
Fax: 01 45 88 36 59

### Chiropractic Center in Saint Germain des Prés
14, rue Guisarde
75006 PARIS
Tel: 01 43 54 26 25
Contact:
Mme Nadine STEINIK-FORESMAN

### Chiropractic for Americans
29, rue de Penthièvre
75008 PARIS
Tel: 01 42 56 63 63
Fax: 01 42 89 35 47

### Chiropractic in Paris
44, rue Laborde
75008 PARIS
Tel: 01 43 87 81 62
Fax: 01 40 08 09 89

### Chiropractic "International Center"
*Back pain, arthritis, sciatica, wry neck? Team of highly-qualified chiropractors from the USA. Specialized in personal treatment. Contact our Paris office for information*
119, rue de l'Université
75007 PARIS
Tel: 01 45 51 38 38
Contacts: Dr CHIAPPINELLI & LEGAGNOUX

### Chiropractic Office Haussmann
*USA licensed chiropractor*
44, rue Laborde
75008 PARIS
Tel: 01 43 87 81 62
Fax: 01 40 08 09 89
Email: 100606.2031@compuserve.com
Contact: M. Marc TOURNEUR

### De Alcantara, Pedro
*Certified teacher of the F.M. Alexander technique*
10, rue Hittorf
75010 PARIS
Tel: 01 42 02 00 17
Email: 100747.3360@compuserve.com

### Godard, Hubert
*Massage therapist: Rolfing*
97, rue de Charenton
75012 PARIS
Tel: 01 43 47 45 53

### Motei, Annie
*Massage therapist: Alexander Technique*
34, Bd de l'Hôpital
75005 PARIS
Tel: 01 47 07 04 72

# HEALTH
SANTÉ

## Reiki
*Relief from stress, pain and illness. Reiki energy strengthens one's capacity to release underlying physical, mental and emotional causes*
62, rue Vasco de Gama
75015 PARIS
Tel: 01 48 28 38 02
Contact: M. Terence COLEMAN

## Reiki, Numerology
*Healing techniques based on philosophy, psychology and holistic sciences*
18, ave Victor Cresson
92130 ISSY LES MOULINEAUX
Tel: 01 46 42 51 20
Fax: 01 41 08 84 17
Contact: Mme Angelika ROMANET

## Sager, Rebecca
*Pre and post natal instruction*
8, rue des Anglais
75005 PARIS
Tel: 01 43 73 68 11

## Shiatsu Massage
*Shiatsu treatment and classes*
23, rue Gazan
75014 PARIS
Tel: 01 45 88 03 42
Contact: M. Carey DOWNER

## Dr. Vigneron, Jeanette Mitchell
*American veterinarian*
58, rue du Cherche Midi
75006 PARIS
Tel: 01 45 44 19 27

## HEALTH-RELATED SERVICES
Divers

184

## Active Relaxation
*Stress reduction through movement, breathing + visualization techniques*
71, rue du Cardinal Lemoine
75005 PARIS
Tel: 01 43 54 91 00
Fax: 01 43 54 98 39
Email: 101367.1402@compuserve.com
Director: Mme Sarah PETLIN

## Anglo-American Pharmacy Swan-Rocher
6, rue de Castiglione
75001 PARIS
Tel: 01 42 60 72 96
Fax: 01 42 60 44 12
Contact: Mme ROCHER

## Bio Rad
94, rue Victor Hugo
94200 IVRY SUR SEINE
Tel: 01 43 90 46 90
Fax: 01 46 71 24 67
Director: M. LUMBROSO

## British and American Pharmacy
1, rue Auber
75009 PARIS
Tel: 01 47 42 49 40
Fax: 01 42 65 29 42

## British Pharmacy
62, ave des Champs Élysées
75008 PARIS
Tel: 01 43 59 22 52

## Centre de Vision
*Optometrists and opticians*
40, rue Saint Honoré
75001 PARIS
Tel: 01 42 33 97 24
Fax: 01 45 08 46 99

## Centre Médico-Social
*Free AIDS testing. For other medical centers consult Minitel 3615 SIDA*
18, rue de Belleville
75020 PARIS
Tel: 01 47 97 40 49
Fax: 01 47 97 38 59

## Confort-Vision
*English-speaking optical house, free tax for import*
95, rue de Passy
75016 PARIS
Tel: 01 42 24 66 80
Contact: M. Guy BONVOISIN

## European Respiratory Society

*Organization of courses & meetings for medical professionals*
60, rue de Vaugirard
75006 PARIS
Tel: 01 45 48 93 10
Fax: 01 45 44 34 11
Email: internet-sec-par@ersnet.org

## Guidant France

*Vascular intervention, Cardiac Rhythm management*
9, rue d'Estienne d'Orves
92504 RUEIL MALMAISON Cedex
Tel: 01 47 14 40 14
Fax: 01 47 49 09 57
President: M. Juan VIDAL

## Jin Shin Jyutsu Ouest

32, rue de la Paroisse
78000 VERSAILLES
Tel: 01 39 51 98 99
Contact: M. Philippe DOUILLARD

## Les Pieds Dans l'Univers

17, ave Corention Cariou
75019 PARIS
Tel: 01 40 35 17 81
Fax: 01 40 35 17 81
Contact:
Mme Mary Thornley PREWITT

## Med Care Domicile

14, rue Rougemont
75009 PARIS
Tel: 01 48 24 55 20
Fax: 01 48 24 38 38
Contact: M. Dallas PATTEN

## Medic'Air International

*Worldwide air-ambulance services*
58, rue Marie-Anne Colombier
93170 BAGNOLET
Tel: 01 43 63 04 04
Hotline: 01 43 63 04 04
Fax: 01 43 63 01 02
Email: aderossi@pratique.fr
Web site: http://www.medicair.starnet.fr
Chairman: M. Arnaud DEROSSI, MD

## Pharmacie "Les Champs"

*Open 24h every day of the year*
84, ave des Champs Élysées
Galerie "Les Champs"
Tel: 01 45 62 02 41
Fax: 01 45 63 83 79
Director: Dr Sylvia DERHY

## Victoire sur le Tabac

*Health center to give up smoking. Personal growth seminar, rebirth and creative thought*
16, rue du Colisée
75008 PARIS
Tel: 01 42 25 66 46
Fax: 01 43 59 53 03
Director: M. Patrice ELLEQUAIN

## Walter's Paris

*Optician - 25% discount on frames and contact lenses for FrancoFile Club Menbers*
107, rue Saint Dominique
75007 PARIS
Tel: 01 45 51 70 08
Fax: 01 45 51 04 42

*LIVING & STUDYING*

# HOME IMPROVEMENT
## TOUT POUR LA MAISON

Need to decorate your apartment, find a king-size bed, repair your refrigerator, or track down an architect that understands your insistence on walk-in closets? You now possess a list of focused contacts.

### ARCHITECTURE
Architecture

### Adams, Robert K., Architect

3, rue Saint Roch
BP 43
28800 BONNEVAL
Tel: 01 37 47 41 19
Fax: 01 37 47 41 19

### Alain Neymarc Architecte

5, rue Scipion
75005 PARIS
Tel: 01 47 07 99 50
Fax: 01 43 37 01 59
Director: M. Alain NEYMARC

### Arc International

96, rue de Rivoli
75004 PARIS
Tel: 01 42 72 00 43
Fax: 01 48 04 87 20

### Bailey et Smith Architectes

14, rue Denis Poisson
75017 PARIS
Tel: 01 45 72 35 59
Fax: 01 45 72 12 01
Email:
Bailey-and-Smith@compuserve.com
Director: M. Martin BAILEY

### Cyril Sweet & Partners

22, ave de Friedland
75008 PARIS
Tel: 01 42 56 00 38
Fax: 01 42 25 26 08
Director: M. Christian BOUCHEL

### Duval, Joséphine & Guy

*Architecture and interior decoration*
54, ave de Saxe
75015 PARIS
Tel: 01 45 67 16 85
Fax: 01 47 83 65 99
Contact: Mme Joséphine DUVAL

### Epstein P.S. & T.

7-9, rue Barbette
75003 PARIS
Tel: 01 48 04 97 30
Fax: 01 48 04 31 81

### Jean-Paul Viguier Architecture

16, rue du Champs de l'Alouette
75013 PARIS
Tel: 01 44 08 62 00
Fax: 01 44 08 62 02
Email: yvesjpv@imaginet.fr
Web site: http://www.planet.fr/viguier
Contact: M. Yves NGUYEN

### Smart Building Engineering

Tour Gamma A
193-197, rue de Bercy
75582 PARIS Cedex 12
Tel: 01 40 04 56 56
Fax: 01 40 04 56 55

### HOME DECORATION/ FURNITURE
Décoration intérieure/ mobilier

### Alkor

*Expertise in researching & buying French antiques*
1, rue Grévin
94100 SAINT MAUR DES FOSSÉS
Tel: 01 43 97 22 80
Fax: 01 48 89 18 75
Director: M. Frank CARROLL

### Artis Flora

*Master-weavers, replicas of famous tapestries*
75, rue Vieille du Temple
75003 PARIS
Tel: 01 48 87 76 18
Fax: 01 48 87 98 60

## Bouchara
*All types of material for fashion and interior decoration*
54, Bd Haussmann
75009 PARIS
Tel: 01 42 80 66 95
Fax: 01 42 85 37 61

## British Import Antiques
Le Louvre des Antiquaires
2-4, allée Topino
2, place du Palais Royal
75002 PARIS
Tel: 01 42 60 19 12
Fax: 01 42 60 54 00

## Christofle
*Quality silverware for the table*
9, rue Royale
75008 PARIS
Tel: 01 49 33 43 00
Fax: 01 49 33 43 08

## Cristalleries de Baccarat
11, place de la Madeleine
75008 PARIS
Tel: 01 42 65 36 26
Fax: 01 42 65 06 64

## Darty
*TV and hi-fi equipment, household appliances*
Place de la Madeleine
75008 PARIS
Tel: 01 42 65 84 71
Fax: 01 40 07 05 62

## Electrorama - La Quincaillerie
11, Bd Saint Germain
75005 PARIS
Tel: 01 40 46 78 10
Fax: 01 40 46 78 15

## Etamine
*Wallpaper*
63, rue du Bac
75007 PARIS
Tel: 01 42 22 03 16

## Franco-Américain du Froid
*American appliances (fridges, air-conditioning)*
183, ave du Maine
75014 PARIS
Tel: 01 45 40 94 10
Fax: 01 45 39 38 33
Director: M. PICARD

## Galerie Robert Four
*Tapestries*
28, rue Bonaparte
75006 PARIS
Tel: 01 43 29 30 60
Fax: 01 43 25 33 95

## Habitat
Forum des Halles
Niveau -2
Porte Rambuteau
75001 PARIS
Tel: 01 40 39 91 06
Fax: 01 42 21 46 36

## Herolia
*Wooden and wrought-iron decorative objects for the home*
75, rue Vieille du Temple
75003 PARIS
Tel: 01 48 87 66 93

## Homelite
*Garden equipment*
Parc du Vert Galant
rue de la Garenne
95310 SAINT OUEN L'AUMONE
Tel: 01 30 37 71 00
Fax: 01 30 37 84 33
Director: M. W. PACINI

## IKEA
*Call for others locations*
202, rue Henri Barbusse
78370 PLAISIR
Tel: 01 30 79 21 21
Fax: 01 30 79 21 11
Minitel: 3615 IKEA

## La Chaise Longue
*Fun objects for the home*
8, rue Princesse
75006 PARIS
Tel: 01 43 29 62 39
Fax: 01 43 29 62 39

## La Maison sur l'Eau Agnès B Voyage
19, rue du Jour
75001 PARIS
Tel: 01 42 33 27 34
Web site: http://www.agnesb.fr

LIVING & STUDYING

187

# HOME IMPROVEMENT
TOUT POUR LA MAISON

## Lalique
11, rue Royale
75008 PARIS
Tel: 01 53 05 12 12
Fax: 01 42 65 59 06

## Le Loft
*English and Scandinavian antique pine furniture*
17 bis, rue Pavée
75004 PARIS
Tel: 01 48 87 46 50
Fax: 01 48 04 02 19
Contact: M. O'Neill

## Le Louvre des Antiquaires
2, place du Palais-Royal
75001 PARIS
Tel: 01 42 97 27 00
Fax: 01 42 97 00 14

## Le Sorbier
*Dried flower and plant arrangements*
70, rue Vieille du Temple
75003 PARIS
Tel: 01 48 87 69 72

## Les Toiles de Mayenne
*Interior decoration, fabrics*
48, rue Linois
75015 PARIS
Tel: 01 45 75 56 02

## Linge des Vosges
*House linen*
94, rue Saint Antoine
75004 PARIS
Tel: 01 42 72 38 26

## Manuel Canovas
*Interior decoration, fabrics*
7, rue de Furstenberg
75006 PARIS
Tel: 01 43 25 75 98

## Mondo
*The Japanese mattress specialist*
85, Bd Beaumarchais
75003 PARIS
Tel: 01 48 04 04 02
Fax: 01 48 04 08 09
Contact: Melle Silvia NILSSON

## Olivier Laederich
*Interior design*
28, rue Barque
75015 PARIS
Tel: 01 43 06 72 62
Fax: 01 45 67 99 68

## Pier Import
40, ave des Champs Élysées
75008 PARIS
Tel: 01 45 61 23 71

## SOF
*Japanese mattresses*
38, Bd Richard Lenoir
75011 PARIS
Tel: 01 49 23 42 02
Fax: 01 49 23 04 92

## Stanhome
*Cleaning products sold privately*
Tour Litwin
10, rue Jean Jaurès
92800 PUTEAUX
Tel: 01 41 26 01 01

## Stephany's House
*English-style furniture, decoration*
7, rue Montenotte
75017 PARIS
Tel: 01 44 09 72 23
Fax: 01 44 09 73 37

## Taï
*Futons*
3, rue Eugène Varlin
75010 PARIS
Tel: 01 40 36 53 98

## Taïr Mercier
*Unusual dinner services, table mats, glasses*
7, Bd Saint Germain
75005 PARIS
Tel: 01 43 54 19 97
Fax: 01 43 25 57 22

## Villa Marais
*Unusual objets d'art for the home*
40, rue des Francs-Bourgeois
75003 PARIS
Tel: 01 42 78 42 40
Fax: 01 42 78 42 65

## Chevalier Conservation
*Specialized in cleaning and restoring carpets and rugs*
64, Bd de la Mission-Marchand
92400 COURBEVOIE
Tel: 01 47 88 41 41
Fax: 01 43 34 08 99
Directors: M. Pierre CHEVALIER

## Deco 64
*Painting and other renovation services*
40, rue des Blancs-Manteaux
75004 PARIS
Tel: 01 48 04 75 31

## Entreprise Murray
*British general contractor: all renovations*
38, rue Servan
75011 PARIS
Tel: 01 43 44 34 47
Fax: 01 43 44 42 47
Email: 100063.1044@compuserve.com
Director: M. Christopher MURRAY

## Foxton, Charles
*Carpentry, electrical and tile work*
Tel: 01 45 25 21 17

## Magon Home Improvements
*Interior decoration and renovation work*
12, rue Corneille
78220 VIROFLAY
Tel: 06 07 36 01 20
Fax: 01 30 24 71 48
Contact: Mme Jasi MAGON

## Rainbow International
*Cleaning specialist for carpets, rugs and upholstery*
40, rue Galilée
77380 COMBS LA VILLE
Tel: 01 60 60 18 16
Fax: 01 60 34 03 54

## The Magic Touch
*Carpet cleaning specialist*
44, ave de Versailles
75016 PARIS
Tel: 01 45 20 60 02

*LIVING & STUDYING*

189

# HOUSING
## LOGEMENT

PARIS-ANGLOPHONE specializes in helping you find apartments, furnished or empty, long-term and short-term, directing you to the agencies that are used to working with anglophones, pointing you to student housing solutions, time-share arrangements, apartment exchanges, and more. Here are the key players. Don't hesitate to check-out the PARIS-ANGLOPHONE online service "Housing in France" at http://www.paris-anglo.com or leave a classified ad by clicking on PICS

### A.A.A. "A Flat in Paris"

A FLAT IN PARIS

*Luxuriously serviced flats in the best parts of the Left Bank and Champs Élysées areas of Paris, available from 14 days*
31, ave de la Motte Picquet
75007 PARIS
Tel: 01 40 61 99 11
Fax: 01 45 66 42 79
Email: flatinparis@easynet.fr
Contact: M. Gérald DE CONCLOIS

### A.B.M. Rent a Flat

ABM RENT A FLAT

*Furnished apartment rentals from studio to 5 rooms in the best areas of Paris. Phone line, dishes, TV...*
12, rue Valentin Haüy
75015 PARIS
Tel: 01 45 67 04 04
Fax: 01 45 67 90 15
Email: abm@abmrentaflat.com
Web site:
http://www.abmrentaflat.paris
Director: M. Laurent MARIONNEAU

### Allô Logement Temporaire
64, rue du Temple
75003 PARIS
Tel: 01 42 72 00 06
Fax: 01 42 72 03 11

### Apalachee Bay International

APALACHEE BAY
RESIDENTIAL PROPERTY

*An extensive range of furnished apartments located in the most pleasant and convenient areas of the city*
56, rue Galilée
75008 PARIS
Tel: 01 40 70 15 03
Fax: 01 40 70 01 37
Email: info@apalachee.com
Web site: http://www.apalachee.com
Contact: Mme Virginia LOMBARDO

### Appartissimmo
PARIS
Tel: 01 42 67 42 42
Fax: 01 42 67 42 03

### ASLOM Company
75, ave Parmentier
75011 PARIS
Tel: 01 43 49 67 79
Fax: 01 47 86 11 11

### At Home in Paris
16, rue Médéric
75017 PARIS
Tel: 01 42 12 40 40
Fax: 01 42 12 40 48

## Century 21 France

*More than 400 offices in France serving your relocation needs*
*(See advertisement)*
Rue des Cévennes, Bâtiment 4
Petite Montagne Sud
CE 1701
91017 ÉVRY Cedex LISSES
Tel: 01 69 11 12 21
Fax: 01 60 86 90 07
Email: cnr21@easynet.fr
Web site: http://www.paris-anglo.com/housing
Contact: M. Frank D. CLUCK

## Citadines Prestige Haussmann

*All suites hotel, furnished studios and apartments*
*(See advertisement)*
131, Bd Haussmann
75008 PARIS
Tel: 01 53 77 07 07
Fax: 01 45 63 46 64
Web site: http://www.citadines.com
Web site: http://www.paris-anglo.com/housing/html/suites.html

## Citadines Trocadéro

*All suites hotel, furnished studios and apartments*
*(See advertisement)*
29 bis, rue Saint Didier
75116 PARIS
Tel: 01 44 34 73 73
Fax: 01 47 04 50 07
Web site: http://www.citadines.com
Or: http://www.paris-anglo.com/housing/html/suites.html

## Collège Franco-Britannique

*Student housing*
9B, Bd Jourdan
75014 PARIS
Tel: 01 44 16 26 58

## Colliers-Auguste-Thouard

24, rue Jacques Ibert
92300 LEVALLOIS PERRET
Tel: 01 47 59 20 00
Fax: 01 47 59 22 69
Web site:
http://www.colliers.auguste.thouard.fr/
Sales Director:
M. Yves DECOURTEUX

## De Circourt Associates

*Short and long-term rental of high standard furnished apartments in and around Paris*
*(See advertisement)*
11, rue Royale
75008 PARIS
Tel: 01 43 12 98 00
Fax: 01 43 12 98 08
email: circourt@easynet.fr
Web site: http://www.paris-anglo.com/housing/decircourt.html
Director: Mme Claire DE CIRCOURT

## Embassy Service

43, ave Marceau
75116 PARIS
Tel: 01 47 20 30 05
Fax: 01 47 20 34 04

## Fondation des États-Unis

*Student housing Residence and cultural center*
Cité Universitaire
15, Bd Jourdan
75690 PARIS Cedex 14
Tel: 01 53 80 68 80
Fax: 01 53 80 68 99
Director: M. Terence MURPHY

# HOUSING
## LOGEMENT

### France Appartements
116, ave des Champs Élysées
75008 PARIS
Tel: 01 44 21 80 20
Fax: 01 44 21 80 21
Contact: F. LECUBIR

### France Lodge Locations
49, rue Lafayette
75009 PARIS
Tel: 01 53 20 09 09
Fax: 01 53 20 01 25

### Gerancia
34, ave des Champs Élysées
75008 PARIS
Tel: 01 43 59 65 81
Fax: 01 40 74 08 59
Email: gerancia@immobilier.ami.fr

### Home Rental
116, ave des Champs Élysées
75008 PARIS
Tel: 01 44 21 82 38
Fax: 01 44 21 81 38
Web site:
http://www.integra.fr/homerental
Director:
M. Claude CHOPARD-LALLIER

### Internet Immobilier
3, rue du Niger
75012 PARIS
Tel: 01 43 07 21 00
Fax: 01 43 07 09 99
Email: webmaster@ani.fr
Web site: http://www.immobilier.ami.fr
Contact: M. Norbert SIMON

### Intervac
*Exchange of lodging in over 40 countries*
230, Bd Voltaire
75011 PARIS
Tel: 01 43 70 21 22
Fax: 01 43 70 73 35
Email: info@intervac.fr

### John Arthur & Tiffen
174, Bd Haussmann
75008 PARIS
Tel: 01 44 21 11 44
Fax: 01 45 63 55 54

### John Taylor
86, ave Victor Hugo
75016 PARIS
Tel: 01 45 53 25 25
Fax: 01 47 55 63 97

### Jones Lang Wootton S.A.
*International consulting on business property*
49, ave Hoche
75008 PARIS
Tel: 01 40 55 15 15
Fax: 01 46 22 28 28
Director: M. Robert WATERLAND
European Partner:
M. Thierry LAROUE-PONT

### KHS Immo
BP 318-16
75767 PARIS Cedex 16
Tel: 01 42 15 04 57
Fax: 01 42 30 53 76
Director: M. Karl SCHABMULLER

### La Grandière Immobilier
79, ave Mozart
75016 PARIS
Tel: 01 42 24 77 00
Fax: 01 42 24 76 77

### La Résidence des Berges de la Seine
1-7, cour du Minervois
75012 PARIS BERCY
Tel: 01 53 02 11 00
Fax: 01 53 02 11 10

### Le Home Bir-Hakeim
3, rue du Docteur Finlay
75015 PARIS
Tel: 01 45 77 09 47
Contact: Mme BLAIN

### Locaflat
63, ave La Motte-Picquet
75015 PARIS
Tel: 01 43 06 78 79
Fax: 01 40 56 99 69
Web site: http://www.locaflat.com

## Maison des Etudiants Canadiens

Cité Universitaire
15, Bd Jourdan
75014 PARIS
Tel: 01 40 78 67 00
Fax: 01 40 78 68 50

## Multiburo

*Office rentals*
17, rue de Galilée
75016 PARIS
Tel: 01 40 69 26 26
Fax: 01 47 23 06 59

## Paris American Academy Housing Service

*Student housing. No agency fee*
9, rue des Ursulines
75005 PARIS
Tel: 01 44 41 99 20
Fax: 01 44 41 99 29

## Paris Appartements Services

*Rental of furnished 1 bedroom & studios in the heart of Paris, selected for their character and charm. Weekly cleaning, 24 hr helpline*
69, rue d'Argout
75002 PARIS
Tel: 01 40 28 01 28
Fax: 01 40 28 92 01
Web site:
http://www.pariserve.tm.fr/paris-apt
Contacts: Hélène & Sabine

## Paris Promo

25, ave Hoche
75008 PARIS
Tel: 01 45 63 25 60
Fax: 01 45 61 10 20
Manager: M. Edmond LEVY

## RayRoth

6, rue Bertin Poirée
75001 PARIS
Tel: 01 40 28 01 19
Tel2: 01 40 28 91 84
Fax: 01 40 26 34 33
Email: intmedia@worldnet.fr
Director: M. Ray LAMPARD

---

### RCI

*International timesharing company with six prime properties in France*
Rue des Cévennes, Bâtiment 4
Petite Montagne Sud
CE 1701
91017 EVRY CEDEX LISSES
Tel: 01 69 11 12 21
Fax: 01 60 86 90 07
Email: cnr21@easynet.fr
Web site:
http://www.paris-anglo.com/housing
Manager: M. Olivier GEQUEL

---

## Richard Ellis

37, rue la Bienfaisance
75008 PARIS
Tel: 01 45 63 08 08
Fax: 01 45 63 54 64

## Servissimo

*Ready-to-live apartments in the heart of Paris for 1 week to 3 months, net prices from 2,940 FF per week*
33, quai de la Tournelle
75005 PARIS
Tel: 01 43 29 03 23
Fax: 01 43 29 53 43
Contact: Mme Catherine GODET

## Studios Dauphine

*Furnished rooms and studios, ex: from 800 F a week for 1 person, from 4400 F a month for 2 persons*
13, rue Dauphine
75006 PARIS
Tel: 01 40 46 93 13
Tel2: 06 07 19 15 55
Manager:
Mme Danielle PETITLAURENT

*LIVING & STUDYING*

193

# HOUSING
LOGEMENT

## Szabo, M. et Mme Z.
7, rue Charles V
75004 PARIS
Tel: 01 42 72 49 02
Fax: 01 42 78 73 63

## Vendome International
*Selected furnished homes
connection*
*Scenario: "Un Américain à Paris"...*
*Our objective: Happy Endings!*
3, rue Duras
75008 PARIS
Tel: 01 42 78 83 30
Fax: 01 42 78 83 40
Executive Officer:
Mme Virginia LOMBARDO

# INSURANCE
ASSURANCES

(See Doing Business & Working: Insurance)

# ADVANTAGE INSURANCE
## •ASSOCIATES•

## INSURANCE MADE EASY... IN ENGLISH

### Dedicated To Serving
### Americans in France

When you call Advantage, you'll find the answers to all your questions about insurance in France. Clear, detailed explanations – in English.

And as we are completely independent, accredited by over 40 French, American and international insurance companies, we can find the best contract at the best price for you.

Your policy documents come complete with full summaries of coverage in English...translations of the claims forms... and information on exactly what to do should the worst happen.

You'll also be able to call on our full claims service which will give you all the back-up and assistance you may need.

Whether you need health, motor, home contents, life, personal injury coverage, business insurance – or simply want an impartial view on your current arrangements, call now at 01 53 20 03 33. And don't hesitate to call before you arrive in France at 33 1 53 20 03 33.

### Advantage Insurance Associates
17, rue Chateaudun
75009 PARIS / France
Tel: 01 53 20 03 33   Fax: 01 44 63 00 97
Email: advantag@easynet.fr
Web site: http://www.paris-anglo.com/housing

# LANGUAGE SCHOOLS
## ÉCOLES DE LANGUES

One of the most highly-sought services in Paris is language schools and methods that can effectively meet your needs, in other words teach you French (or others languages) or help you improve your French for both professional and personal needs. There is a large selection available in Paris today. For a more indepth coverage on selected schools consult http://www.paris-anglo.com/studying.

### Accents of America
9, rue Casimir Delavigne
75006 PARIS
Tel: 01 44 07 05 05
Fax: 01 40 51 74 72
Contact: Mme Sylvie SERIS

### Accord
52, rue Montmartre
75002 PARIS
Tel: 01 42 36 24 95
Fax: 01 42 21 17 91

### Alliance Française
101, Bd Raspail
75006 PARIS
Tel: 01 45 44 38 28
Fax: 01 45 44 89 42
Email: info@paris.alliancefrancaise.fr
Web site:
http://www.paris.alliancefrancaise.fr
Contact: M. Marc BAILLY

### American Dream Center
163, rue de Charenton
75012 PARIS
Tel: 01 43 42 26 00
Fax: 01 43 42 12 00

### American English School
*Private English lessons*
29, rue au Maire
75003 PARIS
Tel: 01 42 72 83 55
Contact: Mme Kathleen SAINT CLARE

### American Lingo
4 bis, ave du Pavillon Sully
78230 LE PECQ
Tel: 01 39 73 00 88
Fax: 01 39 73 52 02
Contact: Mme Barbara HANO

### Americours
8, rue des Acacias
75017 PARIS
Tel: 01 45 74 68 29
Fax: 01 45 74 50 70
Contact: Mme Julie WENGER

### Americours
13 bis, ave de la Motte-Picquet
75007 PARIS
Tel: 01 47 05 32 30
Email: perakita@attmail.com
Contact: Mme Ann ARMOUR

### An American in Paris
25, Bd de Sébastopol
75001 PARIS
Tel: 01 40 26 22 90

### BBC Omnivox
8, rue de Berri
75008 PARIS
Tel: 01 45 62 44 24
Fax: 01 42 56 39 85

## Blue Bird

*Learn French with a friendly flexible team, program tailored to individual needs and multicultural program*
24, rue Léon Frot
75011 PARIS
Tel: 01 43 70 63 63
Fax: 01 43 70 63 63
Contact: M. Souad MAATZATE

## British Institute in Paris

11, rue de Constantine
75007 PARIS
Tel: 01 45 55 71 99
Fax: 01 45 50 31 55
Director: M. Christophe CAMPOS

## Business Talk France

134, Bd Haussmann
75008 PARIS
Tel: 01 49 53 91 83
Fax: 01 49 53 91 83
Email: btf@worldnet.fr
Contact: M. M. BALKE

## Business Talk France

10, rue des Ponchettes
Tel: 04 93 80 12 97
06300 NICE
Email: btf@worldnet.fr

## Centre Culturel International

5, rue de Garches
92210 SAINT CLOUD
Tel: 01 46 02 64 33
Tel2: 01 47 71 61 03
Fax: 01 47 71 91 05
Contact: Mme BICKERT

## Centre d'Échanges Internationaux

1, rue Gozlin
75006 PARIS
Tel: 01 40 51 11 71
Director: M. DUFRENNE

## Centre de Langue Tomatis

*Languages Department*
6, place de la République Dominicaine
75017 PARIS
Tel: 01 42 12 83 70
Fax: 01 42 12 83 79

## Centre International d'Enseignement de la Langue Française

15, rue d'Hauteville
75010 PARIS
Tel: 01 48 00 06 93
Fax: 01 42 46 92 62

---

Chambre de Commerce et d'Industrie de Paris (C.C.I.P.)

CHAMBRE DE COMMERCE ET D'INDUSTRIE DE PARIS

*Language courses*
2, rue Viarmes
75001 PARIS
Tel: 01 45 08 35 00
Web site: http://www.ccip.fr

---

## Cours de Civilisation Française de la Sorbonne

47, rue des Ecoles
75005 PARIS
Tel: 01 40 46 22 11
Fax: 01 40 46 32 29

## CPFP

25, rue de Trévise
75009 PARIS
Tel: 01 45 23 35 68
Fax: 01 42 46 87 85

## Ecola

111, ave Victor Hugo
75016 PARIS
Tel: 01 45 53 76 97
Fax: 01 47 27 61 87
Email: 101567.1602@compuserve.com
Contacts: M. & Mme HOEHN

## École Nickerson

26, rue de la Tremoille
75008 PARIS
Tel: 01 47 23 36 03
Fax: 01 40 70 12 71
Director: Mme CHILTON

*LIVING & STUDYING*

197

# LANGUAGE SCHOOLS
## ÉCOLES DE LANGUES

### Eiffel (International School of French for Foreigners)
3, rue Crocé-Spinelli
75014 PARIS
Tel: 01 43 20 37 41
Fax: 01 43 20 49 13
Contac: M. JOUET

### Élysées Business International
66, ave des Champs Élysées
75008 PARIS
Tel: 01 46 22 54 83
Fax: 01 46 22 54 11
Director: Mme Monique ORSAT

### Eurocentres
13, passage Dauphine
75006 PARIS
Tel: 01 40 46 72 00
Fax: 01 40 46 72 06
Public Relations:
Mme Elisabeth ALBRECHT

### Executive Language Services
20, rue Sainte Croix de la Bretonnerie
75004 PARIS
Tel: 01 44 54 58 88
Fax: 01 48 04 55 53
Director: Mme Dorothy POLLEY

### Executive Link
16, rue Christophe Colomb
75008 PARIS
Tel: 01 44 43 88 37
Fax: 01 44 43 58 10

### Fondation Postuniversitaire International
11, rue Tiquetonne
75002 PARIS
Tel: 01 40 28 04 03
Fax: 01 40 28 49 22

### Formalangues
87, rue la Boétie
75008 PARIS
Tel: 01 53 93 67 89
Fax: 01 53 93 67 80
Director: M. Philippe MAREC

### France Langue
2, rue de Sfax
75116 PARIS
Tel: 01 45 00 40 15
Fax: 01 45 00 53 41
Web site: http://www.france-langue.fr
Director: M. Bertrand PIOT

### Franco-British Chamber of Commerce
41, rue de Turenne
75003 PARIS
Tel: 01 44 59 25 10
Fax: 01 44 59 25 15

### George V Langues
7, rue Marbeuf
75008 PARIS
Tel: 01 47 20 81 25
Fax: 01 40 70 02 30
Email: dchirst@msn.com
Contact: Mme. Mireille CORDELIER

### Groupe IPESUP
16, rue du Cloître Notre Dame
75004 PARIS
Tel: 01 43 25 63 30

### I.E.L.P.
95, Bd Sébastopol
75002 PARIS
Tel: 01 42 33 35 84
Fax: 01 42 21 04 66
Contact: Mme Austin GWENAËLLE

### Idefle
66, rue René Boulanger
75010 PARIS
Tel: 01 42 03 00 25
Fax: 01 42 03 27 40

### Inca Languages
17, rue de Turbigo
75002 PARIS
Tel: 01 40 26 35 32
Fax: 01 40 26 35 03
Email: 71001.674@compuserve.com
Director: M. Richard NEEL

### Inlingua Rive Gauche
109, rue de l'Université
75007 PARIS
Tel: 01 45 51 46 60
Fax: 01 47 05 66 05

## Institut Catholique De Paris (I.L.C.F.)

12, rue Cassette
75270 PARIS Cedex
Tel: 01 44 39 52 68
Fax: 01 44 39 52 09
Email: ilcf@icp.fr
Director: M. Alex CORMANSKI

## Institut de Langue Française

3, ave Bertie Albrecht
75008 PARIS
Tel: 01 45 63 24 00
Fax: 01 45 63 07 09
Director: M. Alain BOIS

## Institut Parisien de Langue et de Civilisation Françaises

*A wide variety of high quality French courses for international students of all ages. Noted for its flexible hours of courses and dates ranging from one week to a year*

87, Bd de Grenelle
75015 PARIS
Tel: 01 40 56 09 53
Fax: 01 43 06 46 30
Email:
institut.parisien@dial.oleane.com
Director:
Mme Marie-Christine SIMON
Contact: Mme BLOSTIN

## Institute of Applied Languages

41, rue de Turenne
75003 PARIS
Tel: 01 44 59 25 12
Fax: 01 44 59 25 15
Email: ial@calva.net
Manager: Mme Claire OLDMEADOW

## Inter Cambio

15, ave de Ségur
75007 PARIS
Tel: 01 40 62 68 30
Fax: 01 40 62 68 21
Director: Mme BERQUO

## Konversando

*Conversation in different languages*
Tel: 01 47 70 21 64

## L'Étoile

*Établissement Libre d'Enseignement Supérieur*
38, Bd Raspail
75007 PARIS
Tel: 01 45 48 00 05
Fax: 01 45 48 62 05
Director: Mme Rosine GILLARD-SIRE

## La Ferme

*The residential school of French for adults on the sunny south Atlantic coast since 1978!*
La Petite Eguille
17600 SAUJON
Tel: 05 46 22 84 31
Fax: 05 46 22 91 38
Email: fer@filnet.fr
Web site:
http://www.edunet.com/laferme
Director:
Mme Mireille RICHARDSON

## Language of International Insurance Institute

3, rue de l'Arrivée
BP 74
75749 PARIS Cedex 15
Tel: 01 43 21 20 23
Fax: 01 43 35 21 20
Partner: Mme Ann P. LEEDS

*LIVING & STUDYING*

199

# LANGUAGE SCHOOLS
## ÉCOLES DE LANGUES

## Language Studies International
350, rue Saint Honoré
75001 PARIS
Tel: 01 42 60 53 70
Fax: 01 42 61 41 36
Director: Mme Christine VILLANOUX

## Langue Onze
15, rue Gambey
75011 PARIS
Tel: 01 43 38 22 87
Fax: 01 43 48 36 01
Director: Mme CLAUDIA

## Langues Plus
15, rue d'Hauteville
75010 PARIS
Tel: 01 48 00 06 93
Fax: 01 42 46 92 62

## Lingua Club/Euro-Irish Summer School
7 bis, rue Decrès
75014 PARIS
Tel: 01 45 39 28 28
Fax: 01 45 39 15 38
Director: Mrs Nadine BARBER

## McCann, Patrick
62, ave de Wagram
75017 PARIS
Tel: 01 47 63 09 21
Fax: 01 47 63 09 18
Email: 106141.3103@compuserve.com

## Metropolitan Languages
151, rue Billancourt
92100 BOULOGNE BILLANCOURT
Tel: 01 46 04 57 32
Fax: 01 46 04 57 12
Contact: Mme Violette HUMBERT

## Nanterre English Language Center
38, rue Salvador Allende
92000 NANTERRE
Tel: 01 41 37 06 89

## New Directions for Teaching and Learning
21, rue Manin
75019 PARIS
Tel: 01 42 01 08 97
Director: Mme Béatrice SOSS

## Paris École des Roches Langues
8, rue Spinoza
75011 PARIS
Tel: 01 47 00 99 98
Fax: 01 43 57 14 46

## Paris Langues
30, rue Cabanis
75014 PARIS
Tel: 01 45 65 05 28
Fax: 01 45 81 26 28

## Promolangue International
8, rue Blanche
75009 PARIS
Tel: 01 42 85 19 45
Fax: 01 45 26 39 68

## Quai d'Orsay Language Center
67, quai d'Orsay
75007 PARIS
Tel: 01 44 11 10 50
Fax: 01 45 51 87 14
Director: Mme Barbara CURTIN

## Ressources Humaines Formation (RHF)
152 bis, ave Gabriel Péri
93400 SAINT OUEN
Tel: 01 49 18 55 55
Fax: 01 40 12 02 84
Contact: Mme Aline REILLY

## Télélangue Systèmes
65 bis, rue du Rocher
75008 PARIS
Tel: 01 64 46 05 77
Tel2: 06 07 34 95 41
Fax: 01 69 28 06 15
Contact: M. Joseph SCHOCK

The American University
of Paris
(Continuing Education)
102, rue Saint Dominique
75007 PARIS
Tel: 01 47 20 44 99
Fax: 01 47 20 45 64
Email: 104076,705@compuserve.com
Web site: http://www.aup.fr

Transfer
20, rue Godot de Moroy
75009 PARIS
Tel: 01 42 66 14 11
Fax: 01 42 66 31 89
Manager: Mme Isabelle COURT

USA Language Services
75, rue Claude Decaen
75012 PARIS
Tel: 01 43 47 30 42
Director: M. Shams SYED

# LAWYERS/LAW FIRMS
## CABINETS D'AVOCATS

See Doing Business/Working: Lawyers/Law Firms

LIVING & STUDYING

# LIBRARIES
## BIBLIOTHÉQUES

The role of books in Paris goes without saying. But doing research in English requires a relationship with a library. Here are your main choices.

## American Library in Paris

90,000 books, 450 periodicals, computerized periodicals research center, author evenings, children's story hours
10, rue du Général Camou
75007 PARIS
Tel: 01 53 59 12 60
Fax: 01 45 50 25 83
Minitel: 3611 AMERICAN LIBRARY
Email:
100142.1066@compuserve.com
Web site: http://ourworld.
compuserve.com/homepages/alp/
Director: Mme Kay RADER

## American University of Paris Library

9 bis, rue Montessuy
75007 PARIS
Fax: 01 45 56 92 89

## Benjamin Franklin Documentation Center

*9000 volumes in English, by appointment only*
US Consulate
2, rue Saint Florentin
75042 PARIS Cedex 08
Tel: 01 42 96 33 10

## Bibliothèque Nationale (B.N.)

*One of the world's most important and complete collections of books, periodicals, manuscripts and archives*
58, rue de Richelieu
75002 PARIS
Tel: 01 47 03 81 26

## Bibliothèque Nationale de France (BNF)

*Newly opened national library*
11, quai François Mauriac
75013 PARIS
Tel: 01 53 79 59 59
Fax: 01 53 79 43 70

## Bibliothèque Sainte Geneviève

*Public interuniversity and encyclopaedic library*
10, place du Panthéon
75005 PARIS
Tel: 01 44 41 97 97
Fax: 01 44 41 97 96

## Bibliothèques et Discothèques de la Ville de Paris

*Main branch of the City of Paris' municipal public libraries*
31, rue des Francs-Bourgeois
75004 PARIS
Tel: 01 42 76 67 75
Fax: 01 42 76 65 33

## British Council Library

9-11, rue de Constantine
75007 PARIS
Tel: 01 49 55 73 00
Fax: 01 47 05 77 02
Minitel: 3615 BRITISH
Head Librarian: Mme Frances SALINIE

# LIBRAIRES
## BIBLIOTHÉQUES

Cité Internationale
Universitaire de Paris -
Library
19, Bd Jourdan
75014 PARIS
Tel: 01 44 16 65 20
Fax: 01 44 16 64 11

English Language Library for
the Blind
*Books on tape in English*
35, rue Lemercier
75017 PARIS
Tel: 01 42 93 47 57
Director: Mme Penelope TROUPE

La Documentation Française
29, quai Voltaire
75007 PARIS
Tel: 01 40 15 70 00
Fax: 01 40 15 72 30

Vidéothèque de Paris
*Video library with more than 4000
films on Paris*
Forum des Halles
2, Grande Galerie
75001 PARIS
Tel: 01 44 76 62 00

# MINITEL DIRECTORY
## SERVEURS MINITEL

PARIS-ANGLOPHONE has grouped here a selection of Minitel services related to living and studying in Paris. For other Minitel services see the Travel & Tourism or Doing Business & Working sections.

### 3614 BBC
*British and international news in English by the BBC*

### 3614 DOC USA
*Benjamin Franklin Documentation Center, US Embassy*

### 3614 PARIS
*Activities taking place in Paris*

### 3615 ACTIONCV
*Information on how to find a job: offers and requests, free classified ads*

### 3615 AMEX
*American Express services and products*

### 3615 ARTS
*One year of detailed listings of cultural events all over France*

### 3615 ATTICA
*Catalogs of teaching manuals & videos available from the Attica bookstore*

### 3615 BASKETUSA
*Information about US basketball: games, results (NBA, NCAA)*

### 3615 BBCVIDEO
*Presents video English teaching methods*

### 3615 BOX OFFICE
*Tickets for shows in Europe and in New York*

### 3615 CAPITAL
*Economical & financial information*

### 3615 CENTURY21
*Century 21 real estate agency network in France*

### 3615 CINEMA
*Cinema news: current shoots, casting calls, reviews*

### 3615 ELECTRE
*Provides information on books and publishers*

### 3615 FNAC
*Ticket booking service for concerts, theater, and opera*

### 3615 INFOPARIS
*Entertainment and home delivery services in and around Paris*

### 3615 INTERNET
*International English-speaking electronic mail network*

### 3615 JAP
*Information on French studies*

### 3615 LETUDIANT
*Service aimed at the student community (accommodation, studies, exams, jobs, courses...)*

### 3615 MINIKID
*Baby sitting service*

### 3615 NEWS
*Comprehensive coverage of French and international news: politics, weather reports, Stock Exchange, strikes*

### 3615 PARIS
*Information and services concerning the French capital*

### 3615 PARISCOPE
*Weekly guide to entertainment and cultural events in the Paris region (comes out on Wednesday)*

### 3615 PARTYLINE
*Information about night clubs and private parties in Paris*

### 3615 ROCKINFO
*Information on rock music performances all over France: concerts, festivals*

### 3615 VIRGIN
*Ticket booking service for concerts, theater, and opera, or call:*
*01 44 68 44 08*

### 3616 ALTERN
*Access to the international Internet network*

### 3617 FAX
*Send faxes & emails by Minitel*

### 3617 FOR SALE
*Real estate*

### 3617 TO LET
*Real estate to rent*

### 3619 USA1
*English-speaking access to the North American videotex network*

# MOVING
## DÉMÉNAGEURS

Have a trunk of books to ship back to San Francisco? Ready to move your family to France? Need to get your household belongings from Paris to Nice? PARIS-ANGLOPHONE offers a host of handy solutions.

## SHIPPING
### Agents maritimes

## See Doing Business & Working

## MOVERS
### Déménageurs

### Access
*Self-storage, self-stockage*
221, Bd Macdonald
75019 PARIS
Tel: 01 44 65 88 88
Fax: 01 44 65 88 87
Marketing Director: M. COURCELLE

### Access
73, rue Noël Pons
92000 NANTERRE
Tel: 01 46 49 32 32
Fax: 01 47 82 45 59

### AGS
9-11, Bd Galliéni
92230 GENNEVILLIERS
Tel: 01 40 80 20 20
Tel2: 01 40 80 20 22

### Allied / Arthur Pierre

*The Professional Movers*

*Worldwide network of professional movers. (See advertisement)*
ZI du Petit Parc
78920 ECQUEVILLY
Tel: 01 34 75 92 92
Fax: 01 34 75 92 87
Email: arthur.p.@wanadoo.fr
Web site:
http://www.paris-anglo.com
Director: M. Ludovic DELAEY
Commercial Dir: M. TRAULLE

### Allship "Home without a Hitch"
*Also car shippers*
62, rue Saint Lazare
75009 PARIS
Tel: 01 48 74 60 70

### American Worldwide Movers
201, ave Jean Lolive
Bâtiment F
93500 PANTIN
Tel: 01 48 46 00 72
Fax: 01 48 43 97 32

### Delahaye Moving
ZI des Amandiers
165, rue de Bezons
78420 CARRIERES SUR SEINE
Tel: 01 39 13 46 82
Fax: 01 39 13 48 55
General Manager: Mme DELAHAYE

# MOVING
### DÉMÉNAGEURS

## Desbordes International

14, rue de la Véga
75012 PARIS
Tel: 01 44 73 84 84
Fax: 01 43 42 51 48
President: M. PIRIOU

## Ecotrans

*Removals, errands 7 days a week*
33, rue du Professeur Calmette
94400 VITRY SUR SEINE
Tel: 01 46 70 76 36
Fax: 01 49 60 60 29
Contact: Mme SASSI

## European Cedars Service

38, rue de Berri
75008 PARIS
Tel: 01 47 74 59 83
Fax: 01 45 06 51 11
Contact: M. Joseph BECHARA

## France Transport Express

34, rue du Puisard
92230 GENNEVILLIERS
Tel: 06 07 94 36 54
Contact:
Mme Laurence DESMORTREIX

## Global Silverhawk

Tour Litwin
10, rue Jean Jaurès
92800 PUTEAUX Cedex
Tel: 01 41 97 09 09
Fax: 01 47 76 35 90

## Grospiron International

15, rue Danielle Casanova
93300 AUBERVILLIERS
Tel: 01 48 11 71 71
Fax: 01 48 11 71 70
President: M. Jean-Luc HADDAD

## Homeship ASM Transeuropean

*International transport/removal/shipping*
BP 360
93616 AULNAY SOUS BOIS Cedex
Tel: 01 48 65 21 61
Fax: 01 48 65 29 59
Director: M. André BERGER

## Interdean

515, rue Hélène Boucher
ZI
78530 BUC
Tel: 01 39 20 14 00
Fax: 01 39 56 30 28
Manager: M. Ara KORKIDIAN

## Mory Worldwide Moving

53, rue du Port
92000 NANTERRE
Tel: 01 47 24 14 14
Fax: 01 47 24 14 15

## Neer Service Déménagements

2, rue Désiré Lemoine
93300 AUBERVILLIERS
Tel: 01 48 35 47 00
Fax: 01 48 35 47 01
Email: paulin@neerservice.fr
Contact: M. PAULIN

## T.L.R. Claude ROSIER

# T . L . R

BP 33
93101 MONTREUIL SOUS BOIS
Cedex
Tel: 01 42 87 08 95
Fax: 01 48 57 63 67
Contact: Mme Agnès GUILLOU

## Trans Euro Worldwide Movers

22, rue du Gros Murger
BP 210
95614 CERGY PONTOISE Cedex
Tel: 01 34 48 97 97
Fax: 01 34 48 93 22

## Transpaq International

116 bis, ave des Champs Élysées
75008 PARIS
Tel: 01 45 63 43 00
Fax: 01 45 63 03 42
Contact: M. DEBBAS

## Ulysse

25, ave Gabriel Péri
95870 BEZONS
Tel: 01 39 47 89 89

## United Professional Movers

Chemin des Chaudronniers
94310 ORLY
Tel: 01 48 92 34 15
Fax: 01 48 53 96 66
Fax2: 01 48 53 04 34
Director: Mme BOURDON

*LIVING & STUDYING*

209

# ORGANIZATIONS/CLUBS
## ASSOCIATIONS/CLUBS

The Americans, Canadians, English, Scottish, Irish, Australians, Welsch, New Zealanders, South Africans, Indians, Franco-American and other anglophone communities in Paris each have created service and cultural organizations catering to the specific needs of their constituencies. For everything from friendship to taxes, you'll find the group you'll want to belong to. Remember that in France the non-profit organization is called an *Association Loi 1901.*

### Accueil d'Irlande
18, rue Neuve des Boulets
75011 PARIS
Tel: 01 43 48 08 60
Fax: 01 43 48 08 36

### Africa Regional Services
USIS
2, rue Saint Florentin
75001 PARIS
Tel: 01 43 12 46 90
Director:
Mme Yolande VERON-SULLIVAN

### African Development
86, rue Ranelagh
75016 PARIS
Tel: 01 42 24 59 62
Fax: 01 40 50 03 87

### American Battle Monuments Commission
*Upkeeps WWI and WWII cemeteries in Europe*
68, rue du 19 Janvier
92380 GARCHES
Tel: 01 47 01 19 76
Fax: 01 47 41 19 79
Director: Colonel Merlin PUGH

### American Car Club de France
15, Fontaine du Perlan
78920 ECQUEVILLY
Tel: 01 34 75 57 79
Fax: 01 34 75 50 69
Contact: M. Jean-Claude PETITPRE

### American Catholic Women's Group
St. Joseph's Church
50, ave Hoche
75008 PARIS
Tel: 01 42 27 28 56
Contact: Mme Anita MALLICK

### American Club
The Mona Bismarck Foundation
34, ave de New York
75016 PARIS
Tel: 01 47 23 64 36
Fax: 01 47 23 66 01

### American Friends of Blérancourt
*Promotion and renovation of the French National Museum of Franco-American Cooperation at Blérancourt*
The Mona Bismarck Foundation
34, ave de New York
75016 PARIS
Tel: 01 47 23 38 88
Fax: 01 42 61 11 18
President: M. Russel PORTER

### American Overseas Memorial Day Association
34, ave de New York
75016 PARIS
Tel: 01 42 61 55 77

### American Women's Group in Paris
22 bis, rue Pétrarque
75116 PARIS
Tel: 01 47 55 87 50
Fax: 01 47 55 87 51
Contact: Mme ROCHARD

## Americans Against the Death Penalty

24, rue des Carmes
BP 88
75005 PARIS
Tel: 01 69 28 66 30
Email: linda-aadp@calva.net
President: Mme Linda LUCASEY

## Amherst College Alumni Association

c/o Hughes Hubbard & Reed
47, ave George Mandel
75116 PARIS
Tel: 01 44 05 80 00
Fax: 01 45 53 15 04
Contact: M. Axel BAUM

## Amis du Jardin Shakespeare du Pré Catelan

1, place de Wagram
75017 PARIS
Tel: 01 42 27 39 54
Chairman: M. L. HEMPHILL

## Amnesty International

4, rue de la Pierre Levée
75011 PARIS
Tel: 01 49 23 11 11
Fax: 01 43 38 26 15
Minitel: 3615 AMNESTY

## Anglo-American Business and Culture Center

20, rue Godot de Mauroy
75009 PARIS
Tel: 01 42 66 14 11
Fax: 01 42 66 31 89

## Anglophones in Aquitaine

*Social club of Anglophones in south-west France*
Chemin de Petit
64160 BUROS
Tel: 05 59 30 47 68
Fax: 05 59 30 47 68
Email: marc.artzrouni@univ-pau.fr
Contact: M. Marc ARTZROUNI

## Art Musique Échange

*Concerts and cultural events in private homes to foster greater Franco-American understanding*
17, rue Maître Albert
75005 PARIS
Tel: 01 43 29 65 91
Contact: Mme Linda DE NAZELLE

## Association Franco-Ecossaise

5, rue de l'Alboni
75016 PARIS
Tel: 01 42 22 30 78
President: M. Georges DICKSON

## Association Frank

*Publishes the literary journal Frank*
32, rue Édouard Vaillant
93100 MONTREUIL SOUS BOIS
Tel: 01 48 59 66 58
Fax: 01 48 59 66 68
Email: david@paris-anglo.com
Web site: http://www.paris-anglo.com/frank
Director: M. David APPLEFIELD

## Association Linguistique et Culturelle Franco-Britannique

5, place de l'Etape
78200 MANTES LA JOLIE
Tel: 01 30 92 72 00
Fax: 01 30 92 35 28

## Association of American Wives of Europeans (AAWE)

*Activities for members and their children, publishes AAWE Guide to Education for 35 years*
BP 127
92154 SURESNES Cedex
Tel: 01 47 28 46 39
Contact: Hollie

## Association of Americans Resident Overseas (AARO)

BP 127
92154 SURESNES Cedex
Tel: 01 42 04 09 38
Fax: 01 42 04 09 12
Email: aaro@aol.com
Web site: http://members.aol.com/aaroparis/aarohome.htm
President: M. Gregory GOOD

*LIVING & STUDYING*

211

## Association of Irish Women in France (AIWF)

*Promoting social and cultural contacts and providing friendly and professional help to Irish women in France*

24, rue de Grenelle
75007 PARIS
Tel: 01 42 22 51 08
Fax: 01 42 22 51 08
President: Mme Patricia BLACK

## Australian University Center

32, rue Saint Marc
75002 PARIS
Tel: 01 42 60 14 15

## B'nai Brith Youth Organization

5 bis, rue de Rochechouart
75009 PARIS
Fax: 01 40 82 95 75

## Blue Note Studio

*Organizes shows combining poetry, dance, music, mime and theater*

19, ave de Saint Cloud
78000 VERSAILLES
Tel: 01 39 50 27 46
Artistic Director: Mme Denise REVE

## Boy Scouts of America

Embassy of the United States
2, ave Gabriel
75382 PARIS Cedex 8
Tel: 01 43 12 20 55
Contact: M. Don TERRY

## British & Commonwealth Women's Association (BCWA)

8, rue de Belloy
75116 PARIS
Tel: 01 47 20 50 91
President: Mme Ann PERRY

## British Diplomatic Spouses Association

British Embassy
35, rue du Fbg Saint Honoré
75008 PARIS
Tel: 01 44 51 31 00
Contact: M. Arthur PLAXY

## British Legion

8, rue Boudreau
75009 PARIS
Tel: 01 47 42 19 26

## Canadian Women's Association

*Social & cultural association of Canadian women and handicapped adults*

5, rue de Constantine
75007 PARIS
Tel: 01 44 05 01 66
President: Mme Nadine SAMMON

## Centrale Franco-Britannique

19, rue Saulnier
75009 PARIS
Tel: 01 48 01 25 77
Fax: 01 48 01 25 90

## Children's Academy on Tour

*A children's organization for cultural awareness*

66, ave des Champs Élysées n° 74
75008 PARIS
Tel: 01 44 95 14 31
Fax: 01 42 89 87 37
Contact: Mme Sabrina SCOTT

## Club des Poètes

30, rue de Bourgogne
75007 PARIS
Tel: 01 47 05 06 03
Fax: 01 45 55 75 79
Minitel: 36 15 CLP
Email: poesie@micronet.fr
Web site: http://www.franceweb.fr/poésie
Contact: M. ROSNAY

## Columbia Business Club France France-Amérique

*Columbia University Business School Alumni Association*

c/o OCMI
10, rue Chardin
75016 PARIS
Tel: 01 42 24 62 62
Fax: 01 45 20 70 06

## Comité La Fayette

*Franco-American association twin-*
*ned with the Lafayette Memorial and*
*the Lafayette Society in Boston*
177, rue de Lourmel
75015 PARIS
President:
Comte de PUSY LA FAYETTE

## Commission Franco-Américaine d'Echanges Universitaires

*Exchange to US university programs*
9, rue Chardin
75016 PARIS
Tel: 01 45 20 46 54
Fax: 01 42 88 04 79

## Community Liaison Office

Embassy of the United States
2, ave Gabriel
75008 PARIS
Tel: 01 43 12 22 15
Contact: Mme Suellen VITTITOW

## Community Liaison Office

Australian Embassy
4, rue Jean Rey
75015 PARIS
Tel: 01 40 59 35 61
Fax: 01 40 59 33 10

## Community Liaison Office

British Embassy
35, rue du Fbg Saint Honoré
75383 PARIS Cedex 08
Tel: 01 44 51 31 00

## Contact B

*Helps young people to find jobs*
c/o Terrell
10, rue Rodier
75009 PARIS
Tel: 01 45 26 81 34
Contact: Mme Bridget TERRELL

## Cornell Club of France

*Meetings among alumni and with*
*alumni of other schools*
85, rue de Courcelles
75017 PARIS
Tel: 01 42 67 14 89
Fax: 01 42 67 06 08
E-mail: 100451.3613@compuserve.com
President: M. Richard MEADE

## Culture Crossings Ltd

*Cultural adaptation seminars for*
*foreign executives and their spouses*
51, rue de Bellechasse
75007 PARIS
Tel: 01 45 56 04 62
Fax: 01 45 55 91 86
Email: platt@club-internet.fr
Director: Mme Polly PLATT

## Daughters of the American Revolution

c/o Mme Alain MAITROT
118, ave Félix Faure
75015 PARIS
Tel: 01 45 54 64 19
President: Mme MAITROT

## Democrats Abroad

16, rue Vieille du Temple
75004 PARIS
Tel: 01 48 04 51 75
Fax: 01 48 04 51 17
Contact: M. Allin SEWARD

## Domino's News - Conviviality Cocktails

*Outings and fun activities for*
*dynamic epicurean singles*
8, rue Duvergier
75019 PARIS
Tel: 01 42 05 95 47
President: M. Dominique DUPRE

## Duke University Club

5, rue Bargue
75015 PARIS
Fax: 01 45 66 49 05
Contact: M. Joseph SMALLHOOVER

## Échange France-Amérique du Nord-Australie (EFANA)

*Exchanges between French and*
*American Senior High Schools*
20, rue Louis David
75116 PARIS
Tel: 01 45 03 12 77
Fax: 01 40 72 62 49
Email: 100536,2241@compuserve.com
Contact: Mme. Monique CARLIER

## Educational Foundation for Foreign Study (EFFS)

4, rue Duphot
75001 PARIS
Tel: 01 42 86 81 94
Fax: 01 42 61 75 44

## English Juniors' Club

*English & computer courses for children aged 3 to 12*

3, rue Faustin Hélie
75116 PARIS
Tel: 01 42 03 66 87
Contact: Mme Monique IFERGAN

## English Speaking Union France

*Promoting understanding and friendship worldwide*

21, rue Michel Ange
75016 PARIS
Tel: 01 46 51 55 24
Fax: 01 46 51 55 24
President: Mme Beatrix
DE MONTGERMONT-KEIL

## Fondation Franco-Américaine

*Awards, scholarships and grants*

54, Bd Raspail
75006 PARIS
Tel: 01 49 54 22 07
Fax: 01 49 54 21 61

## Fondation Soros (Paris)

38, Bd Beaumarchais
75011 PARIS
Tel: 01 48 05 24 74
Fax: 01 40 21 65 41
Email: sorosparis@gn.apc.org
Contact: Mme Annette LABOREY

## Foundation Azazel

11300 PAULIGNE
Fax: 04 68 31 88 01
Email: Azazel@world-net.sct.fr
Contact: Mme Kate PARRIOH

## France Louisiane-Franco Américaine

28, Bd de Strasbourg
75010 PARIS
Tel: 01 42 40 68 78
Fax: 01 42 40 68 80

## France-Amérique

9, ave Franklin Roosevelt
75008 PARIS
Tel: 01 43 59 51 00
Fax: 01 40 75 00 97
President: M. André ROSS

## France-Canada

5, rue de Constantine
75007 PARIS
Tel: 01 45 55 83 65

## France-États-Unis

6, Bd de Grenelle
75015 PARIS
Tel: 01 45 77 48 92
President: M. Jacques MAISONROUGE

## France-Québec

24, rue Modigliani
75015 PARIS
Tel: 01 45 54 35 37
Fax: 01 45 57 69 44
President: M. Georges POIRIER

## Franco-American Community Center

*Newcomer orientation series in October (Bloom Where You're Planted)*

Women of the American Church
65, quai d'Orsay
75007 PARIS
Tel: 01 40 62 05 00
Fax: 01 40 62 05 11

## French-American Center

*An educational and cultural center in the South of France*

10, montée de la Tour
30400 VILLENEUVE LÈS AVIGNON
Tel: 04 90 25 93 23
Fax: 04 90 25 93 24
Director: M. Jerôme Henry RUDES

## Friends of Vieilles Maisons Françaises

91, rue du Fbg Saint Honoré
75370 PARIS Cedex 08
Tel: 01 42 66 00 12
Fax: 01 49 24 95 99
Contact: Mme Suzanne ESTABLIE

## Georgetown University Club

24 bis, rue Greuze
75016 PARIS
Tel: 01 47 27 48 43

## Groupe d'Amitié France - Etats Unis

126, rue de l'Université
75007 PARIS
Tel: 01 40 63 86 26
Fax: 01 40 63 86 80
Intl Affairs Director:
Mme GIBEL-DEBURGE

## Groupe d'Amitié France- Etats Unis du Sénat

*Maintains relations with U.S. Senate and House of Representatives*

Palais du Luxembourg
75291 PARIS Cedex 06
Tel: 01 42 34 27 73
Fax: 01 42 34 21 69
Contact: M. Pierre DE FLEURIEU

## Harvard Business School Club of France

9, ave Franklin Roosevelt
75008 PARIS
Tel: 01 42 56 20 98
Fax: 01 45 62 39 08

## Indian Women's Association

11, rue Sainte Anne
75001 PARIS
Tel: 01 47 49 28 25
President: Mme Iyer RUGMINI

## Interalliée Club

33, rue du Fbg Saint Honoré
75008 PARIS
Tel: 01 42 65 96 00

## International Council of Scientific Unions

51, Bd Montmorency
75008 PARIS
Tel: 01 45 25 03 29
Fax: 01 42 88 94 31

## International League for the Protection of Horses

3, rue de Lyon
75012 PARIS
Tel: 01 44 67 95 76
Fax: 01 44 67 00 57

## International Student & Au Pair Bureau

38, rue Daumesnil
75012 PARIS
Tel: 01 43 46 04 67

## International Welcome to Paris

*Helps anglophones feel at home in Paris*

119, rue de Longchamp
BP 232
92205 NEUILLY SUR SEINE Cedex
Tel: 01 47 22 77 55
Tel2: 01 47 47 40 45
Fax: 01 47 22 31 60
Fax2: 01 47 22 45 02
Directors: Mmes F. DE CREMIERS & D. MUELINE

## Jamaican Group

19, rue du Docteur Blanche
75016 PARIS
Tel: 01 42 88 85 37
Contact: Mme Paula THOMAS

## Junior Service League of Paris

*Aiming to improve the community through trained volunteers in areas such as health, the arts and child welfare*

34, ave de New York
75016 PARIS
Tel: 01 45 77 09 78
President: Mme Caroline ROBERT

## L'Europe des Arts

75, rue du Fbg Saint Honoré
75008 PARIS
Tel: 01 47 42 27 79
Fax: 01 47 42 55 48
President: Mme Janet GREENBERG

## La Leche League France

*Information and advice on breastfeeding*

BP 18
78620 L'ÉTANG LA VILLE
Tel: 01 39 58 45 84
Fax: 01 48 94 70 97
Contact: Mme DIDIERJEAN

*LIVING & STUDYING*

215

## Le Régine's Club

Rue de Ponthieu
75008 PARIS
Tel: 01 43 59 21 13
Fax: 01 42 89 35 06

## Lions Club International

295, rue Saint Jacques
75005 PARIS
Tel: 01 46 34 14 10
Fax: 01 46 33 92 41

## Maxim's Business Club

5, rue Royale
75008 PARIS
Tel: 01 42 65 34 41
Fax: 01 40 07 00 46

## MIT Club of France

8, rue Dupleix
75015 PARIS
Tel: 01 40 56 03 23
President: M. David ZNATY

## Mustang Club de France

8, ave des Hameaux
91130 RIS ORANGIS
Tel: 01 69 06 32 58
President: M. C. VESNAT

## Notre Dame Club of France

*Alumni club of University of Notre Dame*

7, ave des Ternes
75017 PARIS
Tel: 01 44 09 02 03
Fax: 01 44 09 02 03
Director:
M. Stéphane RONSIN-EDWARDS

## PAN The Paris Alumnae/i Network

*Professional and social network of graduates of US colleges and universities*

Rotating address
Tel: 01 43 28 63 40
Email: 101506.41@compuserve.com
President:
Mme Julia MAKRIS-FRENCIA

## Paris American AIDS Committee

Tel: 01 42 27 45 75
Fax: 01 42 27 45 75

## Paris Welsh Society

10, rue de l'Armée d'Orient
75018 PARIS
Tel: 01 46 06 76 13
President: M. Boyd WILLIAMS

## Paris Writers' Workshop

WICE
20, Bd Montparnasse
75015 PARIS
Tel: 01 45 66 75 50
Fax: 01 40 65 96 53

## Péril - Europe

*Solves problems of language hegemony*

4, rue de la Monnaie
30400 VILLENEUVE LES AVIGNON
Tel: 04 90 25 43 77
Contact: M. Alexandre ROUSSET

## Point de Vue Canada

5, rue Pecquay
75004 PARIS
Tel: 01 40 27 91 36
Fax: 01 42 77 76 69
Director: Mme Lynda CADIEUX

## Princeton Paris Research Corporation

7 bis, rue Edmond Valentin
75007 PARIS
Tel: 01 45 55 96 96

## Reid Hall Film Committee

4, rue de Chevreuse
75006 PARIS
Tel: 01 43 20 64 65

## Republicans Abroad (France)

c/o Mme Habourdin
87, ave Mozart
75016 PARIS
Tel: 01 42 88 77 78
President: Mme Phyllis MORGAN

## Retired Officers' Association

The Mona Bismarck Foundation
34, ave de New York
75016 PARIS
Tel: 01 47 23 38 88

## Rotary Club of Paris

40, Bd Emile Augier
75116 PARIS
Tel: 01 45 04 14 44
Fax: 01 45 04 93 98

## Société des Cincinnati de France

2 bis, rue Rabelais
75008 PARIS
Tel: 01 45 61 45 40
Fax: 01 45 61 45 40

## Sons of the American Revolution

52, ave des Champs Élysées
75008 PARIS
Tel: 01 43 59 10 31
Fax: 01 45 62 59 02
President: M. Helie DE NOAILLES

## The Mona Bismarck Foundation

*Promotes French-American culture and art*
34, ave de New York
75016 PARIS
Tel: 01 47 23 38 88
Fax: 01 42 86 94 07
Director: Mme DUNHAM

## The Travellers Club

25, ave des Champs Élysées
75008 PARIS
Tel: 01 43 59 75 00
Fax: 01 45 62 95 16

## Tips on Trips and Camps

*Summer camps and youth travel*
Conseils Loisirs Culturels USA
15, rue Georges Lafenestre
92340 BOURG LA REINE
Tel: 01 46 83 04 66
Fax: 01 46 83 04 66
Email: anteby@club-internet.fr
Contact: Mme Suzanne ANTEBY

## TOC'H Association

*Charity association for English-speaking senior citizens*
14, ave de Joinville
94130 NOGENT SUR MARNE
Tel: 01 48 73 48 37
Contact: Mme Doris LECK

## Trinity College Dublin Association France

22, rue de Navarin
75009 PARIS
Tel: 01 48 74 09 71
Fax: 01 30 53 26 21
Hon. Secretary: Mme Denise PHELAN

## UC Berkeley Alumni Club

Tel: 01 47 55 74 12
Tel: 01 43 54 55 71
Email: tholter@vantive.com
Contacts: Mmes Tamelyn HOLTER & Elena JEUNG

## Union Chrétienne de Jeunes Filles (YWCA)

*Residential foyers for young women (18-24)*
22, rue de Naples
75008 PARIS
Tel: 01 45 22 23 49
Fax: 01 42 94 81 24
Directors: Mme Anne-Marie BONEU

## United Service Organization Inc.

20, rue de la Tremoille
75008 PARIS
Tel: 01 40 70 99 68
Fax: 01 40 70 99 53
Director: Mme Beverley CERCHIO

## Volunteers of the American Hospital of Paris

*Services, library for patients, sale of Le Cookbook to aid hospital*
63, Bd Victor Hugo
92200 NEUILLY SUR SEINE
Tel: 01 46 41 25 48
Contact: Mme SCHRIEBER

## Wine Business Club

138, rue du Fbg Saint Honoré
75008 PARIS
Tel: 01 42 89 14 14
Fax: 01 42 89 15 40
President: M. Alain MARTY

## ORGANIZATIONS/CLUBS
### ASSOCIATIONS/CLUBS

### World Federation of Americans Abroad
BP 27
92154 SURESNES
Tel: 01 42 04 05 24
Tel2: 01 42 22 21 36
Fax: 0142 04 09 12
President: M. Gregory GOOD

### World Monuments Fund
The Mona Bismarck Foundation
34, ave de New York
75116 PARIS
Tel: 01 47 20 71 99
Fax: 01 47 20 71 27

### Yale Club of Paris
16, rue Vieille du Temple
75004 PARIS
Tel: 01 48 04 51 75
Fax: 01 48 04 51 17
President: M. Allin SEWARD

### YMCA/UCJG
5, place de Vénétie
75013 PARIS
Tel: 01 45 83 62 63
Fax: 01 45 86 64 92
Secrétaire Général:
M. François SEIDENBINDER

### Youth for Understanding
30, place Saint Georges
75009 PARIS
Tel: 01 45 26 37 38
Fax: 01 45 26 35 25
Contact: Mme Luce MARTEL

# PRESS/MEDIA
## PRESSE/MÉDIA

See Doing Business & Working: Press/Media.

# PUBS/BARS
## PUBS/BARS

See Living & Studying: Wining & Dining/Pubs, Bars.

See also Travel & Tourism: Restaurants/Bars.

*Marianne & André*
*invite you to*

# Chez Marianne

Restaurant
Caterer
*Salon de thé*
Kosher Deli

*The heart & soul*
*of the*
*rue des Rosier*
*in the Marais*

2, rue des Hospitalières Saint
Gervais
75004 Paris
Tel: 01 42 72 18 86

# RELIGION
## RELIGION

Almost all major religions are represented in Paris with English-language services and activities.

## Adath, Shalom

*Jewish conservative congregation*
22 bis, rue des Belles Feuilles
75116 PARIS
Tel: 01 45 53 84 09
Fax: 01 45 53 45 02

## American Cathedral

*Episcopalian and Anglican Pro-Cathedral Church of the Holy Trinity*
23, ave George V
75008 PARIS
Tel: 01 47 20 17 92
Dean: Rev. E. HUNT

## American Church in Paris

*Religious service for all Protestant denominations*
65, quai d'Orsay
75007 PARIS
Tel: 01 47 05 07 99
Fax: 01 45 50 36 96
Pastor: Dr Larry KALAJAINEN
Associate Pastor:
Dr Richard SOMMERS

## Christ Church - Anglican Episcopal Fellowship in Auvergne

*Worship in English in Anglican Episcopal tradition*
Ave du Dr Juan Hietz
63130 ROYAT
Tel: 04 73 38 41 59

## Christian Science Church

36, Bd Saint Jacques
75014 PARIS
Tel: 01 47 07 26 60

## Church of Christ

4, rue Déodat-de-Severac
75017 PARIS
Tel: 01 42 27 50 86

## Church of Jesus Christ of Latterday Saints

23, rue du 11 Novembre
78110 LE VÉSINET
Tel: 01 39 76 68 84
Leader: M. Charles E. JONES

## Consistoire Israélite de Paris

*Synagogue*
17, rue Saint Georges
75009 PARIS
Tel: 01 40 82 26 26

## Emmanuel Baptist Church of Paris

56, rue des Bons Raisins
92500 RUEIL MALMAISON
Tel: 01 47 51 29 63
Fax: 01 47 14 02 31
Pastor: Dr Bill Clark THOMAS

## Great Synagogue

44, rue de la Victoire
75009 PARIS
Tel: 01 45 26 95 36

## Holy Trinity Church (Anglican)

15, ave Camot
78600 MAISONS LAFITTE
Tel: 01 39 62 34 97
Contact: Rev. Ben EATON

## Hope International Church of Paris at Hotel Orion

*Christian workshop and fellowship, service in English Sundays, 9h30*
8, Bd de Neuilly
92800 PARIS LA DEFENSE
Tel: 01 43 33 04 06
Pastor: Rev. Doulas MILLER

## Kehilat Gesher, The French Anglophone Jewish Community

10, rue de Pologne
78100 SAINT GERMAIN EN LAYE
Tel: 01 39 21 97 19
Email: RabbenuTom@compuserve.com
Rabbi: M. Tom COHEN

## La Mosquée

*Moslem mosque*
Place du Puits de l'Ermite
75005 PARIS
Tel: 01 45 35 97 33
Fax: 01 45 35 16 23

## Orthodox Church

*Orthodox Priest*

26, rue de Sartrouville
95240 CORMEILLES EN PARISIS
Tel: 01 39 78 71 54
Priest: M. Andrew PHILLIPS

## Reformed Church of France

47, rue de Clichy
75009 PARIS
Tel: 01 48 74 90 92

## Religious Society of Friends (Quakers)

114 bis, rue de Vaugirard
75006 PARIS
Tel: 01 45 48 74 23

## Saint Mark's Church

*English church offering Christian fellowship & pastoral care*

31, rue du Pont Colbert
78000 VERSAILLES
Tel: 01 39 02 79 45
Fax: 01 39 50 97 29
President Chaplain:
Rev. David MARSHALL

## St. Michael's Anglican Church

*Sunday services in English*

5, rue d'Aguesseau
75008 PARIS
Tel: 01 47 42 70 88
Fax: 01 47 42 70 11
Contact: Rev. Andrew WARBURTON

## St. George's Anglican Church

7, rue Auguste Vacquerie
75116 PARIS
Tel: 01 47 20 22 51
Chaplain: Rev. Martin DRAPER

## St. Joseph's Roman Catholic Church

50, ave Hoche
75008 PARIS
Tel: 01 42 27 28 56
Fax: 01 42 27 86 49
Contact: Fr. Paul Francis SPENCER

## The Scots Kirk - Church of Scotland

*Sunday service*

10, rue Thimmonier
75009 PARIS
Tel: 01 48 78 47 94
Contact: Rev. Bill REID

## Union Libérale Israélite de France

*Services on Fridays at 18h00 and Saturdays at 10h30*

24, rue Copernic
75116 PARIS
Tel: 01 47 04 37 27
Contact: Rabbi Michael WILLIAMS

## Unitarian Universalist Fellowship of Paris

*Monthly services in English*

7, rue Geoffroy l'Angevin
75004 PARIS
Tel: 01 42 77 96 77
Fax: 01 69 41 16 21
Contact: Mme Jenni SPENCER

## Women of the American Church

*Neighborhood coffee meetings*

American Church of Paris
65, quai d'Orsay
75007 PARIS
Tel: 01 47 05 07 99
Tel2: 01 44 19 77 48
Contact: Mme Meribeth WITHROW

*LIVING & STUDYING*

221

# RELOCATION SERVICES
## BIENVENUE EN FRANCE !

See Doing Business & Working:
Relocation Services.

# RESTAURANTS
## RESTAURANTS

See Staying and Studying: Wining & Dining/
Restaurants/American Eateries/Tex-Mex.

See also Travel & Tourism: Restaurants/Bars

## SHOPPING/BOUTIQUES

Recently surveyed tourists gave shopping as their Number One reason for visiting Paris! Shopping is the Number Two activity of permanent residents. Here you'll find a great selection of boutiques, department stores, fashion outlets, jewelry stores, music shops, cosmetics counters, sporting goods, and gift items offered by both anglophones and those who cater to the English-speaking community. PARIS-ANGLOPHONE is ready to hear about and reward you for your great finds.

### DEPARTMENT STORES
Grands magasins

### Bazar de l'Hôtel de Ville (BHV)
52, rue de Rivoli
75004 PARIS
Tel: 01 42 74 90 00
Fax: 01 42 74 96 79

### Galeries Lafayette
40, Bd Haussmann
75009 PARIS
Tel: 01 42 82 34 56
Fax: 01 48 82 30 51

### La Samaritaine
19, rue de la Monnaie
75001 PARIS
Tel: 01 40 41 20 20

### Le Bon Marché Rive Gauche
5, rue de Babylone
75007 PARIS
Tel: 01 44 39 80 00
Fax: 01 44 39 80 50

### Le Printemps
64, Bd Haussmann
75009 PARIS
Tel: 01 42 82 50 00
Fax: 01 42 82 61 22

### Les Trois Quartiers
23,Bd de la Madeleine
75008 PARIS
Tel: 01 42 97 80 12

### Marks & Spencer
35, Bd Haussmann
75009 PARIS
Tel: 01 47 42 42 91
Fax: 01 42 66 59 92

### FASHION BOUTIQUES
Mode

### Agnès B Femme
6, rue du Jour
75001 PARIS
Tel: 01 45 08 56 56
Web site: http://www.agnesb.fr

### Agnès B Homme
3, rue du Jour
75001 PARIS
Tel: 01 42 33 04 13
Web site: http://www.agnesb.fr

### Agnès B Lolita
10, rue du Jour
75001 PARIS
Tel: 01 45 08 49 89
Web site: http://www.agnesb.fr

### Ann Taylor
102, rue Réaumur
75002 PARIS
Tel: 01 42 33 72 42

### Anna Lowe
104, rue du Fbg Saint-Honoré
75008 PARIS
Tel: 01 42 66 11 32
Fax: 01 40 06 00 53
Web site: http://www.solers.fr/anna lowe

### Aramis
*Clothes for men*
36, rue du Fbg Saint Honoré
75008 PARIS
Tel: 01 42 65 73 76
Fax: 01 40 17 07 78

*LIVING & STUDYING*

223

# SHOPPING/BOUTIQUES
SHOPPING/BOUTIQUES

## Borsalino
*Hatter*
368, rue Saint Honoré
75001 PARIS
Tel: 01 49 26 00 75
Fax: 01 42 96 12 41

## Bally Chaussures
4-6, rue du Havre
75009 PARIS
Tel: 01 44 53 75 75
Fax: 01 44 53 75 87

## British House
162, rue du Fbg Saint Honoré
75008 PARIS
Tel: 01 42 56 37 42

## British Shoes
8, rue de Prague
75012 PARIS
Tel: 01 43 41 98 18

## Burberry's of London
8, Bd Malesherbes
75008 PARIS
Tel: 01 40 07 77 77
Fax: 01 40 07 77 48

## Burton of London
14-16, Bd Poissonnière
75009 PARIS
Tel: 01 47 70 55 19
Fax: 01 42 47 10 63

## Calvin Klein
176, ave Charles de Gaulle
92522 NEUILLY SUR SEINE Cedex
Tel: 01 47 45 93 00
Fax: 01 47 45 93 23
Director: Mme FAURE

## Caroline Rohmer
14, ave Victor Hugo
75116 PARIS
Tel: 01 45 01 24 95

## Céline
38, ave Montaigne
75008 PARIS
Tel: 01 49 52 12 01
Fax: 01 49 52 12 00

## Cerruti 1881
3, place de la Madeleine
75008 PARIS
Tel: 01 53 30 18 81
Fax: 01 42 65 00 54

## Chanel
135, ave Charles de Gaulle
92521 NEUILLY SUR SEINE Cedex
Tel: 01 46 43 40 00
Fax: 01 47 47 60 34

## Chantal Thomass
*Designer clothes and lingerie*
1, rue Vivienne
75001 PARIS
Tel: 01 40 15 02 36

## Chevignon
49, rue Etienne Marcel
75002 PARIS
Tel: 01 40 28 05 77
Fax: 01 40 28 04 67

## Christian Dior
30, ave Montaigne
75008 PARIS
Tel: 01 40 73 54 44
Fax: 01 40 73 57 95

## Christian Lacroix
73, rue du Fbg Saint Honoré
75008 PARIS
Tel: 01 42 68 79 04
Fax: 01 49 24 99 41

## Church's
4, rue des Petits Pères
75002 PARIS
Tel: 01 40 20 94 67
Fax: 01 47 05 14 73
Commercial Director: Mme DEBAIG

## Claude Montana Boutique
131, rue Saint Denis
75001 PARIS
Tel: 01 44 76 87 00
Fax: 01 40 26 19 48

## Cordonnerie Anglaise
*Sells Goodyear shoes and accessories, shoe repairs*
28, rue des Archives
75004 PARIS
Tel: 01 44 54 57 90
Fax: 01 44 54 57 99
Director: M. BONNET

## Daniel Hechter

146, Bd Saint Germain
75006 PARIS
Tel: 01 43 26 96 36
Fax: 01 40 51 03 57
Director: M. Charles JACOB

## Dorothée Bis

33, rue de Sèvres
75006 PARIS
Tel: 01 42 22 00 45

## Electre Paris

*Women clothes*
2, rue de Sèvres
75006 PARIS
Tel: 01 45 44 89 87

## Emmanuel Ungaro

2, ave Montaigne
75008 PARIS
Tel: 01 53 57 00 00
Fax: 01 47 23 82 31

## Emmanuelle Khanh

64, rue François 1er
75008 PARIS
Tel: 01 47 20 38 30
Fax: 01 47 20 39 20

## Finsbury Chaussures

17, rue des Petits-Champs
75001 PARIS
Tel: 01 40 15 92 99

## Fruit of the Loom

112 ter, rue Cardinet
75017 PARIS
Tel: 01 55 65 14 14
Fax: 01 55 65 14 15
Contact: M. Alan WADE

## GAP International

3 bis, Cité Hauteville
75010 PARIS
Tel: 01 48 00 00 11
Fax: 01 48 00 92 50

## Givenchy

3, ave George V
75008 PARIS
Tel: 01 44 31 50 00
Fax: 01 47 20 44 96

## Gucci

2, rue du Fbg Saint Honoré
75008 PARIS
Tel: 01 42 96 83 27
Fax: 01 42 97 41 00
Director: M. PAZ

## Guy Laroche

29, ave Montaigne
75008 PARIS
Tel: 01 40 69 69 50
Fax: 01 47 23 48 99

## Hanae Mori

17-19, ave Montaigne
75008 PARIS
Tel: 01 47 23 52 03

## Harley-Davidson

48, rue de la Chapelle
75018 PARIS
Tel: 01 46 07 81 31
Fax: 01 42 05 96 49

## Hermès

24, rue du Fbg Saint Honoré
75008 PARIS
Tel: 01 40 17 47 17
Fax: 01 40 17 47 18

## Hugo Boss

12-14, Rond-Point des Champs Élysées
75008 PARIS
Tel: 01 45 62 57 57
Fax: 01 44 17 16 80

## Jean Paul Gaultier

6, rue Vivienne
75002 PARIS
Tel: 01 42 86 05 05
Fax: 01 42 86 03 82

## Jean-Louis Scherrer

51-53, ave Montaigne
75008 PARIS
Tel: 01 42 99 05 79
Fax: 01 42 99 05 30

## Joan & David

6, Fbg Saint Honoré
75008 PARIS
Tel: 01 42 65 03 28
Fax: 01 47 42 02 27

*LIVING & STUDYING*

225

# SHOPPING/BOUTIQUES
SHOPPING/BOUTIQUES

## Johann

106, rue de Turenne
75003 PARIS
Tel: 01 40 27 03 06
Fax: 01 40 27 90 30

## John Baillie Real Scotch Tailor

5, place de l'Opéra
75009 PARIS
Tel: 01 47 42 49 24
Fax: 01 47 42 23 39

## Kenzo

3, place des Victoires
75001 PARIS
Tel: 01 40 39 72 00
Fax: 01 40 39 72 05

## Lacoste

95, ave des Champs Élysées
75008 PARIS
Tel: 01 47 23 76 00
Fax: 01 47 23 09 25

## La Vogue

*Fashion for men*
38, Bd des Italiens
75009 PARIS
Tel: 01 47 70 83 06

## Lanvin

15, rue du Fbg Saint Honoré
75008 PARIS
Tel: 01 44 71 33 33
Fax: 01 44 71 33 91

## Laura Ashley

94, rue de Rennes
75006 PARIS
Tel: 01 44 39 20 69
Fax: 01 44 39 20 79

## Les Dessous...de Vignon

25, rue Vignon
75008 PARIS
Tel: 01 42 68 09 12
Contact: Mme Josette LAMENT

## Louis Féraud

88, rue du Fbg Saint Honoré
75008 PARIS
Tel: 01 42 65 27 29
Fax: 01 40 07 01 16
President: Mme BOIVIN

## Louis Vuitton

54, ave Montaigne
75008 PARIS
Tel: 01 45 62 47 00
Fax: 01 45 62 90 43

## Manfield

94, rue du Bac
75007 PARIS
Tel: 01 42 84 32 61

## Maximilien

93-95, ave des Champs Élysées
75008 PARIS
Tel: 01 47 23 68 37
Fax: 01 47 23 08 70

## Mephisto Shoes

101, rue de la Convention
75015 PARIS
Tel: 01 40 60 10 57
Fax: 01 40 60 10 57
Contact: M. Gérard MARDIROSSIAN

## Miss "Griffes"

19, rue de Penthièvre
75008 PARIS
Tel: 01 42 65 10 00

## Old America

51, rue Saint Denis
75001 PARIS
Tel: 01 45 08 18 46

## Old English Tailors

12, Bd des Capucines
75009 PARIS
Tel: 01 47 42 81 89
Fax: 01 47 42 39 30

## Paco Rabanne

7, rue du Cherche-Midi
75006 PARIS
Tel: 01 40 49 08 53
Fax: 01 45 44 93 41

## Peter Hadley

6 bis, place des Petits Pères
75002 PARIS
Tel: 01 42 86 83 73

## Pierre Balmain

44, rue François Ier
75008 PARIS
Tel: 01 47 20 35 34
Fax: 01 47 23 40 11

226

## Pierre Cardin

82, rue du Fbg Saint Honoré
75008 PARIS
Tel: 01 42 65 26 88
Fax: 01 42 66 04 51

## Playtex

6, rue de Penthièvre
75008 PARIS
Tel: 01 42 66 90 91
Fax: 01 42 66 66 91
President: M. Gaby FERTOUT

## Polo Ralph Lauren

2, place de la Madeleine
75008 PARIS
Tel: 01 44 77 53 50
Fax: 01 47 03 38 37

## Réciproque

*Second-hand high fashion*
95, rue de la Pompe
75116 PARIS
Tel: 01 47 04 30 28
Fax: 01 47 04 81 33
Director: Mme Nicole MOREL

## Rodier

35, rue de Sèvres
75006 PARIS
Tel: 01 45 48 49 15
Fax: 01 45 49 16 56

## Sabbia Rosa

*Lingerie*
73, rue des Saints Pères
75006 PARIS
Tel: 01 45 48 88 37
Fax: 01 45 48 73 16

## Sara Lee Personal Products

6, rue Marius Aufan
92300 LEVALLOIS PERRET
Tel: 01 41 49 50 00
Fax: 01 41 49 50 10

## Stride Rite Europe

215, rue Saint Honoré
75001 PARIS
Tel: 01 44 86 03 09
Fax: 01 44 86 03 00
General Manager: M. Michel ROUEAU

## Ted Lapidus

35, rue François Ier
75008 PARIS
Tel: 01 44 43 49 90
Fax: 01 47 23 06 41

## Tehen

*Knitwear for women*
5 bis, rue des Rosiers
75004 PARIS
Tel: 01 40 27 97 37

## Warner's Aiglon

66, rue du Fbg Saint Honoré
75008 PARIS
Tel: 01 42 68 31 00
Fax: 01 42 66 14 15
Director France: M. François KLOTZ

## Yves Saint Laurent

38, rue du Fbg Saint Honoré
75008 PARIS
Tel: 01 42 65 74 59
Fax: 01 42 65 23 16

## Yves Saint Laurent

5, ave Marceau
75116 PARIS
Tel: 01 44 31 64 00
Fax: 01 44 31 65 82

## JEWELRY/COSMETICS
Bijoux/Cosmétiques

## Beauté Prestige International

18, ave Matignon
75008 PARIS
Tel: 01 42 68 09 29
Fax: 01 49 24 07 61

## Beautyssima

6, rue Chevert
75007 PARIS
Tel: 01 47 05 99 50
Contact: M. Thierry ROUSSEAUX

## Boucheron

26, place Vendôme
75001 PARIS
Tel: 01 42 61 58 16
Fax: 01 40 20 95 39

*LIVING & STUDYING*

227

# SHOPPING/BOUTIQUES
SHOPPING/BOUTIQUES

### Cartier
13, rue de la Paix
75002 PARIS
Tel: 01 42 61 58 56
Fax: 01 42 18 53 75

### Centre Franco-Américain Parfumerie
*Duty-free and discount perfume*
49, rue d'Aboukir
75002 PARIS
Tel: 01 42 36 77 46
Fax: 01 40 39 09 41
Director: Mme ANDRE

### Chaumet
12, place Vendôme
75001 PARIS
Tel: 01 44 77 24 00
Fax: 01 44 77 29 89

### Christian Dior Parfums
33, ave Hoche
75008 PARIS
Tel: 01 49 53 85 00
Fax: 01 49 53 85 01

### Colette
*Exclusive distributor of Kiehl's products in France*
213, rue Saint Honoré
75001 PARIS
Tel: 01 42 21 15 60

### Courrèges Parfums
28, rue de la Trémoille
75008 PARIS
Tel: 01 47 23 93 76
Fax: 01 47 23 86 46

### Crabtree & Evelyn
177, Bd Saint Germain
75007 PARIS
Tel: 01 45 44 68 76
Fax: 01 40 49 00 67

### France Tax Free Shopping
4, place de l'Opéra
75002 PARIS
Tel: 01 42 66 24 14
Fax: 01 42 66 24 41

### Guerlain
2, place Vendôme
75001 PARIS
Tel: 01 42 60 68 61

### Harry Winston of New York
29, ave Montaigne
75008 PARIS
Tel: 01 47 20 03 09
Fax: 01 47 23 92 97
Director: M. Philippe SCHAEFFOR

### J.D. International
30, rue Édith Cavell
92411 COURBEVOIE
Tel: 01 41 37 00 63
Fax: 01 41 37 00 63
Contact: M. Jean-Dominique ORTELLI

### Marley
19, rue de la Paix
75002 PARIS
Tel: 01 42 65 68 71
Fax: 01 49 24 04 69

### Mauboussin
20, place Vendôme
75001 PARIS
Tel: 01 44 55 10 86
Fax: 01 44 55 10 05

### Michel Swiss Perfumes & Cosmetics
16, rue de la Paix
75002 PARIS
Tel: 01 42 61 61 11
Fax: 01 49 27 94 47
Director: Mme LEMBERGER

### Nina Ricci Parfums
17, rue François Ier
75008 PARIS
Tel: 01 49 52 56 00
Fax: 01 49 52 59 59

---

### Orlane

*Beauty salon*
163, ave Victor Hugo
75116 PARIS
Tel: 01 47 04 65 00

### Rochas Parfums

33, rue François Ier
75008 PARIS
Tel: 01 53 57 22 00
Fax: 01 53 57 22 09

### Puiforcat

2, ave Matignon
75008 PARIS
Tel: 01 45 63 10 10
Fax: 01 42 56 27 15

### Ralph Lauren Parfums

2, place de la Madeleine
75001 PARIS
Tel: 01 44 77 53 00
Fax: 01 47 03 38 37

### Shiseido

Salons du Palais Royal
142, Galerie de Valois
75001 PARIS
Tel: 01 49 27 09 09
Fax: 01 49 27 92 12

### The Body Shop

150, rue de Rivoli
75001 PARIS
Tel: 01 40 15 05 04
Fax: 01 40 15 04 60

### Van Cleef & Arpels

22, place Vendôme
75001 PARIS
Tel: 01 53 45 45 45
Fax: 01 53 45 45 00

### MUSIC SHOPS
### Boutiques de musique

### Electrica for Sony

11, 13-24, rue des Halles
75001 PARIS
Tel: 01 42 21 11 11
Fax: 01 42 21 15 15

### FNAC Étoile

26-30, ave des Ternes
75017 PARIS
Tel: 01 44 09 18 00
Fax: 01 44 09 18 20
Web site: http://www.fnac.fr
Contact: Mme Catherine BAILLY

### FNAC Forum

1, rue Pierre Lescot
Porte Lescot, Niveau -3
75001 PARIS
Tel: 01 40 41 40 00
Fax: 01 40 41 40 86
Web site: http://www.fnac.fr

### FNAC Montparnasse

136, rue de Rennes
75006 PARIS
Tel: 01 49 54 30 00
Fax: 01 49 54 31 11
Web site: http://www.fnac.fr
Contact: Mme Maryse DIALL

### FNAC Musique

24, Bd des Italiens
75009 PARIS
Tel: 01 48 01 02 03
Fax: 01 48 01 05 20
Web site: http://www.fnac.fr

### GTR Communication

*Specialized in AOR and
West Coast music*

112, Route de Fourqueux
78100 SAINT GERMAIN EN LAYE
Tel: 01 34 51 44 70
Fax: 01 34 51 44 70
President: Mme Jee JACQUET

### House of Guitar

7, rue Douai
75009 PARIS
Tel: 01 45 26 55 10

### Librairie Musicale de Paris

*700 square meters of sheet music*

68 bis, rue Réaumur
75003 PARIS
Tel: 01 42 72 30 72
Fax: 01 42 72 77 80

### O'CD

26, rue des Écoles
75005 PARIS
Tel: 01 43 25 23 27
Fax: 01 43 25 26 74

### Oldies but Goodies

16, rue du Bourg Tibourg
75004 PARIS
Tel: 01 48 87 14 37

### Prowest

*West coast music press promotion*
35, rue Dalou
Bât. C
94400 VITRY SUR SEINE
Fax: 05 53 09 46 90
Email: prowest@perigord.com
Web site: http://www.perigord.com/west-coast
Contact: M. Jean-Luc RAYMOND

### Virgin Megastore

52-60, ave des Champs Élysées
75008 PARIS
Tel: 01 49 53 50 00
Fax: 01 49 53 50 40
Email: postmaster@virgin.fr
Web site: http://www.virgin.fr
Contact: Mme Patricia SUIGNARD

### SPORTing goods
### Équipements sportifs

### Adidas

3, rue du Louvre
75001 PARIS
Tel: 42 60 34 83
Fax: 42 86 98 05
Free call: 0 800 01 10 01

### Au Vieux Campeur

*Everything for camping, hiking and climbing enthusiasts*
48, rue des Écoles
75005 PARIS
Tel: 01 43 29 12 32
Fax: 01 46 34 14 16

### Chattanooga Surf Skateboard Shop

53, ave Bosquet
75007 PARIS
Tel: 01 45 51 76 65
Fax: 01 47 53 01 50

### Cyclic

*Sells, rents and repairs cycles*
19, rue Monge
75005 PARIS
Tel: 01 43 25 63 67
Fax: 01 43 25 63 67

### Decathlon

26, ave de Wagram
75008 PARIS
Tel: 01 45 72 66 88
Fax: 01 45 72 44 88
Web site: http://www.decathlon.fr

### Decathlon

*Sporting equipment*
4, rue Louis Armand
75015 PARIS
Tel: 01 45 58 60 45
Fax: 01 45 54 35 29
Web site: http://www.decathlon.fr

### Everlast

17, rue Beaurepaire
75010 PARIS
Tel: 01 42 08 44 00
Fax: 01 42 08 45 00

### Foot Locker

*Sporting clothes and shoes*
Les Bureaux du manoir
18, chemin du Fond de Chêne
78620 L'ÉTANG LA VILLE
Tel: 01 39 16 01 01
Fax: 01 39 16 02 08
Regional Director: M. Guy SPRUYT

### Foot Locker

22, ave du Général Leclerc
75014 PARIS
Tel: 01 40 44 99 01

### Go Sport

Forum des Halles
Porte Lescot niveau - 3
75045 PARIS Cedex 01
Tel: 01 40 13 73 50
Fax: 01 40 13 73 60

## Le Comptoir du Golf

22, ave de la Grande Armée
75017 PARIS
Tel: 01 43 80 15 00
Fax. 01 47 63 89 91
Sales Manager: Mme Valérie TOUBA

## Maison du Vélo

*Bicycle rentals, sales and repairs*
11, rue Fénelon
75010 PARIS
Tel: 01 42 81 24 72

## P.C. American Sport

*American baseball and football equipment*
14, rue Beaugrenelle
75015 PARIS
Tel: 01 45 75 37 00
Fax: 01 43 31 38 00

## Repetto

*Dance and gym clothes*
22, rue de la Paix
75002 PARIS
Tel: 01 44 71 83 00
Fax: 01 44 71 83 01

## Roller Station Bastille

107, Bd Beaumarchais
75003 PARIS
Tel: 01 42 78 33 00

## Roller Station Montparnasse

140, ave du Maine
75014 PARIS
Tel: 01 43 20 82 27

## Roller Station Trocadéro

60, ave Raymond Poincarré
75116 PARIS
Tel: 01 47 27 21 21

## Sport USA

*American sporting equipment and clothes*
40, rue de la Croix Nivert
75015 PARIS
Tel: 01 45 67 59 16

## GIFTS/MISCELLANEOUS
Cadeaux/divers

## A Blagues City

1, Bd Saint Denis
75003 PARIS
Tel: 01 42 72 94 95

## Atelier d'Ink

*Handmade greetings cards (Christmas, Valentine)*
1, passage Rauch
75011 PARIS
Tel: 01 43 79 96 04
Contact: Nalitt KAPLAN

## Au Nom de la Rose

*Compose bouquets of roses*
4, rue de Tournon
Tel: 01 46 34 10 64
Fax: 01 44 07 15 72

## Axis Boutique

*Original stationery, gadgets and tableware*
13, rue de Charonne
75011 PARIS
Tel: 01 48 06 79 10
Fax: 01 46 78 54 19

## Azul Trading France

*Imports products from Canadian Indians*
Le Pont Lege
85600 LA BOISSIERE DE MON-
TAIGU
Tel: 02 51 42 26 26
Fax: 02 51 42 29 71
Manager: Mme Martine FOURNET

## Bains-Plus

*Clothing, accessories, scented soaps and salts for the bathroom*
51, rue des Francs Bourgeois
75004 PARIS
Tel: 01 48 87 83 07
Fax: 01 48 87 19 12

LIVING & STUDYING

231

## Barneys of New York

33-35, rue de Valois
75001 PARIS
Tel: 01 47 03 41 30
Fax: 01 42 96 20 45
Managers: Mmes Jessica BRATT &
Sandra SHOWLEY

## Blooms

*Florist*
20, rue Muller
75018 PARIS
Tel: 01 42 58 22 71

## Catherine Feff Création

*Figurative paintings*
7 ter, rue du Dr Arnaudet
92190 MEUDON
Tel: 01 45 07 85 66
Fax: 01 45 34 87 56
Director: Mme Catherine FEFF

## Christian Tortu

*Imaginative flowers*
6, Carrefour de l'Odéon
75006 PARIS
Tel: 01 43 26 02 56

## Diptyque

34, Bd Saint Germain
75005 PARIS
Tel: 01 43 26 45 27
Fax: 01 43 54 27 01

## Epona

*New French ceramics and
sculptures*
40, rue Quincampoix
75004 PARIS
Tel: 01 42 77 36 90
Contact: M. BRUNEAU

## Forever Living Products

*Natural products*
14, rue Pergolèse
75116 PARIS
Tel: 01 45 00 05 50
Orders: 01 45 00 81 00
Fax: 01 45 00 05 65
Director: M. DE LA POTERIE

## Interflora

*Worldwide flower service*
45, rue Vivienne
BP 6426
75064 PARIS Cedex 02
Tel: 01 44 82 28 21
Fax: 01 44 82 28 57

## La Kermesse

37, Bd de la Chapelle
75010 PARIS
Tel: 01 42 05 03 66

## Le Chat Huant

*Gift boutique (ceramics, objets d'art,
jewelry)*
50-52, rue Galande
75005 PARIS
Tel: 01 46 33 67 56

## Le Comptoir Irlandais

*Irish clothing and gifts*
153, Bd Voltaire
75011 PARIS
Tel: 01 43 71 25 81

## Le Jardin Moghol

53, rue Vieille du Temple
75004 PARIS
Tel: 01 48 87 41 32
Fax: 01 48 87 44 45

## Les Mille Feuilles

*Splendid bric-à-brac flower shop
(books, vases, pots)*
2, rue Rambuteau
75003 PARIS
Tel: 01 42 78 32 93
Fax: 01 42 78 17 90

## Namaste

52, rue des Francs Bourgeois
75003 PARIS
Tel: 01 42 77 76 35
Fax: 01 42 77 76 35

## Panasonic AEI

27, rue Raymond Losserand
75014 PARIS
Tel: 01 43 35 44 00
Fax: 01 40 47 05 46

### Paris American Art
*Sells painting accessories & frames*
2-4, rue Bonaparte
75006 PARIS
Tel: 01 43 26 79 85
Fax: 01 43 54 33 80

### Pioneer AEI
10, rue Lebon
75017 PARIS
Tel: 01 45 74 97 28
Fax: 01 45 72 67 70

### Potala
*Tibetan handcrafted goods*
1, rue Greffulhe
75008 PARIS
Tel: 01 42 66 55 58
Contact: Mme Sonam THONDUP

### Seiko France
83, rue du Temple
75003 PARIS
Tel: 01 44 54 57 30
Fax: 01 42 71 27 99

### The Disney Store
44, ave des Champs Élysées
75008 PARIS
Tel: 01 45 61 45 25
Fax: 01 45 61 45 26

### The FiloFax: Center
32, rue des Francs Bourgeois
75003 PARIS
Tel: 01 42 78 67 87
Fax: 01 42 78 67 88

### Thorp of London
*Fabrics*
8, ave de Villars
75007 PARIS
Tel: 01 47 53 76 37
Fax: 01 45 55 97 81

### Toys-R-Us
Centre Commercial «Les Quatre Temps»
92092 PARIS LA DÉFENSE
Tel: 01 47 76 29 78
Admin: 01 60 76 83 00

### Toys-R-Us
Forum des Halles
Porte Lescot
Niveau - 1
75001 PARIS
Tel: 01 53 00 93 33

### Tumbleweed
*Contemporary American craftwork*
19, rue de Turenne
75004 PARIS
Tel: 01 42 78 06 10

### Welcome to Paris
*Paris souvenir shop*
106, Bd Clichy
75018 PARIS
Tel: 01 46 06 13 21

*LIVING & STUDYING*

233

# SPECIAL SERVICES
## SERVICES DIVERS

Special Services are services that do not fit into one of PARIS-ANGLOPHONE's 68 subject headings. Here you will find mail order offerings, home deliveries, English-speaking photographers, and private tutors. If you have something to offer to other Paris anglophones, let's hear from you!

### A Carnaval et Fêtes
*Costume rental for special occasions*
22, ave Ledru Rollin
75012 PARIS
Tel: 01 43 47 06 08

### ADV Conseils
*Revamp your image with a Paris fashion specialist!*
32, rue Etienne Marcel
75002 PARIS
Tel: 01 42 36 27 07
Fax: 01 42 21 40 59
Contact: Mme Anne WAGNER

### Allostop-Provoya
*Hitchhiking service*
8, rue Rochambeau
75009 PARIS
Tel: 01 53 20 42 42
Fax: 01 53 20 42 44
Minitel: 36 15 ALLOSTOP
Email: allostop@ecritel.fr
Web site: http://www.ecritel.fr/allostop/

### Angels et Bermans
*Costume makers*
196, Bd Voltaire
75011 PARIS
Tel: 01 43 67 43 92
Fax: 01 43 67 16 16

### Atelier Pergolèse
*Cleaning and ironing service for delicate fabrics*
15, rue Pergolèse
75116 PARIS
Tel: 01 45 00 31 47
Fax: 01 42 25 12 47

### Au Clown de la République
*Costume rental for special occasions, make-up, masks, fireworks*
11, Bd Saint Martin
75003 PARIS
Tel: 01 42 72 73 73
Fax: 01 42 78 03 72
Contact: M. François GENTILE

### Au Réparateur de Bicyclettes
*Cycle repairs*
44, Bd Sébastopol
75003 PARIS
Tel: 01 48 04 51 19

### Bedford
*Professional shoe care and repairs*
5, rue Chauveau Lagarde
75008 PARIS
Tel: 01 42 65 08 57
Contact: M. PULIN

### Bella Voce International

*Realize your dream of singing! American classical singer, doctorate. All styles/levels. Learn to read music. Call for free introduction*
10, place de la Bastille
75011 PARIS
Tel: 01 43 41 36 80
Director:
Mme Marie-Christine ALLEN

### Camps de Luca
*Tailor for men*
11, place de la Madeleine
75008 PARIS
Tel: 01 42 65 42 15
Fax: 01 42 65 40 03

### Cash Converters
*Buy and sell second-hand goods*
15-17, ave Simon Bolivar
75019 PARIS
Tel: 01 42 40 93 03
Fax: 01 42 40 93 88

## Cyclic
*Sells, rents and repairs cycles*
19, rue Monge
75005 PARIS
Tel: 01 43 25 63 67
Fax: 01 43 25 63 67

## Dad
*Pet food and litter home delivery service*
32, rue de Mainville
91210 DRAVEIL
Tel: 01 69 03 20 48

## Delta Services Organizations
*Dinners, galas, hostesses, etc.*
127, rue Amelot
75011 PARIS
Tel: 01 48 44 96 67
Fax: 01 48 44 08 01

## E.N. Productions
*Purchasing office (textiles/fashion)*
21, rue Henry Monnier
75009 PARIS
Tel: 01 53 20 09 70
Fax: 01 53 20 09 71
Email: enprod@imaginet.fr
Contact: M. Yves DUMORA

## Edwards & Edwards
*Booking service for shows in Paris*
Maison de la Grande-Bretagne
19, rue des Mathurins
75009 PARIS
Tel: 01 42 65 39 21
Fax: 01 42 65 39 10

## El Paëlla
*Home delivery paella*
26, rue Louis Braille
75012 PARIS
Tel: 01 43 41 61 61
Contact: M. Robert PASCAL

## Esso
*Gas station open all night
7 days a week*
338, rue Saint Honoré
75001 PARIS
Tel: 01 42 60 49 37
Contact: M. MOULIERE

## Fashion Gradation International
*Patterns and sizes for clothing*
23, rue des Jeûneurs
75002 PARIS
Tel: 01 45 08 17 16
Fax: 01 45 08 00 46

## Fehrenbach Driving School
*New highway code book in English*
53, Bd Henri Sellier
92150 SURESNES
Tel: 01 45 06 31 17
Fax: 01 47 28 81 89
Director: M. Michel FEHRENBACH

## Fleurilège
*Plants, real and fake flowers, floral arrangements for special events*
Place de l'Eglise
78290 CROISSY SUR SEINE
Tel: 01 39 76 80 08
Fax: 01 39 76 21 42

### Françoise D'Abrigeon

"LA TUILERIE" ★★★

PENSION POUR CHIENS & CHATS

*"Pension" for dogs and cats*
"La Tuilerie"
77160 SAINT HILLIERS
Tel: 01 64 00 15 45

## Garage Parking Saint Honoré
*Car park management 24 h/24*
336, rue Saint Honoré
75001 PARIS
Tel: 01 42 61 50 60
Fax: 01 42 61 53 91

## Hargrove, Jeff
*Photographer*
40, Bd de Bercy
75012 PARIS
Tel: 01 43 42 34 01

LIVING & STUDYING

235

# SPECIAL SERVICES
SERVICES DIVERS

### Herbier du Diois
*Sells herbs*
Le Perrier
26150 DIE
Tel: 04 75 22 12 07
Fax: 04 75 22 18 60
Email: 106151.745@compuserve.com
Contact: M. Ton VINK

### Hygreckos, Helen
*Paints portraits and restores
paintings*
15, ave Porte d'Asnières
75017 PARIS
Tel: 01 43 80 50 08

### Kolar, Courtney
*Freelance photographer/
photojournalist*
50, rue Godefroy Cavaignac
75011 PARIS
Tel: 01 44 64 78 18
Email: ckolar@aol.com

### La Redoute
*Mail-order catalog for clothes
and accessories*
Service Relations Clients
59081 ROUBAIX Cedex 2
Tel: 03 20 69 86 00
Fax: 03 20 26 43 75

### Le Médaillier Franklin
*Mail-order sales for decorative
objects (dolls...) and medals*
BP 525
59022 LILLE Cedex
Tel: 01 39 33 29 00
Fax: 01 34 19 72 10
Commercial Director:
Mme Muriel SESTA

### Mail Boxes Etc.
*Handles all your postal, business
and communications needs*
208, rue de la Convention
75015 PARIS
Tel: 01 44 19 60 20
Fax: 01 44 19 60 29

### Mufti, Sharjeel Assad
*Indian astrology, palmistry and
counseling*
18, ave Victor Cresson
92130 ISSY LES MOULINEAUX
Tel: 01 41 08 84 17
Fax: 01 41 08 84 17

### Nelson
*Designer fashion shows, make-up
shows & shopping service*
11, rue d'Arcole
75004 PARIS
Tel: 01 40 46 85 14
Fax: 01 43 25 93 44
Director: Mme Brenda NELSON

### Officers Group Security
*Surveillance, protection*
12, rue Dugommier
75012 PARIS
Tel: 01 43 44 61 07
Fax: 01 43 42 39 50

### Palace Mobile
*Professional DJ for your party*
48, rue de la Glacière
75013 PARIS
Tel: 01 43 31 94 53

### Picto Bastille
*Custom photography lab*
53 bis, rue de la Roquette
75011 PARIS
Tel: 01 53 26 21 21
Fax: 01 53 36 21 00
Sales Manager: M. Michel COLLIOT

### Rent a Cell
*Cellular phone rental*
116 bis, ave des Champs Élysées
75008 PARIS
Tel: 01 53 93 78 00
Fax: 01 53 93 78 09
Contact: M. Michael DANA

### Saint Clare and Son
*Picture frames*
29, rue au Maire
75003 PARIS
Tel: 01 42 72 83 55
Contact: Mme Kathleen SAINT CLARE

### Shell
*Gas station open all night*
6, Bd Raspail
75007 PARIS
Tel: 01 45 48 43 12
Fax: 01 42 84 28 67

### Speedy France
*Car repair shop*
72-78, ave Georges Clémenceau
92022 NANTERRE
Tel: 01 41 20 30 40
Fax: 01 41 20 30 68
President: M. Gilles CHAUVEAU

### Studio B. Esclapez
*Commercial photographer*
1, rue Gutenberg
75015 PARIS
Tel: 01 45 75 21 01
Fax: 01 45 77 23 99
Agent: Mme T. SMITH

### Taylor Home Service
*Tailor-made suits and shirts for men*
18 bis, rue Berteaux Dumas
92200 NEUILLY SUR SEINE
Tel: 01 47 47 55 82
Fax: 01 47 47 15 37

### Theatrix
*Custom Pictures/Specialty Painting*
2, rue Gagnié
94400 VITRY SUR SEINE
Tel: 01 45 21 41 53

### Top Boy
*Costume and wig rental*
35, Bd de Strasbourg
75010 PARIS
Tel: 01 47 70 40 78
Fax: 01 42 46 43 90
Director: Mme Sophie GLASMAN

### Top Retouches
*Alterations*
8, rue Gramme
75015 PARIS
Tel: 01 48 42 55 05

### Trois Suisses
*Clothing for the whole family by mail-order*
Tel: 08 36 67 36 36

### Voices Choeur International
*High-level amateur choir. Music by American composers, traditional folk songs and spirituals*
2, rue de Paradis
75010 PARIS
Tel: 01 48 00 96 84
Fax: 01 42 47 12 34
Email: 103374.456@compuserve.com
Contact: Mme Bonnie WOOLEY

**LIVING & STUDYING**

# SPORTS
## SPORTS

There are just too many municipal swimming pools, tennis courts, and basketball courts these days to list them all, but PARIS-ANGLOPHONE has put together the contact addresses for the respective sports associations, clubs, and points of information for many sports activities and facilities in Paris. In addition, here are the major health clubs that offer memberships popular with English-speakers. Aerobics, work-outs, squash matches, and step-master, here you come!

### ASSOCIATIONS
### Fédérations

### Baseball Club de France
29, rue la Quintinie
75015 PARIS
Tel: 01 42 50 50 01

### Fédération Française d'Escrime
*National Fencing Federation*
14, rue Moncey
75009 PARIS
Tel: 01 44 53 27 50
Fax: 01 40 23 96 18

### Fédération Française de Football Américain (F.F.F.A.)
79, rue Rateau
93120 LA COURNEUVE
Tel: 01 43 11 14 70
Fax: 01 43 11 14 71
President: M. Frédéric PAQUET

### Fédération Française de Golf
69, ave Victor Hugo
75783 PARIS Cedex 16
Tel: 01 44 17 63 00
Fax: 01 44 17 63 63
General Director:
M. Hubert CHESNEAU

### Fédération Française de Rugby
*Comité Ile de France*
56, ave de Saint Mandé
75012 PARIS
Tel: 01 43 42 51 51

### Fédération Française des Sports de Glace
*National Ice Skating Federation*
35, rue Félicien David
75016 PARIS
Tel: 01 53 92 81 81
Fax: 01 53 92 81 82

### Fédération Française de Tennis
2, ave Gordon Bennett
75016 PARIS
Tel: 01 47 43 48 00
Fax: 01 47 43 04 94
Minitel: 3615 FFT
Web site: http://www.fft.fr

### Fédération Française de Voile
*National Sailing Federation*
55, ave Kléber
75016 PARIS
Tel: 01 44 05 81 00
Fax: 01 47 04 90 12
Web site: http://www.ffv.fr

### Ligue de Paris Ile De France de Squash
14, rue Ernest Renan
75015 PARIS
Tel: 01 40 56 03 22
Fax: 01 40 56 00 58
Minitel: 36 15 IDF SQUASH

### Paris Université Club (PUC)
17, ave Pierre de Coubertin
75013 PARIS
Tel: 01 44 16 62 62
Fax: 01 44 16 62 90

## Aerobics, American-Style
*Paris fitness professionals*
65, quai d'Orsay
75007 PARIS
Tel: 01 40 62 05 00
Contact: Mme Alison BENNEY

## Aqua Boulevard/Forest Hill
*Water sports center. Call for other Forest Hill locations*
4, rue Louis Armand
75015 PARIS
Tel: 01 40 60 10 00

## Aqualand
*Outdoor pool with waves*
91190 GIF SUR YVETTE
Tel: 01 60 12 25 90

## Club Quartier Latin
19, rue de Pontoise
75005 PARIS
Tel: 01 43 54 82 45
Fax: 01 43 25 15 06

## Espace Vit'Halles
*Health club popular with americans*
48, rue Rambuteau
75003 PARIS
Tel: 01 42 77 21 71
Fax: 01 42 77 50 25

## Gymnase Club Champs-Elysées
*Many locations in Paris*
26, rue de Berri
75008 PARIS
Tel: 01 43 59 04 58
Fax: 01 42 56 76 28

## Ritz Health Club
Hôtel Ritz
15, place Vendôme
75041 PARIS Cedex 01
Tel: 01 43 16 30 60
Fax: 01 43 16 37 06

## Shape and Physical Condition
*Weights, stretching, cardio, diet. All Paris + around in gyms or at home. American + French licence.*
*100FF/class*
*Private Training in Gym or at Home*
8, rue Édouard Manet
94000 CRÉTEIL
Tel: 01 43 99 27 14
Personal Trainer: Mme Tatiana DUPRES

## Standard Athletic Club
*Cricket, squash, tennis, football, rugby, hockey, snooker, bridge*
Route Forestière du Pavé de Meudon
92360 MEUDON LA FORÊT
Tel: 01 46 26 16 09
Fax: 01 45 07 87 63

## Golf du Paris Country Club
1, rue Camp Canadien
92210 ST CLOUD
Tel: 01 47 77 39 22
Fax: 01 47 71 00 50

## Paris Country Club
121, rue du Lt. Colonel de Montbrison
92500 RUEIL MALMAISON
Tel: 01 47 77 64 00
Fax: 01 47 32 19 80
President: M DALIA
Director: M Selim LEVY

LIVING & STUDYING

239

# THEATER/DANCE
## THÉÂTRE/DANSE

On any given night you'll be able to see scores of contemporary and classical theatrical and musical performances, opera and dance at one of the numerous venue in and around Paris. Listed here though are the English-language theater companies and theaters in which performances are in English. Lastly, listed here are theater and dance companies offering courses and classes for anglophones. For performance schedules consult *L'Officiel des Spectacle*s or *Pariscope*.

## THEATERS
Théâtres

### ACT
*Professional English theater*
84, rue Pixérécourt
75020 PARIS
Tel: 01 40 33 64 02
Fax: 01 40 33 64 03
Email: COMING
Contacts: Mme Anne WILSON

### Acting International
148, rue du Temple
75019 PARIS
Tel: 01 42 00 06 79
Contact: Mme Lesley CHATTERLEY

### Actor's Institute
42, rue du Fbg Saint Denis
75010 PARIS
Tel: 01 42 46 66 66
Fax: 01 42 46 69 97

### Actorat
16, rue des Grands Augustins
75006 PARIS
Tel: 01 43 25 43 63
Fax: 01 43 25 43 32
Contact: Mme VUILLIN

### Brace, Cindy
*Artistic agent*
31, rue Milton
75009 PARIS
Tel: 01 45 26 33 49
Fax: 01 48 74 51 42

### Break A Leg
23, rue Gazan
75014 PARIS
Tel: 01 45 88 03 42
Fax: 01 44 73 92 92
Contact: Mme Marie CAMPBELL

### Company Oz
4, rue Georges Saché
75014 PARIS
Tel: 01 45 43 05 26
Contact: Mme Michèle MATHIEU

### D.P.I.
*Bilingual production management*
80, rue de Lagny
75020 PARIS
Tel: 01 43 79 81 46
Fax: 01 43 79 81 46
Email: 100416.573@compuserve. com
Contact: M. Dominic PEISSEL

### Dear Conjunction Theatre Company
6, rue Arthur Rozier
75019 PARIS
Tel: 01 42 41 69 65
Fax: 01 42 06 26 94
Contact: Mme Patricia KESSLER

### FACT (Franco-Américaine Cinéma Théâtre)
65, rue de Reuilly
75012 PARIS
Tel: 01 43 44 76 98
Artistic Director:
Mme Sarah EIGERMAN

## On Stage

27, rue de la Beaune
93100 MONTREUIL SOUS BOIS
Tel: 01 48 59 41 50
Email: mikey@club-internet.fr
Contact: M. Nick CALDERBANK

## Pichot, Elizabeth

104, rue Bobillot
75013 PARIS
Tel: 01 53 62 15 33
Fax: 01 53 62 15 34

## Théâtre de Nesle

*In the heart of Saint Germain des Prés, the Théâtre de Nesle offers an enticing theater program in English*

8, rue de Nesle
75006 PARIS
Tel: 01 46 34 61 04
Fax: 01 43 25 00 00
President: M. Jacques BONNAUD

## DANCE
Danse

## Aidohouedo, l'Arc-en-Ciel

*African dance workshops*

127, rue d'Avron
75020 PARIS
Tel: 01 43 56 75 80
Fax: 01 43 56 27 83
President: M. Jean-Fortuné DE SOUZA

## Body Sparks

*Dance, Salsa, Latin America*

23, rue de Turenne
75003 PARIS
Tel: 01 42 71 03 46
Fax: 01 43 46 57 17
Director: Mme Suzanne SPARKS

## Cours de Danse Etiennette Morgan

Salle Pleyel
Studio 617
252, rue du Fbg Saint Honoré
75008 PARIS
Tel: 01 45 63 32 90

## K-Danse

14, Bd Raspail
75007 PARIS
Tel: 01 46 33 93 43
Contact: Mme GODEBSKI

## Studio Aline Roux

92bis, Bd Montparnasse
75014 PARIS
Tel: 01 43 20 44 39
Administrator:
Mme Jacqueline DE PERCEVAL

**LIVING & STUDYING**

241

# UNIVERSITIES/SCHOOLS
## UNIVERSITÉS/ÉCOLES

There are some 50 American university local and exchange programs operating in Paris, offering undergraduate and graduate programs in everything from French civilization to Masters of Business Administration. There are also French institutions offering programs of interest to English-speaking students. Organized as a sub-heading, please find private high schools, junior high schools, elementary schools, and pre-schools with English or bilingual programs. Finally, special schools such as culinary programs, art academies, and others have been listed for your convenience.

## UNIVERSITIES
### Universités

### A.I.M. Hotel Administration
*International hotel management school*
31, quai de Grenelle
75015 PARIS
Tel: 01 45 75 65 75
Fax: 01 40 59 03 02
Email: aimparis@worldnet.fr
Director: M. O. DOGRAMACI

### American Business School
12, rue Alexandre Parodi
75010 PARIS
Tel: 01 40 03 15 49
Fax: 01 40 03 15 05
Email: jdillon@groupe-igs.org
Web site: http://www.groupe-igs.org
Contact: Mme Arlene MLODZIK

### American Business School
*BS/BA and MBA programs*
19, rue Roux-de-Brignoles
13006 MARSEILLE
Tel: 04 91 81 97 97
Fax: 04 31 81 97 98
Director: Mme Barbara VAHANIAN

### American Graduate School of International Relations and Diplomacy
6, rue de Lubeck
75116 PARIS
Tel: 01 39 73 13 40
Fax: 01 39 73 13 40
Email: info@agsird.edu
Web site: http://www.agsird.edu
Contact: Mme Joyce THOMSON

### American School of Modern Music
117, rue de la Croix Nivert
75015 PARIS
Tel: 01 45 31 16 07

### Art School
7, rue d'Hautpoul
75019 PARIS
Tel: 01 42 49 10 15
Fax: 01 42 06 71 17

### Atelier de Sèvres
47, rue de Sèvres
75006 PARIS
Tel: 01 42 22 59 73
Fax: 01 45 44 01 93
Email: mgb@club-internet
Directeur: M. Michel BOURGEOIS

### Boston University - Paris
*Master of Arts in international relations, internship program*
15, rue de Pondichéry
75015 PARIS
Tel: 01 45 66 59 49
Tel2: 01 42 19 98 92
Fax: 01 45 66 64 68
Contact: Mme Karlene WALLACE

### C.E.M.H.I.
*European Center for Hotel Management*
52, rue Saint Lazare
75009 PARIS
Tel: 01 45 26 59 28
Fax: 01 45 26 59 29
Email: ipsa@imaginet.fr
Director of Studies:
Mme Véronique SOURNIES

## Center for University Programs Abroad
19-21, rue Cassette
75006 PARIS
Tel: 01 42 22 87 50
Fax: 01 45 48 23 24
Email: cupa@magic.fr
Directors: Mmes Elliot CHATELIN & Pascale BESSIERES

## Columbia University
Reid Hall
4, rue de Chevreuse
75006 PARIS
Tel: 01 43 20 24 83
Fax: 01 43 20 52 96
Director of Studies: Mme Brunhilde BIEBUYCKX

## Ecole Nationale Supérieure des Arts Décoratifs
*National School of Decorative Arts*
31, rue d'Ulm
75240 PARIS Cedex 05
Tel: 01 42 34 97 21
Fax: 01 42 34 97 57
Email: bolle@ensad.fr
Office of Admissions:
Mme Danielle BOLLE

## École Nationale Supérieure des Beaux-Arts
*Painting, sculpture, engraving, drawing classes, art exhibits, publishing*
14, rue Bonaparte
75006 PARIS
Tel: 01 47 03 50 00
Fax: 01 47 03 50 80
Email: @ensb-a.culture.fr
Dean of Academic Affairs:
Mme MINOT

## Educo
23, rue du Montparnasse
75006 PARIS
Tel: 01 42 22 34 66
Fax: 01 45 48 24 86
Director: Mme Shelby OCANA

## E.I.C.A.R.
*École Internationale de Création Audiovisuelle et de Reportage, For aspiring directors, journalists, screenwriters, film editors and TV anchormen*
93, ave d'Italie
75013 PARIS
Tel: 01 53 79 10 00
Fax: 01 53 79 16 26

## European Business School
27, Bd Ney
75018 PARIS
Tel: 01 40 36 92 93
Tel2: 01 40 36 16 88
Fax: 01 40 36 40 20
Minitel: 3614 EBS
International Coordinator:
Mme Karine KEMPEN

## European School of Management
*European Masters in International Business*
6, ave de la Porte de Champerret
75017 PARIS
Tel: 01 44 09 33 00
Director: M. Michel RIMBAUD

## European University
Immeuble Norma
20, rue Jean Jaurès
92807 PUTEAUX LA DÉFENSE
Tel: 01 47 67 01 84
Fax: 01 47 62 90 41
Director of Admissions:
M. Marc LARSEN

## Fashion Institute of Technology
20, rue du Commandant Mouchotte
75014 PARIS
Tel: 01 43 35 10 12
Fax: 01 43 35 10 12

## Georgia Institute of Technology
*Architecture school with exchange programs between France and Great Britain*
144, ave de Flandre
75019 PARIS
Tel: 01 40 36 32 57
Fax: 01 40 36 32 57

*LIVING & STUDYING*

243

# UNIVERSITIES/SCHOOLS
UNIVERSITÉS/ÉCOLES

## Groove Music School
54, Bd Clichy
75018 PARIS
Tel: 01 42 55 17 53
Contact: Patrick

## H.E.C. Hautes Études Commerciales
*Bilingual (English-French) MBA program*
Institut Supérieur des Affaires
78351 JOUY EN JOSAS
Tel: 01 39 67 70 00
Fax: 01 39 67 71 31
Minitel: 3616 HEC
Web site: http://www.hec.fr

## Hamilton College
*Junior Year in France*
Reid Hall
4, rue de la Chevreuse
75006 PARIS
Tel: 01 43 20 77 77
Fax: 01 42 79 07 76

## IGS University
12, rue Alexandre Parodi
75010 PARIS
Tel: 01 40 03 15 04
Fax: 01 40 03 15 05
Email: jdillon@groupe-igs.org
Web site: http://www.groupe-igs.org
Director: M. Jarlath DILLON

## IMHI - Cornell University/ Groupe ESSEC
*Graduate studies in international hotel management (Master's level)*
BP 105
ave Bernard Hirsch
95021 CERGY PONTOISE Cedex
Tel: 01 34 43 31 75
Fax: 01 34 43 17 01
Email: williams@edu.essec.fr
Office of Admissions:
Mme Marilyn WILLIAMS

## INSEAD
*Ten-month graduate MBA program*
Bd de Constance
77305 FONTAINEBLEAU Cedex
Tel: 01 60 72 40 00
Fax: 01 60 74 55 00
Web site: http://www.insead.fr
Head of Admissions:
Mme Carole GIRAUD

## Institut Britannique de Paris
9-11, rue de Constantine
75340 PARIS Cedex 07
Tel: 01 44 11 73 79
Fax: 01 45 50 31 55
General Secretary: M. Simon STONE

## Institut Européen de Management International
Hotel management
52, rue Saint Lazare
75009 PARIS
Tel: 01 45 26 59 28
Fax: 01 45 26 59 29
Contact: Mme. Véronique SOURNIES

## Institut Franco-Américain de Management
*Associated with Hartford, Northeastern, Boston and Pace Universities*
19, rue Cépré
75015 PARIS
Tel: 01 47 34 38 23
Fax: 01 47 83 31 72
Director of Studies:
M. Michel LEMIEUX

## Institute for American Universities
27, place de l'Université
13625 AIX EN PROVENCE Cedex 1
Tel: 04 42 23 39 35
Fax: 04 42 21 11 38
Email: iauadm@univ-aix.fr
Director of Admissions:
Mme Grace ANDERSON

## ISG International School of Business
4-6-8, rue de Lota
75116 PARIS
Tel: 01 53 70 82 22
Fax: 01 53 70 82 24
Email: isg@isg.fr
Web site: http://www.isg.fr
Dean: Mme LEROY

## James Madison University
26, rue Auguste Comte
92170 VANVES
Tel: 01 46 44 57 51

## Kaplan

15, rue de Pondichéry
75015 PARIS
Tel: 01 45 66 55 33

## Les Ateliers - Ecole Nationale Supérieure de Création Industrielle

48, rue Saint Sabin
75011 PARIS
Tel: 01 49 23 12 12
Fax: 01 43 38 51 36

## Lincoln International Business School

65, rue du Théâtre
75015 PARIS
Tel: 01 44 37 05 05
Fax: 01 44 37 05 00
Director of Studies:
M. Renaud BURONFOSSE

## MBA Center

151, ave de Versailles
75016 PARIS
Tel: 01 40 50 38 66
Fax: 01 40 75 02 43
Minitel: 36 15 US Academy
Email: c.european.mba@infonie.fr
Contact: Mme Sandra ETIENNE

## MICEFA Student Exchange

*CUNY, Berkeley, U. of Texas-Austin, U. of Denver Florida Intl, Waterloo, Cal. State, New Jersey, Indiana, Illinois, Puerto Rico, Waterloo (Canada)*
Centre Saint Jacques
26, rue du Fbg Saint Jacques
75014 PARIS
Tel: 01 40 51 76 96
Fax: 01 44 07 18 10
Director: Mme Nancy MERRITT

## Middlebury College

Reid Hall
4, rue de Chevreuse
75006 PARIS
Tel: 01 43 20 70 57

## New York University

56, rue de Passy
75016 PARIS
Tel: 01 53 92 50 80
Fax: 01 53 92 50 81
Director: Prof. Maud WALTHER

## Paris American Academy

*Degrees: BFA/MFA. Fine Arts. Interior Design. Fashion Language. Academic year Oct. through May and/or Jan. through Sept. One month intensive programs throughout the year*
9, rue des Ursulines
75005 PARIS
Tel: 01 44 41 99 20
Fax: 01 44 41 99 29
Founder-Director: M. Richard ROY

## Parsons School of Design

*BFA in Fine Arts, Visual Communication, Fashion*
14, rue Letellier
75015 PARIS
Tel: 01 45 77 39 66
Fax: 01 45 77 10 44
Head of Admissions:
Mme Heather SACCO

## Sarah Lawrence College

Reid Hall
4, rue de Chevreuse
75006 PARIS
Tel: 01 43 22 14 36
Fax: 01 43 22 69 26

## Schiller International University

*S.I.U. is an independent American university offering graduate and undergraduate programs in Europe & the US (See advertisement)*
32, Bd de Vaugirard
75015 PARIS
Tel: 01 45 38 56 01
Fax: 01 45 38 54 30
Email: study@campus.schiller.edu
Web site: http://www.schiller.edu/
http://www.paris-anglo.com
Director: Mme BARODY

# UNIVERSITIES/SCHOOLS
## UNIVERSITÉS/ÉCOLES

### Skidmore College

142, rue de Rivoli
75001 PARIS
Tel: 01 42 36 02 55
Fax: 01 45 08 42 87
Email: 101620.2436@compuserve.com
Director: Dr Norman STOKLE

### Smith College

*Junior Year in Paris*
4, rue de Chevreuse
Reid Hall
75006 PARIS
Tel: 01 43 21 65 54
Fax: 01 45 38 72 20

### Spéos

*Paris Photographic Institute*
7-8, rue Jules Vallès
75011 PARIS
Tel: 01 40 09 18 58
Toll-Free: 1 800 258 84 92
(USA-France)
Fax: 01 40 09 84 97
Web site: http://www.speos.fr
Contact: Mme Karen ARCHER

### Southern Methodist University

Reid Hall
4, rue de Chevreuse
75006 PARIS
Tel: 01 43 20 04 86
Email: smuinparis@compuserve.com
Director: Mme Isabelle REYNIER

### SUNY Brockport/SUNY Oswego

4, rue de Chevreuse
75006 PARIS
Tel: 01 43 22 10 51

246

### Sweetbriar College Junior Year in France

c/o Alliance Française
101, Bd Raspail
75006 PARIS
Tel: 01 45 48 79 30
Fax: 01 45 49 27 52
Director: M. Émile LANGLOIS

### The American University of Paris

Office of Admissions
31, ave Bosquet
75343 PARIS Cedex
Tel: 01 40 62 07 20
Fax: 01 47 05 34 32
Minitel: 3615 AUP
Email: admissions@aup.fr
Web site: http://www.aup.fr

### The Center for Global Business Studies in Association with Hartford University

8, Terrasse Bellini
92807 PARIS LA DÉFENSE 11
Tel: 01 49 00 19 61
Fax: 01 47 76 45 13
Executive Director:
Mme Pamela D. MEADE

---

### The Open University

*UK's largest distance-teaching
university, stand-alone or degree
courses (BA, BSc, MBA, etc.) for
people resident in Europe*
c/o Rosemary Pearson
22, place Georges Pompidou
Boîte 42
92300 LEVALLOIS PERRET
Tel: 01 47 58 53 73
Fax: 01 47 58 55 25
Email: r.pearson@open.ac.uk
Web site: http://www.open.ac.uk
Coordinator:
Mme Rosemary PEARSON

---

### Tufts University

2, rue des Taillandiers
75011 PARIS
Tel: 01 43 38 14 18
Fax: 01 43 55 80 07
Director: Mme Virginia REMMERS

## Tulane University

Reid Hall
4, rue de Chevreuse
75006 PARIS
Tel: 01 43 21 35 85

## Université de Paris III Sorbonne Nouvelle

*French classes for anglophones*

13, rue de Santeuil
Bureau 443
75005 PARIS
Tel: 01 45 87 41 21
Fax: 01 45 87 41 75
Contact: Mme DUMAINE

## Université de Paris IV La Sorbonne

*French classes for anglophones*

47, rue des Écoles
75005 PARIS
Tel: 01 40 46 26 64
Fax: 01 40 46 32 29
Director: M. Pierre BRUNEL

## Wesleyan University Program in Paris

*Study abroad programs for US students*

Reid Hall
4, rue de Chevreuse
75006 PARIS
Tel: 01 43 22 12 47
Fax: 01 43 22 38 51
Email: wesleyan@paris7.jussieu.fr
Contact: Mme Lisa FLEURY

## SCHOOLS
Écoles

## American Boarding Schools Foundation

*Association representing 40 American boarding schools in Paris*

45, rue des Dames
75017 PARIS
Tel: 01 45 22 20 24
Fax: 01 44 70 05 37

## American Kids

PARIS
Tel: 01 43 07 13 88
Fax: 01 40 75 02 43

## American School Harriet Bonelli

*English tuition for 3 to 14 year-olds*

1, rue Crébillon
75006 PARIS
Tel: 01 46 34 78 05
Fax: 01 43 25 52 69

## American School of Paris

*English lessons, all levels, all ages*

BP 82
41, rue Pasteur
92210 SAINT CLOUD
Tel: 01 41 12 82 82
Fax: 01 46 02 23 90
Email: usecole@ibm.net
Web site: http://www.teaser.fr/~cchater/
Director of Admissions: M. GUSE

## Bilingual Montessori School of Paris

*Bilingual Montessori for children aged 2 to 6*

65, quai d'Orsay
75007 PARIS
Tel: 01 45 55 13 27
Fax: 01 45 51 25 12
Director: Mme Barbara PORTER

## British School of Paris

38, quai de l'Ecluse
78290 CROISSY SUR SEINE
Tel: 01 34 80 45 90
Fax: 01 39 76 12 69
Principal: M. HONOUR

## Collège de Sèvres - Section Internationale

Rue Lecoq
92310 SÈVRES
Tel: 01 46 23 96 35
Fax: 01 45 34 76 63
Email: association.sis@wanadoo.fr

## Collège International de Fontainebleau

*Section Internationale*

48, rue Guérin
77300 FONTAINEBLEAU
Tel: 01 64 22 11 77
(Anglophone Section)
Fax: 01 64 23 43 17
Email: 106411.1345@compuserve.com
Head of Section:
Mme Glenys KENNEDY

*LIVING & STUDYING*

247

## Collège-Lycée Honoré de Balzac
*International Section*
119, Bd Bessières
75017 PARIS
Tel: 01 53 11 12 13

## Ecole Active Bilingue

Ecole active Bilingue

*The challenge of the year 2000.*
*The French BAC with European*
*"mention" with international*
*option, SAT, High School diploma,*
*British A level. (See advertisement)*
Administration
117, Bd Malesherbes
75008 PARIS
Tel: 01 45 63 47 00
Tel2: 01 45 63 62 22
Fax: 01 45 63 62 23
Web site: http://www.eab.fr
Public Relations:
Mme Nicole HOURCADE-REDING

## Ecole Active Bilingue Jeannine Manuel
418 bis, rue Albert Bailly
59700 MARCQ EN BAROEUL
Tel: 03 20 65 90 50
Fax: 03 20 98 06 41
Email: 100775.1125@compuserve.com
Director: Mme LUX

## Ecole Active Bilingue Jeannine Manuel
70, rue du Théâtre
75015 PARIS
Tel: 01 44 37 00 80
Email: 100775.1125@compuserve.com
Contact: Mme Shirley BURCHILL

## Ecole Active Bilingue Jeannine Manuel
141, ave de Suffren
75007 PARIS
Tel: 01 47 34 27 72
Email: 100775.1125@compuserve.com

## Ecole Active Bilingue Jeannine Manuel
15, rue Edgar Faure
75015 PARIS
Tel: 01 44 49 09 43
Email: 100775.1125@compuserve.com

## École Bilingue Internationale Privée Mental'Ô
38, ave Louis Pasteur
34470 PEROLS
Tel: 04 67 50 59 38
Fax: 04 67 17 02 64
Presidente: Mme Danièle COUCHAUX

## École Internationale de Marne la Vallée
CREPS de Montry
BP 26 77450 ESBLY
Tel: 01 60 04 34 70
Fax: 01 60 04 34 70

## Être et Découvrir
*Montessori*
10, route de Saint Germain
78860 SAINT NOM LA BRÉTÈCHE
Tel: 01 30 56 62 06
President: Mme Hélène PACAUD

## International School of Paris
*Primary School/Middle School/*
*High school*
6, rue Beethoven
75016 PARIS
Tel: 01 42 24 09 54
Fax: 01 45 27 15 93
Email: 100731,2644@compuserve.com
Head of Admissions:
M. Jones GARETH

## Jardin d'Enfants Montessori d'Auteuil
53, rue Erlanger
75016 PARIS
Tel: 01 46 51 65 87
Fax: 01 45 51 25 12

## "L'École Aujourd'hui - School for Today"
*Bilingual primary education*
24, Bd Edgar Quinet
75014 PARIS
Tel: 01 43 20 61 24
Coordinator: Mme Pierrette KOHEN

## Le Petit Cours
*Bilingual pre-school and primary education for children*
104, rue Ordener
75018 PARIS
Tel: 01 46 06 80 33
Fax: 01 46 06 94 09
Director: M. Daniel MATUL

## Lennen Bilingual School
65, quai d'Orsay
75007 PARIS
Tel: 01 47 05 66 55

## Lycée Franco-Américain Marcel Roby
*Bilingual-bicultural education*
6, rue Giraud Teulon
BP 143
78100 SAINT GERMAIN EN LAYE
Tel: 01 34 51 00 96
Fax: 01 34 51 95 70
Director: M. Don ANDERSON

## Lycée International de Saint Germain en Laye
American Section
Rue du Fer-à-Cheval
BP 230
78104 SAINT GERMAIN EN LAYE
Cedex
Tel: 01 34 51 74 85
Fax: 01 30 87 00 49

## Marymount School
72, Bd de la Saussaye
92200 NEUILLY SUR SEINE
Tel: 01 46 24 10 51
Fax: 01 46 37 07 50
Headmistress:
Sister Genevieve MURPHY

## Thomas Jefferson School
13, rue Clef
75015 PARIS
Tel: 01 43 37 93 31

## United Nations Nursery School
*International bilingual school for children aged 2 to 6*
40, rue Pierre Guérin
75016 PARIS
Tel: 01 45 27 20 24
Fax: 01 45 24 28 54
Director: Mme Brigitte WEILL

## EDUCATIONAL PROGRAMS
Stages/Séjours linguistiques

## Academic Year Abroad
4, rue de Chevreuse
75006 PARIS
Tel: 01 43 20 91 92
Fax: 01 43 20 91 92
Director: Mme Paule SCHNEERSOHN

## A.I.F.S.
*Language-oriented stays in France for US students*
10, rue du Docteur Blanche
75016
PARIS
Tel: 01 46 47 92 74
Fax: 01 40 50 36 38
Director: Mme Martha DWYER

## American School of Paris (The Extension Program)
*English lessons, all levels, all ages*
BP 82
41, rue Pasteur
92210 SAINT CLOUD
Tel: 01 46 02 54 43
Fax: 01 46 02 23 90
Email: 101613,770@compuserve.com
Web site: http://www.teaser.fr/~cchater/
Director ASP Extension Program:
Mme Laurence FENIOU-SALIM

## Aspect Foundation Exchange Programs
53, rue du Fbg Poissonnière
75009 PARIS
Tel: 01 48 00 06 00
Fax: 01 48 00 05 94
Email: 101575.2443@compuserve.com
Director of Admissions:
Mme Véronique BARTET

## Association France-Ontario
Allée de Clotemont
77183 CROISSY BEAUBOURG
Tel: 01 60 06 44 50
Fax: 01 60 05 03 45
Contact: Mme Christine SCARANO

## Association "Les Fauvettes"
10, rue Léon Jouhaux
75010 PARIS
Tel: 01 42 06 25 29
Fax: 01 42 06 51 35

*LIVING & STUDYING*

249

### C.I.E./College Year in America
Route de Droisy
27240 HELLENVILLIERS
Tel: 02 32 58 15 12
Fax: 02 32 58 15 12
Email: 106212.3671@compuserve.com
Contact: M. G. Stephen RYER

### Center for International Education
*Linguistic trips & university studies to the USA*
7, rue Berryer
75008 PARIS
Tel: 02 32 58 15 12
Fax: 02 32 58 15 12
Email: 106212,3671@compuserve.com
Contact: M. G. Stephen RYER

### Collège les Bouvets / Espace Langues
1, rue Félix Pyat
92800 PUTEAUX
Tel: 01 47 74 54 53
Tel2: 01 46 93 92 20
Fax: 01 46 93 92 22

### Council on International Educational Exchange (CIEE)
*International education exchanges*
1, place de l'Odéon
75006 PARIS
Tel: 01 44 41 74 74
Fax: 01 43 26 97 45
Director Europe: M. Guy HAUG

### En Plein Air
*Provence Painting Workshop*
12, rue d'Orchampt
75018 PARIS
Tel: 01 42 54 10 35
Email: 100616.1753@compuserve.com

### Experiment
*Linguistic and cultural visits for au pairs in the USA*
89, rue de Turbigo
75003 PARIS
Tel: 01 44 54 58 00
Fax: 01 44 54 58 01
Director: M. Gilbert GUILLEMOTO

### Franco-American Commission for Educational Exchange
*Administration of Fulbright Scholarship Program France-USA*
9, rue Chardin
75016 PARIS
Tel: 01 45 20 46 54
Fax: 01 42 88 04 79
Minitel: 3617 USAETUDES
Director: M. Pierre COLLOMBERT

### Internships in Francophone Europe
26, rue du Commandant Mouchotte
75014 PARIS
Tel: 01 43 21 78 07
Fax: 01 42 79 94 13
Email: 100662,1352@compuserve.com
Director: M. Thimoty CARLSON

### Paris Center for Critical Studies
*Undergraduate and graduate level courses*
1, place de l'Odéon
75006 PARIS
Tel: 01 46 33 85 33
Fax: 01 43 26 97 45
Email: 100434.2176@compuserve.com
Director: M. Dana POLAN

### The American University of Paris (Continuing Education)
102, rue Saint Dominique
75007 PARIS
Tel: 01 47 20 44 99
Fax: 01 47 20 45 64
Email: 104076,705@compuserve.com
Web site: http://www.aup.fr

### Toastmasters
16, rue Puteaux
75017 PARIS
Tel: 01 42 94 20 59
Fax: 01 42 94 20 49
Minitel: 36 15 SE*toastmaster

## WICE Institute for Continuing Education

**WICE**

*WICE is an international, English-speaking association dedicated to providing high quality educational and cultural courses, including the TEFL certificate program, an professional experience via numerous volunteer opportunities*

20, Bd Montparnasse
75015 PARIS
Tel: 01 45 66 75 50
Fax: 01 40 65 96 53
Email: 101367.433@compuserve.com
Office Manager:
Mme Gunilla GUINAMENT

## World Discovery Agency

*Cultural services: homestays abroad, internships*

7, rue Auguste Simon
94700 MAISONS ALFORT
Tel: 01 43 78 33 74
Fax: 01 43 78 04 25
Contact: Mme Lysiane GALLERON

## CULINARY SCHOOLS
Écoles de cuisine

## Centre d'Information, de Documentation et de Dégustation

30, rue de la Sablière
75014 PARIS
Tel: 01 45 45 32 20
Fax: 01 45 42 78 20
Minitel: 3615 FORMATEL
Minitel: 3615 OENO
Contacts: Mme Melba MAUVIEL &
M. Alain SEGELLE

## La Cuisine de Marie-Blanche

18, ave de la Motte-Picquet
75007 PARIS
Tel: 01 45 51 36 34
Fax: 01 45 51 90 19

## La Toque d'Or

55, rue de Varenne
75007 PARIS
Tel: 01 45 44 86 51
Fax: 01 45 44 63 81
Email: parisgourmet@multicable.fr
Director: Mme Sue YOUNG

## La Varenne

*French culinary school*

Château du Fey
89300 VILLECIEN
Tel: 03 86 63 18 34
Fax: 03 86 63 01 33
Director: Mme Marah STETS

## Le Cordon Bleu

8, rue Léon Delhomme
75015 PARIS
Tel: 01 53 68 22 50
Fax: 01 48 56 03 77 (store)
Fax: 01 48 56 03 96 (school)
Director: Mme Lizabeth NICOL

## Ritz Escoffier École de Gastronomie Française

*Cooking and pastry classes*

38, rue Cambon
75001 PARIS
Tel: 01 43 16 30 50
Fax: 01 43 16 31 50
Manager: Mme Marie-Anne DUFEU

## Wine Business Conseil

*Oenology classes, wine-tasting*

138, rue du Fbg Saint Honoré
75008 PARIS
Tel: 01 42 89 14 14
Fax: 01 42 89 15 40
President: M. Alain MARTY

LIVING & STUDYING

251

# USEFUL NUMBERS
## RENSEIGNEMENTS PRATIQUES

Here is a list of frequently-needed phone and fax numbers for Paris residents and students. Feel free to add your own numbers to this list.

## 08 36 68 92 22*
*National database of bad checks*
Tel: 08 36 68 22 92*

## Allo Sports Service
*Details on Paris' 200 municipal sports activities*
Tel: 01 42 76 54 54

## American Express
11, rue Scribe
75009 PARIS
Tel: 01 47 77 77 00

## American Express Carte France
4, rue Louis Blériot
92561 RUEIL MALMAISON Cedex
Tel: 01 47 77 70 07
Fax: 01 47 77 74 57
President: M. PETRUCCELLI

## American Ticket Agency
*For the French Open*
Tel: 01 43 29 64 45

## AT&T Dial Direct
Tel: 00 00 11
Free Call: 0 800 90 82 93

## Arizona Pizza
*Home delivery of homemade US pizzas, brownies*
Tel: 01 39 18 50 00

## British Telecom
Tel: (00) 00 44

## Central Post Office
*Open 24 hours*
52, rue du Louvre
75001 PARIS
Tel: 01 40 28 20 00

## Cinema Booking Service (Allo Ciné)
*Film programs and booking services by phone*
Tel: 01 40 30 20 10

## Citiphone
*Citibank 24 hour banking service*
Tel: 01 49 05 49 05

## Collect Calls to the US
Tel: 00 00 11

## Diners Club de France
19 Le Parvis
92073 PARIS LA DÉFENSE Cedex 36
Tel: 01 49 06 17 25
Fax: 01 49 06 17 99
Lost: 01 49 06 17 50
Minitel: 3615 DINERS CLUB

## Directory Assistance for the US
Tel: 00 33 12 11

## Directory Information
Tel: 12

## Domino's Pizza National Hotline
Tel: 08 36 67 21 21

## Eurocard-Mastercard
16, rue Lecourbe
75015 PARIS
Tel: 01 45 67 53 53
Minitel: 3615 EM

## FACTS-LINE
*HIV/AIDS help-line in English*
Tel: 01 44 93 16 69

## Fax Service
Tel: 01 40 28 20 00

## Insurance needs
Tel: 01 53 20 03 33

## Local France-Telecom Business Office
Tel: 14

## MCI Direct
Tel: (00) 00 19

## Minitel Directory
Tel: 36 11

## Paris-Anglophone
*To order this book*
Tel: 01 48 59 66 58

## Telephone Prefix for International Calls
Tel: 00

## S+A Satellite TV
*English-language satellite TV*
Tel: 01 42 35 72 47

## SPRINT
Tel: (00) 00 87

## Telephone Prefixes for Paris and Provinces
01 for Paris and suburbs
02 for Northeast
03 for Northwest
04 for Southwest and Corsica
05 for Southeast
08 00 for Toll-free

## Telephone Repairs
Tel: 13

## Time
Tel: 36 99

## VISA-Carte Bleue
41, Bd des Capucines
75002 PARIS
Admin: 01 40 15 00 74
Lost: 01 42 60 25 10
Minitel: 3615 CB VISA

## VoiceMail
*Interactive telephone service in English*
Tel: 08 36 68 09 66

## Wake-up Calls
*Tel: 55+the time in four digits (ex: 0800 = 8 a.m.), then # electronically programmed*

## Weather Information
Paris: 08 36 68 00 00
International: 08 36 70 00 00
Provinces: 08 36 70 00 00

## Note here your useful numbers:

—————————————
—————————————
—————————————
—————————————
—————————————
—————————————
—————————————
—————————————
—————————————
—————————————
—————————————
—————————————
—————————————
—————————————
—————————————
—————————————
—————————————

*LIVING & STUDYING*

253

# WINING & DINING
## À TABLE

This is not the list of great French bistros and brasseries that PARIS-ANGLOPHONE offers its readers. For those listings see the Travel & Tourism section. Here, however, are the Anglo-American eateries frequented by both sentimental anglophones and French worshippers of American myths.

## RESTAURANTS
Restaurants

### Bertie's
*British cuisine*
Hôtel Baltimore
1, rue Léo Delibes
75016 PARIS
Tel: 01 44 34 54 34
Fax: 01 44 34 54 44

### Duke
19, rue de Ponthieu
75008 PARIS
Tel: 01 42 56 19 10

### Hollywood Savoy
44, rue Notre-Dame-des-Victoires
75002 PARIS
Tel: 01 42 36 16 73

### L'Américain à Paris
10, rue Chabanais
75002 PARIS
Tel: 01 42 96 54 69
Fax: 01 49 27 06 77

### Le Restaurant au Tabac Bleu
117, rue du Fbg Saint Martin
75010 PARIS
Tel: 01 42 05 46 02

### Le Western
Hôtel Hilton
18, ave de Suffren
75015 PARIS
Tel: 01 44 38 56 00
Fax: 01 44 38 56 10

### Quai du Blues
17, Bd Vital Bouhot
92200 NEUILLY SUR SEINE
Tel: 01 46 37 31 31

### Sam Pepper
32, rue Brey
75017 PARIS
Tel: 01 43 80 20 52

### The Studio
Société du 41
41, rue du Temple
75004 PARIS
Tel: 01 42 74 10 38
Fax: 01 42 77 19 90
Contacts: Monique & Alex

---

### Woolloomooloo Australian Restaurant-Wine Bar

WoollooMooloo
*restaurant australien*

36, Bd Henri IV
75004 PARIS
Tel: 01 42 72 32 11
Fax: 01 42 72 32 21
Email: woolomoo@worldnet.fr
Manager: M. Ben JOHNSTON

---

## AMERICAN EATERIES/ TEX-MEX
Cafés américains/Tex-Mex

### American Pie & Company
15, rue des Archives
75004 PARIS
Tel: 01 48 04 76 79
Fax: 01 42 71 20 84

### Arriba Mexico
32, ave de la République
75011 PARIS
Tel: 01 49 29 95 40
Fax: 01 42 08 98 38
Manager: M. MIGUEL

## Ay! Caramba!

59, rue de Mouzaïa
75019 PARIS
Tel: 01 42 41 23 80
Fax: 01 42 41 50 34

## Blue Jack Saloon

21, Bd Arago
75013 PARIS
Tel: 01 47 07 01 15

## Cactus Charly

68, rue de Ponthieu
75008 PARIS
Tel: 01 45 62 01 77
Fax: 01 45 62 82 08

## Chesterfield Café

124, rue La Boétie
75008 PARIS
Tel: 01 42 25 18 06
Manager: M. Arnaud DALAIS

## Chi-Chi's

27, Bd des Italiens
75002 PARIS
Tel: 01 42 66 09 57

## Chicago Meatpackers

8, rue Coquillière
75001 PARIS
Tel: 01 40 28 02 33
Fax: 01 40 41 95 84

## Chicago Pizza Pie Factory

5, rue de Berri
75008 PARIS
Tel: 01 45 62 50 23
Fax: 01 45 63 87 56

## Chili's

1, rue Washington
75008 PARIS
Tel: 01 42 89 87 87
Fax: 01 42 89 98 80
Director of Operations:
M. Peter KARAM

## Conway's

73, rue Saint Denis
75001 PARIS
Tel: 01 42 33 22 86
Fax: 01 42 33 22 86

## Elliott

166, Bd Haussmann
75008 PARIS
Tel: 01 42 89 30 50
Fax: 01 42 89 30 57
Director: M. Gérard BINI

## Forest Café

121, rue Mouffetard
75005 PARIS
Tel: 01 43 31 64 64
Fax: 01 43 31 60 70

## Front Page

58, rue Saint Denis
75001 PARIS
Tel: 01 40 26 26 56

## Hard Rock Café

14, Bd Montmartre
75009 PARIS
Tel: 01 42 46 10 00
Fax: 01 42 46 49 70
Sales Dir: Mme Jacqueline WELLER

## Haynes

3, rue Clauzel
75009 PARIS
Tel: 01 48 78 40 63

## Henry's

189, rue de la Pompe
75016 PARIS
Tel: 01 47 27 25 75

## Hollywood Canteen

22, rue de la Roquette
75011 PARIS
Tel: 01 47 00 18 28
Fax: 01 47 00 18 38
Director: M. DESCOUTS

## Indiana Café

130, Bd Saint Germain
75006 PARIS
Tel: 01 46 34 66 31

## Indiana Café

18, rue Quentin Bauchart
75008 PARIS
Tel: 01 40 70 96 89

## Joe Allen

30, rue Pierre Lescot
75001 PARIS
Tel: 01 42 36 70 13
Fax: 01 40 28 06 94

## La Ballena "Taco Loco"

116, rue Amelot
75011 PARIS
Tel: 01 43 57 90 24
Director: M. CAMPOS

## La Cantina

10, rue Papillon
75009 PARIS
Tel: 01 42 47 05 21
Fax: 01 40 22 61 87
Manager: M. DIEGO

## La Cucaracha

31, rue Tiquetonne
75002 PARIS
Tel: 01 40 26 68 36

## La Louisiane

176, rue Montmartre
75002 PARIS
Tel: 01 42 36 58 98
Fax: 01 42 36 05 30
Director: M. Ludovic GRANES

## Le Café Pacifico

50, Bd du Montparnasse
75015 PARIS
Tel: 01 45 48 63 87

## Le Canyon's Café

35, rue du Pont-Neuf
75001 PARIS
Tel: 01 45 08 45 21
Fax: 01 45 08 03 15
Director: M. BENCHABANE

## Le Saloon

47, Bd Richard Lenoir
75011 PARIS
Tel: 01 43 57 06 75

## Manhattan Delicatessen

65, ave Félix Faure
75015 PARIS
Tel: 01 44 26 03 03
Fax: 01 44 26 04 04
Director: M. COLLOTTE

## Mustang Café

84, Bd Montparnasse
75014 PARIS
Tel: 01 43 35 36 12

## Mustang Café

20, rue de la Roquette
75011 PARIS
Tel: 01 49 23 41 41
Fax: 01 49 23 40 74
Manager: M. Éric ANGELVY

## New Haven Café

250, rue du Fbg Saint Antoine
75012 PARIS
Tel: 01 43 72 56 79

## O'Cantina

161, ave Daumesnil
75012 PARIS
Tel: 01 44 74 07 06

## One One Seven

117, rue des Dames
75017 PARIS
Tel: 01 43 87 63 08

## Planet Hollywood

78, ave des Champs Élysées
75008 PARIS
Tel: 01 53 83 78 27

## Restaurant Mexicain Cielito Lindo

33, rue de Charonne
75011 PARIS
Tel: 01 47 00 16 44
Contacts: Maurice & Ana CALMARD

## Sixty Six Café

8, rue de Lappe
75011 PARIS
Tel: 01 43 38 30 20
Fax: 01 43 57 21 96

## Sunset Ice Cream

22, place Saint André des Arts
75006 PARIS
Tel: 01 43 26 29 97

## Susan's Place

51, rue des Écoles
75005 PARIS
Tel: 01 43 54 23 22
Contact: Mme Susan

**E·a·B**

Ecole active Bilingue

- Kindergarten and Primary Classes (age 3 to 11)
  6, av. Van Dyck, 75008 Paris.
  ☎ 33 01 46 22 14 24. Métro: Courcelles.

- Kindergarten and Primary Classes (age 3 to 11)
  123, rue de la Pompe, 75116 Paris.
  ☎ 33 01 45 53 89 36. Métro: Pompe.

- "Collège français" Junior High School (age 11 to 15)
  Cambridge Examinations (K.E.T., P.E.T., First Certificate)
  16, rue Margueritte, 75017 Paris.
  ☎ 33 01 46 22 40 20. Métro: Courcelles.

- "Lycée français" High School (age 15 to 18)
  24 bis, rue de Berri, 75008 Paris.
  ☎ 33 01 45 63 30 73. Métro: Georges V

- American Section: grades 6 to 12, S.A.T., H.S.D., E.F.L.
  52, av. Victor Hugo, 75116 Paris.
  ☎ 33 01 45 00 11 57. Metro: Victor Hugo

- British Section O and A levels, Exams Center for Cambrige,
  Oxford and London universities.
  52, av. Victor Hugo, 75116 Paris.
  ☎ 33 01 45 00 11 57. Métro: Victor Hugo.

Founded in 1954 to provide bilingual education, E.a.B. helps students make a transition to the French System leading to the French "Baccalaureat" (European Endorsement or O.I.B. International Option). The Junior High School Program prepares students for the French "lycée". American Section and British Section (Advanced levels) prepare students for university.

Particular emphasis is placed upon languages - Spanish and German in addition to English in primary classes - Japanese (mother tongue), Chinese. Integration of students into the world and the development of an international view-point are key points at E.a.B.

# Ecole active Bilingue

**PUBLIC RELATIONS:**
117, Bd Malesherbes - 75008 Paris
Tél. 33 01 45 63 47 00 - Fax 33 01 45 63 62 23
http://www.eab.fr

Ecole privée sous contrat d'association avec l'État, à l'exception de certaines classes

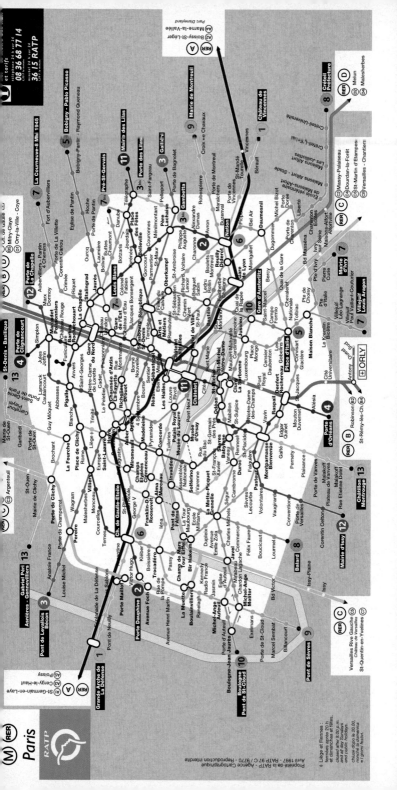

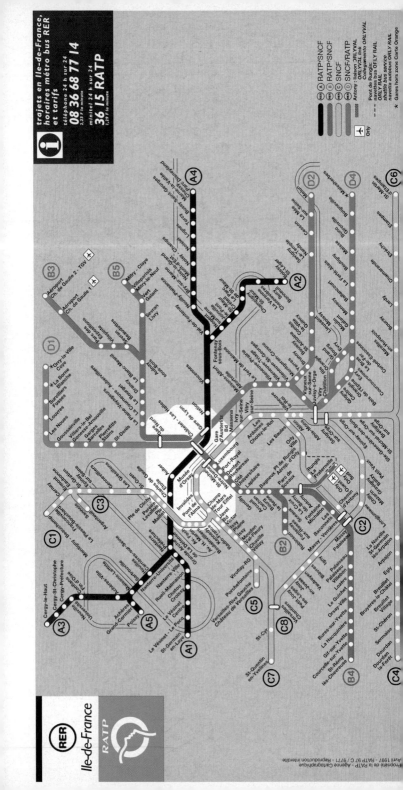

## T.G.I. Friday's
8, Bd Montmartre
75009 PARIS
Tel: 01 47 70 27 20
Fax: 01 42 46 30 07

## Tapas Nocturne
17, rue de Lappe
75011 PARIS
Tel: 01 43 57 91 12

## The American Dream Restaurant
21, rue Daunou
75002 PARIS
Tel: 01 42 60 99 89
Fax: 01 42 61 12 27
Contact: M. Charles LELLOUCHE

## Tropical Café American Restaurant
5, place Parmentier
92000 NEUILLY SUR SEINE
Tel: 01 47 45 15 55
Fax: 01 47 82 24 37

## West Side Café
34, rue Saint Ferdinand
75017 PARIS
Tel: 01 40 68 75 05
Fax: 01 44 09 91 04
Contact: M. Fred ELIAS

## Zuni
2-4, rue de Sabot
75006 PARIS
Tel: 42 84 02 83

## PUBS/BARS
Pubs/Bars

## Bedford Arms
17, rue Princesse
75006 PARIS
Tel: 01 46 33 43 54

## Café Iguana
15, rue de la Roquette
75011 PARIS
Tel: 01 40 21 39 99

## Café Oz
184, rue Saint Jacques
75005 PARIS
Tel: 01 43 54 30 48
Fax: 01 46 33 69 27
Contact: M. Michael KENNEDY

## Cambridge Tavern
17, ave de Wagram
75017 PARIS
Tel: 01 43 80 34 12
Fax: 01 44 09 06 34

## Carr's Restaurant & Bar
1, rue du Mont Thabor
75001 PARIS
Tel: 01 42 60 60 26
Fax: 01 42 60 33 32
Manager: M. Conall CARR

## Cavern
21, rue Dauphine
75006 PARIS
Tel: 01 43 54 53 82
Fax: 01 44 07 31 54

## Charly's Bar
26, rue de la Parcheminerie
75005 PARIS
Tel: 01 43 26 61 23
Fax: 01 46 33 34 54

## Cockney Tavern
39, Bd de Clichy
75009 PARIS
Tel: 01 48 74 80 80
Fax: 01 48 74 36 71
Manager: M. Roger TAILLANDIER

## Connolly's Corner
12, rue Mirbel
75005 PARIS
Tel: 01 43 31 94 22

## Coolin Irish Pub
Marché Saint Germain
15, rue Clément
75006 PARIS
Tel: 01 44 07 00 92
Fax: 01 44 07 00 92

## Cruiskeen Lawn
18, rue des Halles
75001 PARIS
Tel: 01 45 08 99 15

*LIVING & STUDYING*

257

# WINING & DINING
## À TABLE

### Edward & Son's
10, Bd de Clichy
75018 PARIS
Tel: 01 44 92 90 91
Fax: 01 44 92 90 93
Contact: M. EDOUARD

### Finnegan's Wake
9, rue des Boulangers
75005 PARIS
Tel: 01 46 34 23 65

### Hall's Beer Tavern
68, rue Saint Denis
75001 PARIS
Tel: 01 42 36 92 72
Fax: 01 42 33 85 84

### Harry's New York Bar

*Established in 1911 at Sank Roo Doe Noo. Remains today a great meeting place for adopted anglophile Parisians*
5, rue Daunou
75002 PARIS
Tel: 01 42 61 71 14
Fax: 01 42 61 58 99

### Horse's Mouth
120, rue Montmartre
75002 PARIS
Tel: 01 40 39 93 66

### Isa'Bar
12, rue Jean-Jacques Rousseau
75001 PARIS
Tel: 01 40 39 05 22

### Johnny's
55, rue Montmartre
75002 PARIS
Tel: 01 42 33 91 33

### Juveniles
47, rue de Richelieu
75001 PARIS
Tel: 01 42 97 46 49

### Kitty O'Shea's Pub
10, rue des Capucines
75002 PARIS
Tel: 01 40 15 00 30
Manager: M. Dermot TOOLAN

### La Taverne de Cluny
51, rue de la Harpe
75005 PARIS
Tel: 01 43 54 28 88

### Le Baron Rouge
1, rue Théophile Roussel
75012 PARIS
Tel: 01 43 43 14 32

### Le Bistrot Irlandais
15, rue de la Santé
75013 PARIS
Tel: 01 47 07 07 45
Email: 100337,3664@compuserve.com
Owner: M. Spencer SHIDNER

### Le Delano Paris/Miami/ New York
12, rue Delambre
75014 PARIS
Tel: 01 43 21 98 49
Contact: Tony

### Le Doobie's
2, rue Robert Estienne
75008 PARIS
Tel: 01 53 76 10 76
Fax: 01 42 25 21 71

### Le Mayflower
49, rue Descartes
75005 PARIS
Tel: 01 43 54 56 47

### Ministry Hardcore Café
1, rue Mansart
75009 PARIS
Tel: 01 42 82 08 88
Fax: 01 42 82 08 88
Email: a.silverfarb-canicio.wanadoo.fr
Contact:
Mme Ariane SILVERFARB-CANICIO

### Molly Malone Lounge Bar
21, rue Godot de Mauroy
75009 PARIS
Tel: 01 47 42 07 77

## Montecristo Café
68, ave des Champs Élysées
75008 PARIS
Tel: 01 45 62 30 86
Fax: 01 45 62 22 76

## Mulligan's
16, rue de la Verrerie
75004 PARIS
Tel: 01 40 29 03 89
Manager: M. Alain DETALLE

## O'Brien's Irish Pub
77, rue Saint Dominique
75007 PARIS
Tel: 01 45 51 75 87
Fax: 01 45 51 54 00

## O'Kiddy's
15, rue Pottier
78150 LE CHESNAY
Tel: 01 39 55 05 19
Fax: 01 39 55 36 15

## O'Neil
20, rue des Canettes
75006 PARIS
Tel: 01 46 33 36 66

## Oscar Wilde
21, rue des Halles
75001 PARIS
Tel: 01 42 21 03 63

## Pub 64 WE
64, rue de Charenton
75012 PARIS
Tel: 01 44 75 39 55

## Pub Winston Churchill
*The first English pub in Paris*
5, rue de Presbourg
75016 PARIS
Tel: 01 40 67 17 37
Fax: 01 45 00 88 12
Manager: M. TYSSIER

## Roscoes American Bar
47, rue de Ponthieu
75008 PARIS
Tel: 01 43 59 76 77

## Rosebud
11 bis, rue Delambre
75014 PARIS
Tel: 01 43 35 38 54

## Saint John Irish Pub
188 bis, ave Charles de Gaulle
92200 NEUILLY SUR SEINE
Tel: 01 46 24 59 90

## Sous-Bock Tavern
49, rue Saint Honoré
75001 PARIS
Tel: 01 40 26 46 61
Fax: 01 40 26 59 36

## Stolly's Stone Bar
16, rue Cloche-Perce
75004 PARIS
Tel: 01 42 76 06 76

## Sweeney's
18, rue Laplace
75005 PARIS
Tel: 01 46 33 36 37
Contact: Reneta

## The Auld Alliance
80, rue François Miron
75004 PARIS
Tel: 01 48 04 30 40

## The Cricketer
41, rue des Mathurins
75008 PARIS
Tel: 01 40 07 01 45
Fax: 01 42 66 29 85

## The Flann O' Brien Irish Pub
6, rue Bailleul
75001 PARIS
Tel: 01 42 60 13 58
Contact: James

## The Frog & Princess
9, rue Princesse
75006 PARIS
Tel: 01 40 51 77 38
Fax: 01 43 29 12 14

## The Frog & Rosbif
116, rue Saint Denis
75002 PARIS
Tel: 01 42 36 34 73

## The Hairy Lemon
4, rue Caron
75004 PARIS
Tel: 01 42 72 90 40
Owner: M. ADAMS

*LIVING & STUDYING*

259

## WINING & DINING
À TABLE

### The James Ulysses Pub
5, rue du Jour
75001 PARIS
Tel: 01 45 08 17 04

### The Kildare Irish Pub
6, rue du Quatre Septembre
75002 PARIS
Tel: 01 47 03 91 91

### The Lizard Lounge
18, rue du Bourg Tibourg
75004 PARIS
Tel: 01 42 72 81 34

### The Quiet Man
5, rue des Haudriettes
75003 PARIS
Tel: 01 48 04 02 77
Fax: 01 48 04 35 22

### The Teeson Street
5, rue Saint Sulpice
75006 PARIS
Tel: 01 43 54 11 48
Contact: Pat O'CONNOR

### The Tigh Johnny Irish Pub
55, rue Montmartre
75002 PARIS
Tel: 01 42 33 91 33

### Tony's Bar
11, rue du Cygne
75001 PARIS
Tel: 01 42 33 29 82

### Willi's Wine Bar
*Fine dining with extensive wine list*
13, rue des Petits-Champs
75001 PARIS
Tel: 01 42 61 05 09
Fax: 01 47 03 36 93
http://www.aawine.com/willis

260

### CAFÉS/TEA ROOMS
Cafés/Salons de thé

### Antoine's
31, rue de Ponthieu
75008 PARIS
Tel: 01 42 89 44 20

### Bread and Best
10, rue Saint Marc
75002 PARIS
Tel: 01 40 26 56 66
Fax: 01 40 26 58 06
Email: 73631,1672@compuserve.com
Contact: M. Alistair WHATMORE

### Lina's Sandwiches
*Many locations in Paris*
50, rue Etienne Marcel
75002 PARIS
Tel: 01 42 21 16 14
Fax: 01 42 33 78 03
Owner: Mme Lina GOSHN

### Lindsay's Tea Shop
4, rue Yvonne Le Tac
75018 PARIS
Fax: 01 42 52 74 09

### The Bagel Place

6, place Sainte Opportune
75001 PARIS
Tel: 01 40 28 96 40
Fax: 01 40 28 97 94
Email: BagelPlace@aol.com
Contact: M. Barry WILKINSON

### The Tea Caddy
14, rue Saint Julien le Pauvre
75005 PARIS
Tel: 01 43 54 15 56

### FAST FOOD/ SANDWICHES
Fast food/Sandwiches

### Burger King France Holding
*Headquarters,*
*many locations in Paris*
1, place Victor Hugo
92400 COURBEVOIE
Tel: 01 46 91 95 95
Fax: 01 47 68 57 43

## Domino's Pizza

*World leader in home delivery, over 50 stores in France*

65, rue Saint Dominique
75007 PARIS
Tel: 01 47 05 73 73
Recording: 01 36 67 21 21

## France Quick

*Fast food chain headquarters, many locations around Paris*

Les Mercuriales
40, rue Jean Jaurès
93176 BAGNOLET Cedex
Tel: 01 49 72 13 00
Fax: 01 43 63 59 13

## Kentucky Fried Chicken

31, Bd Sébastopol
75001 PARIS
Tel: 01 40 26 61 14
Fax: 01 40 28 91 18

## Lina's Sandwiches

30, Bd des Italiens
75009 PARIS
Tel: 01 42 46 02 06
Fax: 01 42 46 02 40
Owner: Mme Lina GOSHN

## McDonalds

*Headquarters, many locations around Paris*

1, rue Gustave Eiffel
78045 GUYANCOURT Cedex
Tel: 01 30 48 63 00
Fax: 01 30 48 63 00

## Pizza Hut

*For all locations: 01 05 30 30 30*

29, Bd des Italiens
75002 PARIS
Tel: 01 42 65 16 00
Manager: M. CHOUKRI

## Slice Pizza

11, rue de la Roquette
75011 PARIS
Tel: 01 43 57 66 67
Director: Mme Stéphanie SARAF

LIVING & STUDYING

261

# SELECTED INTERNATIONAL
# COUNTRY & CITY CODES

After dialing 00 and reaching the international dial tone, dial the appropriate country code and city code followed by the telephone number.

| | | | | | | |
|---|---|---|---|---|---|---|
| **Australia** | 61 | **Ireland** | 353 | **Portugal** | 351 |
| Canberra | 6 | Dublin | 1 | Lisbon | 1 |
| Melbourne | 3 | | | | |
| Sydney | 2 | **Iceland** | 354 | **Romania** | 40 |
| Perth | 9 | Reykjavik | 55 or 56 | Bucharest | 1 |
| | | | or 58 | | |
| **Austria** | 43 | | | **Russia** | 7 |
| Vienna | 1 | **Israel** | 972 | Moscow | 095 |
| | | Jerusalem | 2 | St. Petersberg | 812 |
| **Belgium** | 32 | Tel Aviv | 3 | | |
| Brussels | 2 | | | **Singapour** | 65 |
| | | **Italy** | 39 | | |
| **Canada** | 1 | Milan | 2 | **Slovenia** | 386 |
| Montreal | 514 | Rome | 6 | | |
| Quebec | 418 | | | **South Africa** | 27 |
| Toronto | 915 or 416 | **Japan** | 81 | Cape Town | 21 |
| Vancouver | 604 | Kyoto | 75 | Johannesburg | 11 |
| | | Tokyo | 3 or 33 | Pretoria | 12 |
| **Czech Rep.** | 42 | | | | |
| Prague | 2 | **Luxembourg** | 352 | **Spain** | 34 |
| | | | | Barcelona | 3 |
| **Denmark** | 45 | **Malta** | 356 | Madrid | 1 |
| Copenhagen | – | | | | |
| | | **Mexico** | 52 | **Sweden** | 46 |
| **Finland** | 358 | Mexico City | 5 | Stockholm | 8 |
| Helsinki | 0 | | | | |
| | | **Monaco** | 337 | **Switzerland** | 41 |
| **Germany** | 49 | | | Geneva | 22 |
| Berlin | 30 | **Netherlands** | 31 | Zurich | 1 |
| Frankfurt | 69 | Amsterdam | 20 | | |
| Hamburg | 40 | | | **UK** | 44 |
| Munich | 89 | **New Zealand** | 64 | Birmingham | 121 |
| | | Auckland | 9 | Edinburgh | 131 |
| **Greece** | 30 | Wellington | 4 | Glasgow | 141 |
| Athens | 1 | | | London | 171 or 181 |
| | | **Norway** | 47 | Manchester | 161 |
| **Hong Kong** | 852 | Oslo | 22 | | |
| | | | | **USA** | 1 |
| **Hungary** | 36 | **Pakistan** | 92 | Boston | 617 |
| Budapest | 1 | Karachi | 21 | Chicago | 312 |
| | | | | Los Angeles | 213 |
| **India** | 91 | **Poland** | 48 | Miami | 305 |
| Bombay | 22 | Warsaw | 2 or 22 | New York | 212 |
| New Delhi | 11 | | | San Francisco | 415 |
| | | | | Wash., D.C. | 202 |

# EMERGENCY NUMBERS
## EN CAS D'URGENCE

**Ambulances de l'Assistance Publique**
*Handles transportation from one hospital to another*
Tel: 01 45 13 67 89

**Anti-Poison Center**
*24-hour service*
Tel: 01 40 37 04 04

**Association des Urgences Médicales de Paris**
*Medical emergencies*
Tel: 01 48 28 40 04

**Burns (severe)**
Tel: 01 42 34 17 58

**Enfance et Partage**
*Hotline for kids in trouble 09h00-21h00*
Tel: 0 800 05 12 34

**Lost Eurocard/Mastercard/Mastercharge**
Tel: 01 45 67 47 67

**Lost Luggage (Roissy)**
Tel: 01 48 62 10 46

**Lost/Stolen American Express Card**
Tel: 01 47 77 72 00

**Lost/Stolen Carte Bleue or Visa Card**
Tel: 01 42 77 11 90

**Lost/Stolen Diner's Club Card**
Tel: 01 47 62 75 75

**Medic'Air International**
*Worldwide air-ambulance services*
Tel: 01 43 63 04 04
Fax: 01 43 63 01 02
Hotline: 01 43 63 04 04
Email: aderossi@pratique.fr
Web site: http://www.medicair.starnet.fr
Chairman: M. Arnaud DEROSSI, MD

**Medical Emergencies**
*Tel: 15*

**Objets Trouvés**
*Lost and Found*
36, rue des Morillons
75015 PARIS
Tel: 01 45 31 14 80

# EMERGENCY NUMBERS

EN CAS D'URGENCE

**Pharma Presto**
*Medicine delivered to your house*
Tel: 01 42 42 42 50

**Police Secours**
Tel: 17

**Pompiers**
*Fire Brigade*
Tel: 18

**Psychiatric Emergencies**
Tel: 01 47 07 24 24

**Rape Crisis Hotline**
Free call: 0 800 05 95 95

**SAMU Ambulances**
*24-hour emergency service*
Tel: 01 45 67 50 50
Tel: 15

**Sida Info Service**
*AIDS help line*
Tel: 0 800 36 66 36

**SOS Attack**
*Assistance to assaulted victims*
Tel: 01 47 04 20 00
Office: 01 45 55 55 55

**SOS Cardiologues**
*Emergency service for heart patients*
Tel: 01 47 07 50 50

**SOS Décès**
*24h funeral assistance*
Tel: 01 42 02 99 99
Fax: 01 42 40 63 52

**SOS Dentistes**
*24 hour emergency dental help*
Tel: 01 43 37 51 00

**SOS Dépannage**
*Household emergencies*
Tel: 01 43 31 14 14
Fax: 01 47 07 21 04

**SOS Dépression**
17, ave de Clichy
75017 PARIS
Tel: 01 44 08 78 78

## SOS Divorce
Tel: 01 45 63 11 13
Tel: 01 45 62 09 62

## SOS Help! Crisis Line
*A friendly listener daily 15h00-23h00*
Tel: 01 47 23 80 80
Contact: Plum LE-TAN

## SOS Locataires
*Help for tenants*
Tel: 01 48 06 82 75

## SOS Locksmith
*24 hours*
Tel: 01 47 07 99 99

## SOS Médecins
*24-hour emergency medical house calls*
Tel: 01 47 07 77 77
Tel2: 01 43 37 77 77
Fax: 01 47 07 20 00

## SOS Médical
Tel: 01 48 28 40 04

## SOS Oeil
*Eye care*
Tel: 01 40 92 93 94

## SOS Pédiatres
*Pediatric assistance*
Tel: 01 43 94 35 01

## SOS Pregnancy
Tel: 01 45 82 13 14

## SOS Vet
*Round-the-clock veterinary home visits*
Tel: 01 47 55 47 00

## Urgences Dentaires Parisiennes
*Round-the-clock emergency dental service*
Tel: 01 45 35 41 41

*EMERGENCY NUMBERS*

# INDEX

# INDEX

# INDEX

# INDEX

274

# INDEX

# INDEX

Manuel Canovas 188
Maraviglia, Paul 105
Marc Delacre 149
Marchal, Dr. 180
Mareuil, Dr. Philippe 179
Maria Galland Institut 147
Marianne (Chez) 34, 219
Marketing Search 120
Marks & Spencer 223
Marley 228
Marois, Dr. Pierre 180
Marymount School 249
Mathijsen, Claire 182
Matra Communication 132
Matrox 71
Mauboussin 228
Maurice Franck 149
Maxim's Business Club 216
Maxim's Restaurant 31
Maximilien 226
May Courier International 78
Mayflower (Le) 258
MBA Center 245
McCann, Patrick 200
McCann-Erikson 58
McClean, Richard 105
McCloud, Cory 91
McDonalds 261
McElhearn - Benini 139
McGraw Hill Publications
115
MCI Direct 253
MCI International France 132
McKinsey & Company 76
Meade & Nabias 97
Med Care Domicile 185
Médaillier Franklin (Le) 236
**MÉDECINS 178**
Média Sid 116
Mediaplay International 92
Médiathèque 167
Mediatime 107
Medic'Air International 185,
263
Medical Emergencies 263
Mephisto Shoes 226
Mercedes-Benz 155
Mercure 27
Méridien Hotels (Le) 25
Merrill Lynch, Pierce, Fenner
& Smith 80
MESSAGE Mother Support
Group 163
Metropolitan Languages 200
Metropolitan Models 120
Mexi & Co. 173
MICEFA Student Exchange
245
Michel Brosseau 149
Michel Swiss Perfumes &
Cosmetics 228
Michèle & Heinz Coiffeurs
149

Michelin 30
Micro Université 167
Microsoft France 68
Middlebury College 245
Midland 62
Mille Break-First 177
Mille Fêtes 160
Mille Feuilles (Les) 232
Millesimes 35
Minerve Intérim 120
Ministère de l'Économie et
du Budget 82
Ministère de l'Éducation
Nationale 83
Ministère de l'Équipement,
du Logement, des Transports
et du Tourisme 83
Ministère de l'Industrie 83
Ministère de l'Intérieur 83
Ministère de la Culture 82
Ministère de la Défense 83
Ministère de la Jeunesse et
des Sports 83
Ministère de la Justice 83
Ministère des Affaires Étran-
gères 83
Ministère des Petites et
Moyennes Entreprises, du
Commerce et de l'Artisanat
83
Ministère du Travail et des
Affaires Sociales 83
Ministères (Les) 33
Ministry Hardcore Café 258
**MINITEL DIRECTORY
29, 100, 205**
Miss "Griffes" 226
Mistral B&B (Le) 28
MIT Club of France 216
Mixteca (La) 173
Mobilier 186
Mod's Hair 149
Mode 223
Moët-Hennessy 176
Molly Malone Lounge Bar
258
Mona Bismarck Foundation
(The) 217
Monaco Tourist Office 40
Mondial Moquette 189
Mondo 188
Mont Blanc Helicopters 171
Montecristo Café 259
Montessori 247, 248
Moore France 111
Moquet, Borde, Dieux, Geens
& Associés 97
Morel, Patrick 196
Morgan, Phyllis 216
Morgan Stanley 62
Morocco Tourist Office 40
Mory Worldwide Moving 208
Mosquée (La) 220

Motei, Annie 183
Moulin de la Galette (Le) 33
Mousquetaires (Les) 36
**MOVERS 207**
MP Bureau Business 128
MSN Microsoft France 90
MTV Europe 109
Mufti, Sharjeel Assad 236
Mulligan's 259
Multi Services International
76
Multiburo 193
Multimedia 91
Multimédia Investissement 93
Multimedia-related
Companies 93
Muniche (Le) 33
Murphy, Terence 191
Musée de la Curiosité et de la
Magie 160
Musée en Herbe 160
Music Shops 229
Mustang Café 256
Mustang Club de France 216

# N

Nadine Lennox 113
Nagpal International
Translation 139
Nagpal, Dr. H.R.S. 182
Namaste 232
Nannies 157
Nannies Incorporated 157
Nanterre English Language
Center 200
Nataf, Florence 139
Natali, Dr. Robert 180
Natalys 158
National Bank of Canada 62
National Geographic
Magazine 115
Natura-Diet 150
Naturalia 150
NDH Conseil 124
Neal, Michael 152
Nectar des Bourbons Fine
Wines 176
Neer Service
Déménagements 208
Nelson 236
Netherlands (The) -
Embassy 20
Netherlands (The) Tourist
Office 40
Netscape Communications 90
Netter, Dr. Laurence 180
Neuer, Jean-Jacques 97
New Directions for Teaching
and Learning 200
New Haven Café 256
Newman, Rebecca 129

# INDEX

# French Toast

*Harriet Welty Rochefort*

•

## what it's really like
## to pick up
## and move
## to Paris

•

**Told with humor
by a woman from Iowa
who left home for the City of Light
25 years ago
and didn't return.**

*"I read the book on the EuroStar between
Paris and London and wished the train
had not reached its top speed of 300 km/h!"*
*Leslie Caron*

*"Harriet Welty Rochefort's amusing portrayal
of life with the French hits the bull's eye."*

**To Order, see page 288!**